First World War
and Army of Occupation
War Diary
France, Belgium and Germany

29 DIVISION
87 Infantry Brigade
South Wales Borderers
2nd Battalion
1 March 1916 - 5 April 1919

WO95/2304/2

The Naval & Military Press Ltd
www.nmarchive.com
Published in association with The National Archives

Published by

The Naval & Military Press Ltd

Unit 10 Ridgewood Industrial Park,
Uckfield, East Sussex,
TN22 5QE England
Tel: +44 (0) 1825 749494

www.naval-military-press.com

www.nmarchive.com

This diary has been reprinted in facsimile from the original. Any imperfections are inevitably reproduced and the quality may fall short of modern type and cartographic standards.

© Crown Copyright
Images reproduced by permission of The National Archives, London, England, 2015.

Contents

Document type	Place/Title	Date From	Date To
Heading	WO95/2304/2		
Heading	29th Division 87th Infy Bde 2nd Bn Sth Wales Bordrs Mar 1916-Apr 1919 To U K 23		
Heading	29th Division. 87th Infantry Brigade. Arrived Marseilles from Egypt 15.3.16 2nd Battalion South Wales Borderers March 1916 Dec 18		
War Diary	Suez	01/03/1916	08/03/1916
War Diary	Alexander	09/03/1916	10/03/1916
War Diary	Marseilles	15/03/1916	18/03/1916
War Diary	Domart	18/03/1916	31/03/1916
Heading	29th Division. 87th Infantry Brigade. 2nd Battalion South Wales Borderers. April 1916 Appendices attached:- Report on Raid 29/30.4.16		
War Diary	Amplier	01/04/1916	04/04/1916
War Diary	Firing Line	05/04/1916	08/04/1916
War Diary	Mailly Maillet	09/04/1916	13/04/1916
War Diary	Louvencourt	14/04/1916	30/04/1916
Miscellaneous	Raiding Scheme Appendix I	00/04/1916	00/04/1916
Map	Line held by Battalion from 3rd May 1916		
Map	App I.A.		
Miscellaneous	Report on Raid Scheme of 29th 30th April 1916 Appendix II	29/04/1916	29/04/1916
Heading	29th Division. 87th Infantry Brigade. 2nd Battalion South Wales Borderers May 1916		
War Diary	Mailly Maillet	01/05/1916	03/05/1916
War Diary	Firing Line	03/05/1916	13/05/1916
War Diary	Englebelmer	14/05/1916	18/05/1916
War Diary	Acheux Wood	19/05/1916	28/06/1916
War Diary	Firing Line	29/05/1916	31/05/1916
Heading	29th Division 87th Infantry Brigade. 2nd Battalion South Wales Borderers June 1916 Appendices attached:- Patrol Report. Instruction for Attack		
War Diary	Firing Line	01/06/1916	07/06/1916
War Diary	Englebelmer	08/06/1916	15/06/1916
War Diary	Louvencourt	16/06/1916	23/06/1916
War Diary	Firing Line	24/06/1916	30/06/1916
Miscellaneous	87th Bde Appendix I	28/06/1916	28/06/1916
Miscellaneous	Report on Patrol Appendix II	30/06/1916	30/06/1916
Miscellaneous	Orders For the Attack Appendix III	22/06/1916	22/06/1916
Miscellaneous	Gas Discharge		
Miscellaneous	Programme of art Bombardment & Infantry advance		
Miscellaneous	Scheme for Attack on German Trenches 31/6/16 Appendix IV	30/06/1916	30/06/1916
Miscellaneous	OC Coy Previous Arrangements For Y2 Night Cancelled and the following Substituted Appendix V	30/06/1916	30/06/1916
Heading	29th Division 87th Infantry Brigade. 2nd Battalion South Wales Borderers. July 1916		
Heading	War Diary Of 2nd Bn. South Wales Borderers for July 1916		
Miscellaneous	DAG G.H.Q. 3rd Echelon	07/08/1916	07/08/1916

War Diary	Firing Line	01/07/1916	31/07/1916
Heading	29th Division 87th Infantry Brigade. 2nd Battalion South Wales Borderers. August 1916		
Heading	2 Battn The South Wales Borderers War Diary from 1st August 1916 to 31st August 1916 Volume 19 Vol 6		
War Diary		01/08/1916	31/08/1916
Heading	29th Division. 87th Infantry Brigade. 2nd Battalion South Wales Borderers September 1916		
Heading	War Diary 2nd Battalion The South Wales Borderers. For September 1916 Volume 20		
War Diary		01/09/1916	30/09/1916
Miscellaneous	2nd Battn The South Wales Borderers Appendix I	07/09/1916	07/09/1916
Heading	29th Division 87th Infantry Brigade. 2nd Battalion South Wales Borderers. October 1916		
Heading	War Diary of 2nd Battalion The South Wales Borderers, PP.209 To 220 Volume 22. October 1916		
War Diary		01/10/1916	21/10/1916
War Diary	Gueudecourt	21/10/1916	31/10/1916
Heading	29th Division 87th Infantry Brigade. 2nd Battalion South Wales Borderers November 1916		
Heading	War Diary of the 2nd Battalion The South Wales Borderers, From 1st November 1916 to 31st November 1916 Vol 9 Pages 221 to		
War Diary	Fricourt	01/11/1916	03/11/1916
War Diary	Airaisnes	04/11/1916	14/11/1916
War Diary	Citadel Camp	15/11/1916	15/11/1916
War Diary	Les Boeufs	16/11/1916	23/11/1916
War Diary	Carnoy	24/11/1916	26/11/1916
War Diary	Guillemont	27/11/1916	28/11/1916
War Diary	Les Boeufs	29/11/1916	30/11/1916
Heading	29th Division 87th Infantry Brigade. 2nd Battalion South Wales Borderers. December 1916		
Heading	War Diary of 2nd Battalion The South Wales Borderers, From 1/12/16-31/12/16 Volume 25 Nos.228 To 231. Vol 10		
War Diary	Les Boeufs	01/12/1916	02/12/1916
War Diary	Guillemont	03/12/1916	03/12/1916
War Diary	Carnoy	04/12/1916	09/12/1916
War Diary	Ville	10/12/1916	11/12/1916
War Diary	Corbie	12/12/1916	12/12/1916
War Diary	Ribecourt	13/12/1916	16/12/1916
War Diary	Le Quesnoy	17/12/1916	31/12/1916
Heading	War Diaries Of 2nd South Wales Borderers Volume I January 1917 Vol XI		
War Diary	Le Quesnoy	01/01/1917	11/01/1917
War Diary	Bresle	12/01/1917	12/01/1917
War Diary	Carnoy	13/01/1917	13/01/1917
War Diary	Guillemont	14/01/1917	14/01/1917
War Diary	Morval	15/01/1917	17/01/1917
War Diary	Carnoy	18/01/1917	21/01/1917
War Diary	Les Boeufs	22/01/1917	24/01/1917
War Diary	Guillemont	25/01/1917	26/01/1917
War Diary	Morval	27/01/1917	27/01/1917
War Diary	Les Boeufs	28/01/1917	29/01/1917
War Diary	Guillemont	30/01/1917	30/01/1917
War Diary	Carnoy	31/01/1917	31/01/1917

War Diary		27/01/1917	27/01/1917
Heading	2nd South Wales Borderers War Diary February 1917 Vol 12		
War Diary	Carnoy	01/02/1917	01/02/1917
War Diary	Carnoy To Guillemont	02/03/1917	02/03/1917
War Diary	Guillemont to Trenches	03/02/1917	05/02/1917
War Diary	In The Line	06/02/1917	06/02/1917
War Diary	Carnoy To Meaulte	07/02/1917	14/02/1917
War Diary	Meaulte	15/02/1917	17/02/1917
War Diary	Maltzhorn	18/02/1917	18/02/1917
War Diary	Trenches	19/02/1917	21/02/1917
War Diary	Bronfay	22/02/1917	23/02/1917
War Diary	Hardecourt	24/03/1917	24/03/1917
War Diary	Sailly Saillisel	25/02/1917	26/02/1917
War Diary	Bouleaux Area	27/02/1917	27/02/1917
War Diary	Bronfay	28/02/1917	28/02/1917
Heading	War Diary of 2nd South Wales Borderers for Month of March 1917 Vol 13		
War Diary	Bouleaux Area	27/02/1917	27/02/1917
War Diary	Bronfay	28/02/1917	01/03/1917
War Diary	Meaulte	02/03/1917	02/03/1917
War Diary	Bonnay	03/03/1917	05/04/1917
War Diary	Bonnay	06/03/1917	13/03/1917
War Diary	Le Quesnoy	19/03/1917	29/03/1917
War Diary	Le Quesnoy	22/03/1917	30/03/1917
War Diary	Vignacourt	29/03/1917	29/03/1917
War Diary	Montrelet	30/03/1917	31/03/1917
Heading	War Diary of 2nd South Wales Borderers Month of April 1917 Volume No 26 Vol 14		
War Diary	Occoches	01/04/1917	01/04/1917
War Diary	Lucheux	02/04/1917	05/04/1917
War Diary	Etree-Wamin	05/04/1917	07/04/1917
War Diary	Monchiet	08/04/1917	12/04/1917
War Diary	Monchy In The Line	12/04/1917	17/04/1917
War Diary	Arras	19/04/1917	19/04/1917
War Diary	Monchy Le Preux	23/04/1917	30/04/1917
War Diary	Casualties	13/04/1917	17/04/1917
War Diary	In Attack on	23/04/1917	30/04/1917
Heading	War Diary Of 2nd Battn. South Wales Borderers From 1-5-17 To 31-5-17 Volume No. 27 Vol 15		
War Diary	St Amand	01/05/1917	01/05/1917
War Diary	Wanquetin	02/05/1917	02/05/1917
War Diary	Arras	03/05/1917	03/05/1917
War Diary	Observation Ridge	04/05/1917	04/05/1917
War Diary	Arras	05/05/1917	07/05/1917
War Diary	Duisans	07/05/1917	13/05/1917
War Diary	Arras	14/05/1917	14/05/1917
War Diary	Monchy Le Preux	15/05/1917	21/05/1917
War Diary	Arras	21/05/1917	29/05/1917
War Diary	Brown Line	29/05/1917	29/05/1917
War Diary	Monchy	30/05/1917	31/05/1917
Heading	War Diary of 2nd Battn The South Wales Borderers Volume 28 From June 1st 1917 to June 30th 1917 Vol 16		
War Diary	Monchy	01/06/1917	02/06/1917
War Diary	Arras	03/06/1917	04/06/1917

War Diary	Candas	05/06/1917	26/06/1917
War Diary	Poperinghe	27/06/1917	28/06/1917
War Diary	Brielen	29/06/1917	30/06/1917
Heading	War Diary Of 2nd Battn South Wales Borderers From July 1st 1917 To July 31st 1917 Volume 29 Vol 17		
War Diary	Brielen	01/07/1917	02/07/1917
War Diary	Zwaanhof Sector	02/07/1917	06/07/1917
War Diary	Crombeke	07/07/1917	12/07/1917
War Diary	Woesten	13/07/1917	20/07/1917
War Diary	Crombeke	21/07/1917	25/07/1917
War Diary	Forest Camp (Woesten)	31/07/1917	31/07/1917
Heading	War Diary Of 2nd Battn The South Wales Borderers From 1/8/17 To 31/8/17 Volume No. 30 Vol 18		
War Diary	Forest Camp N: Woestan	01/08/1917	03/08/1917
War Diary	Piccadilly Camp	04/08/1917	07/08/1917
War Diary	Camps No. 1 & 2	08/08/1917	08/08/1917
War Diary	Dublin Camp	09/08/1917	10/08/1917
War Diary	Eton Camp	11/08/1917	14/08/1917
War Diary	Left Support Saules Farm	15/08/1917	15/08/1917
War Diary	Sentier Fm	16/08/1917	17/08/1917
War Diary	Addingly Camp	17/08/1917	20/08/1917
War Diary	Dulwich Camp	20/06/1917	22/08/1917
War Diary	Elverdinghe	22/08/1917	22/08/1917
War Diary	Widjendrift	23/08/1917	27/08/1917
War Diary	Dulwich Camp	28/08/1917	28/08/1917
War Diary	Plumstead Camp	29/08/1917	31/08/1917
Miscellaneous	Account of Operation. 16 Aug 1917	16/08/1917	16/08/1917
Diagram etc	Broembeek		
Map			
Heading	War Diary of 2nd Battalion The South Wales Borderers From 1.9.17 To 30.9.17 Vol 19		
War Diary	Plumstead Camp Proven	01/09/1917	20/09/1917
War Diary	De Hippe Camp	20/09/1917	27/09/1917
War Diary	Rugby Camp	28/09/1917	29/09/1917
War Diary	Front Line	30/09/1917	30/09/1917
Miscellaneous	Roll of Officers With Battn on 30 Sept 1917 Appendix II	30/09/1917	30/09/1917
Heading	War Diary of 2nd Battn South Wales Borderers From 1.10.17 To 31.10.17 Vol 20		
Miscellaneous	87 Brigade	02/11/1917	02/11/1917
War Diary	Front line	01/10/1917	02/10/1917
War Diary	Charter House Camp	03/10/1917	05/10/1917
War Diary	Front Line	06/10/1917	08/10/1917
War Diary	White Mill Camp	09/10/1917	09/10/1917
War Diary	Poodle Camp	10/10/1917	15/10/1917
War Diary	Bellacourt	17/10/1917	28/10/1917
War Diary	Bellacourt	23/10/1917	23/10/1917
War Diary	Bellacourt	25/10/1917	31/10/1917
Map	Appendix 1 A. 1. War Diary Oct 1917		
Miscellaneous	Message Pad.		
Miscellaneous	Training Programme For Week Ending 26/10/17 October Appendix II	26/10/1917	26/10/1917
Miscellaneous	Training Programme Week Ending 3/11/17 Appendix III	03/11/1917	03/11/1917
Heading	War Diary of 2nd Battn South Wales Borderers From 1.11.17 To 30.11.17 Vol 21		

War Diary	Bellacourt	01/11/1917	18/11/1917
War Diary	Haut Allaines	18/11/1917	18/11/1917
War Diary	Fins	19/11/1917	20/11/1917
War Diary	Marcoing	20/11/1917	21/11/1917
War Diary	Masnieres	22/11/1917	23/11/1917
War Diary	Bridge Head Defences	24/11/1917	26/11/1917
War Diary	Marcoing	27/11/1917	28/11/1917
War Diary	Bridge Head Defences	29/11/1917	30/11/1917
War Diary	Marcoing Copse L 29 & 9.1	30/11/1917	30/11/1917
War Diary	Marcoing Copse L 29 & 9.1	20/11/1917	29/11/1917
Miscellaneous	Account of Operation On 20th Nov 1917 Appendix II	20/11/1917	20/11/1917
Miscellaneous	Additional Account Of Operation On 21th Nov 1917. After concerting Fuller Information.	21/11/1917	21/11/1917
Miscellaneous	Account of Operation On 21th Nov 1917. Appendix IV	21/11/1917	21/11/1917
Miscellaneous		24/11/1917	24/11/1917
Map	Appendix VI		
Miscellaneous	Message From		
Heading	War Diary Of 2nd Battalion South Wales Borderers From 1st December 1917 To 31st December 1917 Folio 39 Vol 22		
War Diary	Marcoing Copse L.29.b.9.0	01/12/1917	03/12/1917
War Diary	Ribecourt	03/12/1917	04/12/1917
War Diary	Sorel	05/12/1917	05/12/1917
War Diary	Liencourt	06/12/1917	16/12/1917
War Diary	Liencourt	16/12/1917	16/12/1917
War Diary	Conchy	17/12/1917	17/12/1917
War Diary	Grigny	18/12/1917	18/12/1917
War Diary	Embry	19/12/1917	22/12/1917
War Diary	Embry & Rimboval	25/12/1917	30/12/1917
War Diary	Avroult	31/12/1917	31/12/1917
Miscellaneous	Account of Operation 30th Nov 3 Dec Appendix I	30/11/1917	30/11/1917
Map	December 1917 Appendix II Disposition Taken up by 2/S Wales Borderers		
Miscellaneous	Message Form		
Miscellaneous	Special Order of The Day by Major General St Beauvoir de Lisle, K.O.B. D.S.O. Commanding 29th Division. Appendix III	07/12/1917	07/12/1917
Miscellaneous	Programme Of Work Week Ending 15th Dec. Appendix IV	09/12/1917	09/12/1917
Map	Dotted Blue Line Shows Approve Position Front Line Dispositions of Coys 2/SW Borderers Shown in Blue. Appendix III		
Miscellaneous	Programme Of Work	20/12/1917	20/12/1917
Heading	Appendix V December		
Map	Appendix V Disposition of Bridge Head Defences Front Line 23 Nov 17		
Miscellaneous	Note:- Either Give Map Reference Or Mark Your position By A "X" On the Map On back.		
Miscellaneous	Training Programme Appendix VI	29/12/1917	29/12/1917
Heading	War Diary of Battn South Wales Borderers From 1.1.18 To 31.1.18 Folio 42 Vol 23		
War Diary	Renescures	01/01/1918	01/01/1918
War Diary	Roosendael	02/01/1918	02/01/1918
War Diary	Portsmouth Camp (Proven Area)	03/01/1918	05/01/1918
War Diary	Boesinghe	06/01/1918	17/01/1918
War Diary	Boesinghe	14/01/1918	14/01/1918

War Diary	Brake Camp Brandhoek	18/01/1918	24/01/1918
War Diary	Brake Camp Brandhoek	20/01/1918	25/01/1918
War Diary	Junction Camp St. Jean	26/11/1918	26/11/1918
Heading	War Diary Of 2nd Battn South Wales Borderers From 1/2/18. To 28/2/18 Vol 24		
War Diary	Junction Camp St. Jean	01/02/1918	03/02/1918
War Diary	Bellevue	04/02/1918	07/02/1918
War Diary	Front Line	07/02/1918	09/02/1918
War Diary	Junction Camp	10/02/1918	11/02/1918
War Diary	Hill Camp Watou	12/02/1918	20/02/1918
War Diary	Hill Camp Watou	16/02/1918	16/02/1918
War Diary	Hill Camp Watou	16/02/1918	28/02/1918
Heading	War Diary Of 2nd Battn South Wales Borderers From 1/3/18 To 31/3/18 Folio 44 Vol 25		
War Diary	Poperinghe	01/03/1918	06/03/1918
War Diary	English Camp	06/03/1918	09/03/1918
War Diary	Front Line	10/03/1918	12/03/1918
War Diary	English Camp	13/03/1918	15/03/1918
War Diary	Front Line	16/03/1918	18/03/1918
War Diary	Front Line V. 28 a.65.15 to V.29 A. 60.50	18/03/1918	20/03/1918
War Diary	Front Line	21/03/1918	23/03/1918
War Diary	Red Rose Camp	23/03/1918	30/03/1918
War Diary	Junction Camp	30/03/1918	31/03/1918
Miscellaneous	March 1918 Appendix I	02/03/1918	02/03/1918
Miscellaneous	Trenches Note On Attack	13/03/1918	13/03/1918
Heading	87th Brigade. 29th Division. 2nd Battalion South Wales Borderers April 1918		
Heading	War Diary Of 2nd Battn South Wales Borderers From 1-4-18 To 30-4-18 Vol 26		
War Diary	S. Jean	01/04/1918	03/04/1918
War Diary	Paschendaele	03/04/1918	03/04/1918
War Diary	Bellvue	03/04/1918	03/04/1918
War Diary	Paschendaele	03/04/1918	03/04/1918
War Diary	Paschendaele	03/04/1918	09/04/1918
War Diary	Poperinghe St Janter Biezen	09/04/1918	09/04/1918
War Diary	Watou	10/04/1918	10/04/1918
War Diary	Les Haies Basses	11/04/1918	11/04/1918
War Diary	Doulieu	12/04/1918	12/04/1918
War Diary	Ferme Labis	13/04/1918	13/04/1918
War Diary	Labis	13/04/1918	13/04/1918
War Diary	Casualties	11/04/1918	12/04/1918
War Diary	St Sylvester Cappel	14/04/1918	15/04/1918
War Diary	St Sylvester	16/04/1918	17/04/1918
War Diary	Campagne	18/04/1918	18/04/1918
War Diary	St Sylvester	19/04/1918	20/04/1918
War Diary	La Ht Loge V. 20 d. 6.5	21/04/1918	22/04/1918
War Diary	La Haute Loge Hazebrouck	22/04/1918	26/04/1918
War Diary	Support Bn	27/04/1918	27/04/1918
War Diary		24/04/1918	24/04/1918
War Diary	Support	28/04/1918	01/05/1918
War Diary	Firing Line	02/05/1918	02/05/1918
Map			
Miscellaneous	Special Order Of The Day By Major General D.E.C. Ayley C.M.G., Commanding 29th Division. War Diary App IV	24/04/1918	24/04/1918
Map			

Heading	Raid 1/KOSB 26/27		
War Diary	Support	01/05/1918	02/05/1918
War Diary	Firing Line	03/05/1918	05/05/1918
War Diary	G" Marquette Farm	03/05/1918	08/05/1918
War Diary	D 6 D 99	09/05/1918	14/05/1918
War Diary	E 13 d E 14 C.	14/05/1918	16/05/1918
War Diary	E 9 a g Support Line	17/05/1918	18/05/1918
War Diary	Petit Sec Bois	18/05/1918	20/05/1918
War Diary	Front Line	20/05/1918	21/05/1918
War Diary	Swartenbrouch		
War Diary	Enclosures at E 23 C 2070 E 23 C 20 99	21/05/1918	23/05/1918
War Diary	Bois D'aval	23/05/1918	24/05/1918
War Diary	The Becque	24/05/1918	24/05/1918
War Diary	Vieux Berquin	24/05/1918	26/05/1918
War Diary	E 17 a. 5.8	26/04/1918	26/05/1918
War Diary	E 15 d 7.4 E 21 & 8.1	26/04/1918	26/04/1918
War Diary	E 15 Cent	26/05/1918	28/05/1918
War Diary	Morbecque D 13a 4.3	28/05/1918	31/05/1918
Heading	War Diary Of 2nd Battn. South Wales Borderers From 1-6-18 To 30-6-18 Vol 28		
War Diary	Camp N.W. Morbecque	01/06/1918	01/06/1918
War Diary	Gd Marquette D 12b	02/06/1918	02/06/1918
War Diary	Le Grand Hasard	03/06/1918	14/06/1918
War Diary	E. 14 C 7.0	15/06/1918	18/06/1918
War Diary	Morbecque	18/06/1918	19/06/1918
War Diary	E 14 C 7.0	20/06/1918	22/06/1918
War Diary	Racqinghem B 14 b88	23/06/1918	30/06/1918
Operation(al) Order(s)	Operation Order No. 1 By Lt. Colonel G.T. Raikes D.S.O., Commanding 2nd Battn. South Wales Borderers. Appendix "A"	14/06/1918	14/06/1918
Operation(al) Order(s)	Operation Order No. 2 By Lt. Colonel G.T. Raikes D.S.O., Commanding 2nd Battn. South Wales Borderers. Appendix "B"	14/06/1918	14/06/1918
Miscellaneous	Appendix "C". To 87th Brigade, Headquarters.	15/06/1918	15/06/1918
Miscellaneous	Appendix "D" To Headquarters 87th Brigade.	15/06/1918	15/06/1918
Operation(al) Order(s)	Appendix "D" Notes On Para 6, Of Operation Order No. 7		
Miscellaneous	Appendix "E" O/C., "C" Company. Ref. "Dog" Tonight.		
Miscellaneous	Appendix "F" To NOFA,		
Operation(al) Order(s)	Appendix "G" Operation Order No. 3 By Lt. Colonel G.T. Raikes D.S.O. Commanding 2nd Battn. South Wales Borderers.	17/06/1918	17/06/1918
Miscellaneous	Appendix "H" War Diary, To Headquarters, 87th Brigade.	18/06/1918	18/06/1918
Operation(al) Order(s)	Appendix "E" Operation Order No. 4		
Operation(al) Order(s)	Appendix "K" Operation Order No. 5 By Lt.-Colonel G.T. Raikes D.S.O. Commanding 2nd Battn. South Wales Borderers.	19/06/1918	19/06/1918
Operation(al) Order(s)	Appendix L Operation Order No. 6. By Lt. Colonel G.T. Raikes D.S.O. Commanding 2nd Battn. South Wales Borderers.	21/06/1918	21/06/1918
Miscellaneous	Appendix M. 2nd. Battn. South Wales Borderers.	26/06/1918	26/06/1918
Operation(al) Order(s)	Appendix "N" Operation Order No. 7, By Lt. Colonel G.T. Raikes D.S.O. Commanding 2nd. South Wales Borderers.		

Type	Description	Start	End
Miscellaneous	Appendix O. Nominal Royal Officers June 30th 1918	30/06/1918	30/06/1918
Map	Trenches Corrected From Photos Up to 15.6.18		
War Diary	Racquinghem B14 & 88	01/07/1918	14/07/1918
War Diary	E 3 C 1.8	15/07/1918	18/07/1918
War Diary	Lynde	19/07/1918	19/07/1918
War Diary	Hondeghem	23/07/1918	23/07/1918
War Diary	St Marie Cappel	24/07/1918	31/07/1918
Miscellaneous	2nd. Battn. South Wales Borderers.		
Heading	War Diary Of 2nd Battalion South Wales Borderers. From 1.8.18 To 31.8.18 Volume No. 43 Vol 30		
War Diary	St Marie Capel	01/08/1918	03/08/1918
War Diary	La Kreule V 17 C 9.3	03/08/1918	15/08/1918
War Diary	Front Line Merris Sector	16/08/1918	18/08/1918
War Diary	Outtersteene Ridge	19/08/1918	20/08/1918
War Diary	La Kreule V 17 C 9.3	21/08/1918	25/08/1918
War Diary	Outtersteene Ridge	26/08/1918	31/08/1918
Operation(al) Order(s)	Appendix 11 87th. Infantry Brigade Order No. 125		
Operation(al) Order(s)	Appendix 3 2nd South Wales Borderers Order No. 17	17/08/1918	17/08/1918
Miscellaneous	Appendix I Account of Operation 18th August 1918	18/08/1918	18/08/1918
Miscellaneous	Appendix No. VI Nominal Roll Of Officers. 31.8.18	31/08/1918	31/08/1918
Map	Trenches Corrected To 5.8.18		
Map	T.S. 272. Corps. Section 19.8.18 Trenches Corrected To 14.8.18		
War Diary	Outtersteen Ridge	01/09/1918	02/09/1918
War Diary	Dook Farm A 3a	03/09/1918	04/09/1918
War Diary	Outtersteene	04/09/1918	06/09/1918
War Diary	A 2 d Central	07/09/1918	09/09/1918
War Diary	Erin Cottage	10/09/1918	12/09/1918
War Diary	Wallon Capel U5d	13/09/1918	16/09/1918
War Diary	St Jaenter Bitzen	17/09/1918	18/09/1918
War Diary	Compass Farm 28/H 56 of 3.3	19/09/1918	20/09/1918
War Diary	Ypres	20/09/1918	23/09/1918
War Diary	Road Camp	24/09/1918	26/09/1918
War Diary	Ypres	27/09/1918	30/09/1918
Operation(al) Order(s)	Appendix 1 87th Infantry Brigade Order No. 134	01/09/1918	01/09/1918
Miscellaneous	Appendix 1 Headquarters, 2nd. S.W.B.	02/09/1918	02/09/1918
Operation(al) Order(s)	Appendix No. 2 87th Infantry Brigade Order No. 147	27/09/1918	27/09/1918
Operation(al) Order(s)	2nd South Wales Borderers Order No. 25. Appendix 3		
Map			
Heading	War Diary Of 2nd. Battalion South Wales Borderers From 1.10.18 To 31.10.18 Volume No. 45. Vol 32		
War Diary	Ghelevelt	01/10/1918	01/10/1918
War Diary	N. of Geluwe	02/10/1918	03/10/1918
War Diary	Westhoek	04/10/1918	06/10/1918
War Diary	Ypres	07/10/1918	09/10/1918
War Diary	Westhoek	10/10/1918	10/10/1918
War Diary	Ledeghem	11/10/1918	15/10/1918
War Diary	Salines	16/10/1918	20/10/1918
War Diary	Staceghem	21/10/1918	22/10/1918
War Diary	O. 11	23/10/1918	23/10/1918
War Diary	Steenbrugge	24/10/1918	31/10/1918
Miscellaneous	Account of Operation. 14th-16th Oct 1917	14/10/1918	14/10/1918
Miscellaneous	Account of Operation. 20"-24" Oct 1917	20/10/1918	20/10/1918
Miscellaneous	Appendix 3. Nominal Roll of Officers 31.10.18	31/10/1918	31/10/1918
Map			
Heading	Map A		

Heading	2nd Battn South Wales Borderers War Diary November 1918		
War Diary	St. Andre	01/11/1918	06/11/1918
War Diary	Tourcoing	07/11/1918	14/11/1918
War Diary	Ghoy	15/11/1918	16/11/1918
War Diary	Ollignies	17/11/1918	17/11/1918
War Diary	Steenkerque	18/11/1918	20/11/1918
War Diary	Ittre	21/11/1918	22/11/1918
War Diary	Bousval	23/11/1918	23/11/1918
War Diary	Ernage	24/11/1918	24/11/1918
War Diary	Grand Leez	25/11/1918	26/11/1918
War Diary	Forville	27/11/1918	27/11/1918
War Diary	Stree	28/11/1918	28/11/1918
War Diary	Comblain-Au-Pont	29/11/1918	29/11/1918
War Diary	Winamplanche	30/11/1918	30/11/1918
Miscellaneous	List of Officers.	30/11/1918	30/11/1918
Heading	29th Div. 87th Bde. War Diary 2nd Battn. South Wales Borderers. December 1918		
War Diary	Stavelot	01/12/1918	03/12/1918
War Diary	Nidrum	04/12/1918	04/12/1918
War Diary	Mutzenich	05/12/1918	05/12/1918
War Diary	Nideggen	06/12/1918	06/12/1918
War Diary	Vettweiss	07/12/1918	07/12/1918
War Diary	Kierdorf	08/12/1918	08/12/1918
War Diary	Kriel	09/12/1918	09/12/1918
War Diary	South of Cologne	10/12/1918	11/12/1918
War Diary	Cologne	12/12/1918	13/12/1918
War Diary	Berg	14/12/1918	14/12/1918
War Diary	Gladbach Burscheid	15/12/1918	15/12/1918
War Diary	Bleiding Hausen	16/12/1918	28/12/1918
War Diary	Burscheid	29/12/1918	31/12/1918
Miscellaneous	2nd South Wales Borderers		
Miscellaneous	Appendix 2nd South Wales Borderers.		
Heading	Southern (Late 29th) Divn 87th Infy Bde 2nd Bn 5th Wales Borderers Jan-Apr 1919 To U.K		
Heading	War Diary of The 2nd Battn. South Wales Borderers. From 1st January 1919 To 31st January Volume No. 16 Vol 35		
War Diary	Burscheid	01/01/1919	31/01/1919
Miscellaneous			
Heading	War Diary Of 2nd. Battalion. South Wales Borderers From 1.2.19 to 28.2.19 Volume No. 36		
War Diary	Burscheid	03/02/1919	28/02/1919
Miscellaneous	2nd South Wales Borderers.		
War Diary	Burscheid	03/03/1919	17/03/1919
War Diary	Mulheim Cologne	17/03/1919	17/03/1919
War Diary	Mulheim	24/03/1919	31/03/1919
Miscellaneous	Other Ranks. 46		
War Diary	Dunkirk	01/04/1919	04/04/1919
War Diary	Dover	04/04/1919	04/04/1919
War Diary	Brecon	05/04/1919	05/04/1919
Miscellaneous	On His Majesty's Service.		

M005/2304/2

29TH DIVISION
87TH INFY BDE

2ND BN STH WALES BORDRS
MAR 1916 - DEC APR 1919

To U K

2304

29th Division.
87th Infantry Brigade.

Arrived MARSEILLES from EGYPT 15.3.16.

2nd BATTALION

SOUTH WALES BORDERERS

MARCH 1916

Army Form C. 2118.

WAR DIARY
or
INTELLIGENCE SUMMARY.

XXX DIVH 2/24th from M.E.F.

(141)

117

Place	Date	Hour	Summary of Events and Information	Remarks and references to Appendices
Suez.	1st March	0630	All baggage & men W. of the cavalry 0630, with exception of garrison of No.4 Post which was not relieved by 42nd Division until 0900 — The detachment marched camp at 1700 remainder arriving at 1000 —	
	2nd to 8th		During this period those men who had failed to make a 12 inch knot in rifle through four practices at the recruits' course while these who had passed fired 5 rounds per man individual field firing — 150 rounds S.A.A. and '15 rounds S.A.A.' were also exercised in the attack at Ceremonial, and carried out a route march of nine miles, wearing F.S.M.O. and	
	3rd		On the 3rd 2/Lts C.W. HANNAH and H.S. ADCOCK 13th Sherwood Foresters, and 2/Lts DFDON and F.M. SMITH 14th Sherwood Foresters joined the Battn —	
	4th		On the 4th Capt. D.H.S. SOMERVILLE rejoined from leave	
	6th		On the 6th Lieut. G.W. PHILLIMORE 3rd H.L.I. joined the Battalion	
	7th		Orders received for embarkation of a portion of the Battalion at Alexandria —	
	8th		to leave Suez about 1930 the 2nd Lt. R. BALLANTINE rejoined from Hospital — These orders modified — The whole Battalion proceeded to Alexandria during the night 8/9 March, being allotted a portion of each train took	

Army Form C. 2118.

WAR DIARY
or
INTELLIGENCE SUMMARY.
(Erase heading not required.)

142

Place	Date March	Hour	Summary of Events and Information	Remarks and references to Appendices
Alexandria	9th		Trains and two passenger trains – On arrival at Alexandria the Battalion embarked on the S.S. KAROA and S.S. KINGSTONIAN 21 Officers and 372 other ranks on the former ship and 7 Officers and 275 other ranks on the latter – (viz. H.T. ADCOCK, 13th Shropshire Yeomanry, was disembarked after embarkation, 2/Lt. H.T. ADCOCK, 13th Shropshire Yeomanry) + sent to hospital (ante 10E) Total strength sailing 26 Officers, 1 M.O. 1 Chaplain and 647 other ranks – Sailed from Alexandria – Headquarters on the KAROA –	
	10th		Landed at Marseilles – Troop train left at about 01.00 on the 16E with the half Battalion, in guns + about 160 horses + mules –	
Marseille	15E			
	18th	0600	Arrived PONT REMY 0600 + detrained – Ordered to leave two permanent fatigue parties at PONT REMY, 1 Officer + 34 other ranks for sanitary duties + 1 Officer + 60 others for unloading trains – Marched to DOMART-EN-PONTHIEU about 13 miles – Billets had already been allotted + by the Brigade, + partially told off by the advanced party – The Battalion was the first unit of the 62nd Division to arrive, with the exception of the 1st line transport + Staff sent on in advance –	
DOMART				

Army Form C. 2118.

WAR DIARY
or
INTELLIGENCE SUMMARY.
(Erase heading not required.)

Place	Date	Hour	Summary of Events and Information	Remarks and references to Appendices
DOMART	May 19th		The other half Battalion from the KINGSTONIAN arrived & were billeted in the same village —	
	21st		Fine Officers, the R.M.S. Major & 130 other ranks went on 8 days leave to England	
	22nd		Battalion and 190 Line Transport did a Route March 14 miles in full marching order — Very little ground available for manoeuvring — Have obtained two fields for hill purposes —	
	28th		During the past week the training of machine gunners, Lewis gunners + signallers has proceeded — A Battalion Route March of about 13 miles was carried out on 25th and a Brigade Route March of about 14 miles on the 27th — Ground for tactical training is very limited, the whole surrounding being under cultivation — There was snow for two days & some rain, which interfered with the programme of work — The Officer & 60 men who have been unhorsed trains at PONT REMY rejoined to-day —	

WAR DIARY
or
INTELLIGENCE SUMMARY
(Erase heading not required.)

Army Form C. 2118.

Place	Date	Hour	Summary of Events and Information	Remarks and references to Appendices
DOMART	30	0830	Brigade moved to AMPLIER and went into huts there – Battn. billeted to Brigade's (with the advanced guard – Halted for two hours en route & marched to AMPLIER about 8.15.45. Distance 14 miles – Two men killed and – great difficulty in obtaining boots, and many men got sore feet – Two P Pattern garments have been issued to every man –	
	31		Rest. – So many of the transport & drivers of supplies & stores (many to be been employed with, and we have had to buy them – Lamps & buckets & c.) that have also been purchased to the distance from our DOMART, the supply problem not being likely to trouble us –	

31/3/16.

[signature]
a/lt? 2/Batt.W.div Riflemen

29th Division.
87th Infantry Brigade.

2nd BATTALION

SOUTH WALES BORDERERS.

A P R I L 1 9 1 6

Appendices attached ; - Report on Raid 29/30.4.16.

Army Form C. 2118.

WAR DIARY
or
INTELLIGENCE SUMMARY.
(Erase heading not required.)

2SWB

Place	Date	Hour	Summary of Events and Information	Remarks and references to Appendices
AMPLIER	1st		Companies spent the day practising with gas helmets. Orders received to move to ENGLEBELMER the following day.	
	2nd		Brigade moved out from AMPLIER, Battalion marching off at 1330 and going into billets in ENGLEBELMER, where it arrived at 1920 after a halt meal at 1.5 miles. After going about 4 miles the Brigade was inspected by G.O.C. 8th Corps on the march. Men very tired on reaching billets. Two men who did not arrive with Battn, who came in next day, the remainder arriving with the transport.	
	3rd	1900	Moved up by platoons at 5 minutes interval and took over trenches from 13th E. Yorks A, B, C. Coys holding the line from right to left, D coy in reserve at Battn H.Q. Trenches in very bad state, and much damaged by trench mortar fire. Coy Commanders had spent the previous 36 hours in the trenches to take over. — Length of line held about 1100 yds. — Fairly windy bombarded by two Trench Mortars, which have badly damaged the Left of the Salient with the Retters, of the MARY REDAN. This Op is missed with the latrine galleries running out towards the enemy trenches. One entrance has been blocked and part of the galleries damaged by trench mortars. — Another fired about 30 to 40 rounds.	2September I.A.
	4th			

13T

WAR DIARY or INTELLIGENCE SUMMARY

Army Form C. 2118.

Place: Fauquissart Line
Date: April 5th

Summary of Events and Information:

Several patrols sent out last night to examine wire & found in front – friend C.H. PHILLIMORE 3rd H.L.S. (attached) and a man went out at 8am and hid outside the trenches opposite the point where the two individuals were last seen. About 11am shots to a machine gun were heard from the enemy trenches opposite the point where the two individuals were last seen. Two men were killed and 2Lt A. BALLANTINE wounded (slightly) a trench mortar was knocked out while working on the rear face of the enemy W–. Wire is being pushed out steadily, the first strand, and stakes in Sap which have already been pushed out to a distance (from 40 to 150 yards. They will eventually be connected up by a new firing trench –

G.O.C. 29th Division visited the trenches –

Bn. 2/Lt. W.H. MACON has been appointed Bat'n. Intelligence Officer, his duties being to collect reports from various observers & observers & to compile the daily & weekly Intelligence Summaries – This is to be the subject to the Army –

From 1330 to 1530 the left trenches and its communication trench were shelled by the enemy (right hand shell) with Shrapnel H.E. and minenwerfer shells – Only a few hostile shells were fired, about 15 cm. the remainder were field guns – No casualties were caused –

Army Form C. 2118.

WAR DIARY
or
INTELLIGENCE SUMMARY.
(Erase heading not required.)

Place	Date	Hour	Summary of Events and Information	Remarks and references to Appendices
June 2nd	6th		Patrols went out last night, but could find no trace of Lt. PHILLIMORE & his companion — A quiet day has been shelled in the morning, & some trench mortars in the afternoon. (to the N end of the Salient) 2nd Lt. FILMAYER & 2nd Lt. MAYER offrs and 8 NCOs/men sent in 7 days trench mortar course at VALHEUREUX.	(147)
		2000.	At about 2000 a bombing patrol of 1 officer and 7 men was sent out down a Sap in the centre of the Left Coy (C Coy) — On arrival at the head of the Sap 2 men were sent on in advance to see whether any hostile patrols were moving in the front recent shewn 50 yards in advance. They came back & reported a patrol extended order — Patrol weilded some time to verify this, it then retired — About this time some bombing & rifle grenades Going on further to the NORTH —	
		2100	At 2100, just as this patrol got in, the enemy opened a heavy bombardment with minenwerfer and H.E. and shrapnel. The whole sector held by the Battn came under fire, but the greatest concentration was on the right half of the left Coy & on the communication trenches leading up to it — The line was first driven in on the line of saps & then in to the fire trench, and then in to the Support line. A slip of mine in front of the right of the line was lifted from the front line and which the damage on the parapets and entire company was entirely levelled and destroyed mainly by the minenwerfer — When the fire was lifted from the front line and while the enemy entered the front line held by the right half of the Left company, a party of the enemy entered the front line held by the night half of the Left company — Most of these were killed they brother of the line	

1577 Wt.W10791/1773 500,000 1/15 D. D. & L.   A.D.S.S./Forms/C. 2118.

WAR DIARY or INTELLIGENCE SUMMARY

Army Form C. 2118.

Place	Date	Hour	Summary of Events and Information	Remarks and references to Appendices
Firing Line	6th (cont.)		had been with drawn into PICCADILLY (support line), but there were still men in the dug outs — and two who were burned down under some fallen timbers — A party of 2 officers & some grenadiers were holding BOND STREET, drawing rifle shots from the hut, when a fatty sporting lieutenant was heard of [?] them. The ladies Officer challenged them, as shown thought that it was a party from our men reply was a loud "Jawohl" — A brisk fight ensued, several bombs [?] to them [?] at the enemy, who then retired — The leading German carried an white tank — They were white arm badges on both arms. Bombardment suddenly ceased — Our guns had been firing very hard on the German front trenches in case an attack to [?] was intended, & also on his rear lines —	
		2130	Our guns ceased firing at the same time as the enemy — Half [?] the reserve company was pushed up to hunt the barrage ceased, and it was found the Germans had evacuated the trench — No damage was done except to a slight to the track which was very much damaged at the point where the Germans had entered and at the tip of the salient. The tank was strewn with unexploded stick grenades, by a area was also left with a dagger — A tiny safe leading was made & some German prisoners, showing the many got our wounded men was seen at dawn lying close on top — An officer was dragging his dead [?] man dressed his wounds & carrying out to see who was [?] , & together with another man dressed his wounds & carrying/W	

WAR DIARY or INTELLIGENCE SUMMARY

Army Form C. 2118.

Place	Date	Hour	Summary of Events and Information	Remarks and references to Appendices
Firing Line	April 7	7 (cont)	him in. They were in full view of the enemy but were not fired at by them. The man stated that he had seen a dugout with 14 others when the Germans entered the trench the night before. They thought already into the dugout which killed one man and woke the remainder up. The rest were then taken prisoner & taken out of the trench. As they were retiring they came under our shell fire to the remainder, who were kept in it for quite a [while?], was left behind with the wounded & later managed to crawl back. [The officer is now sometime in the middle & sometimes left.] The bodies of 3 dead Germans were seen lying out among the remains of our wire. They were brought in & in the night of the 7th. They had been murdered almost by Stills fire, presumably their own. — No identification marks could be found on them, other than bullets blown out by the shell are believed to prevent identification of the Regiment. A small station light was seen in the enemy's trenches. It was first observed at 2150 & went out at 2155, which seems to show that it was used as a signal to the enemy's artillery. Red, White & the rockets were observed to have been seen very nightly have been the signal to the infantry to retire and leave our trenches. 	

WAR DIARY or INTELLIGENCE SUMMARY

Army Form C. 2118.

Place	Date	Hour	Summary of Events and Information	Remarks and references to Appendices
Fivy Lines	April 7		The German lines were left before the bombardment and also between 2145 and 2215 — The men appeared to mount with extend matches — (This had previously been reported by some other units) —

N.B.
1. This was evidently a pre-arranged raid very carefully planned and very well executed and the communication trenches had been registered on previous days by the minenwerfer & guns, see diary for 5th & 6th.
2. The trench raided and the minenwerfer emplacement & guns destroyed appear to be objectives of this raid — The minenwerfer was estimated to be 50 yards behind their front. The minenwerfer was reported to its destruction —
3. There was almost certainly a covering party of Germans in No Man's Land outside, the slope of the ground which made the infantry advance easy, without being seen.
4. The raiding party were armed with pistols, daggers, stick grenades and had no hand grenades in their pockets — They wore white bands on each arm — no rifles or bayonets were seen.
5. Telephone communication was cut almost at once — The left company's line was inside 5 minutes, the Brigade line 1 hour, & all line, including the Artillery, inside 1½ an hour.

Casualties:
Capt. F.S. BLAKE 1st K.S.L.I. (attached) wounded (at duty) Lieut O.C. BODLEY, T.C. LLEWELLIN, 2/Lt. F.T. DICKINSON and H.S. POWELL wounded —
Other ranks 23 killed 1/15 D.D.&L., 3 died of wounds, 21 missing, 31 wounded — Total 50 (Must 18 other ranks later found buried & dead. Total Thompson 2 killed 18 missing)| |

1577 Wt.W10791/1773 500,000 1/15 D.D.&L. A.D.S.S./Forms/C.2118.

Army Form C. 2118.

WAR DIARY
or
INTELLIGENCE SUMMARY.
(Erase heading not required.)

(151)

Instructions regarding War Diaries and Intelligence Summaries are contained in F.S. Regs., Part II. and the Staff Manual respectively. Title pages will be prepared in manuscript.

Place	Date April	Hour	Summary of Events and Information	Remarks and references to Appendices
Front Line	8th		Worked parties from Bn. in R. of W. and Somewhere helped to repair trenches last night — One man wounded this morning. All working in PICCADILLY – Shipshape.	
		1700–2000	Relieved by 1/R Irish Fusiliers and moved back to Brigade Reserve H.Q. with C and D Coys in MAILLY MAILLET, A and B Coys in AUCHONVILLERS. Good billets — Weather rather a trouble before we left firing line, as the shelling had smashed up the Tanks.	
MAILLY MAILLET.	9th to 10th 11th		Started on a new to various fatigues, working on communication trenches from Reserve to firing line, defences of villages, fatigues to Artillery &c. Rain today, first time for a week. Orders received for a move to Divisional Reserve in LOUVENCOURT tomorrow. — Men in MAILLY MAILLET have all had a lot of life lately of underclothing — No boots left, and no mule shoes —	
	12th	21.00	Moved to LOUVENCOURT. Inspected by 2/R. and Fusiliers and 4/Worcesters. Rain all day, but fine during our march — Good billets in LOUVENCOURT.	
	13th		Reorganised the Bombers, formed a Grenadier Company of 8 Squads, as we lose the Peninsula — Also started fresh training in G.M. and Signalling classes — Obtained about 14 tons of straw for purchase, to billets in billets.	

Army Form C. 2118.

WAR DIARY
or
INTELLIGENCE SUMMARY.
(Erase heading not required.)

152

Place	Date	Hour	Summary of Events and Information	Remarks and references to Appendices
LOUVENCOURT	14⁵		Classes at work, also Sqn Major & Coy Commander. Practising Patrols – Inlying 60 men in outside fatigues on blanket for men withdrawn & handed in to Advance – Weather still cold.	
	15⁵		Work as yesterday – Very cold with showers of sleet & snow – Reminder of Rather hard through shower gas chambers. Outside fatigue 60 men – Weather warmer – high wind. Heavy firing last night about 23.00. Aeroplane passed over during the night. W. obtained 200 screw stakes & 50 coils barbed wire in readiness for putting up & cutting entanglements –	
	16⁵			
	17⁵		Lecture by R.E. Officer on wire entanglements – Commenced practice in putting up another wild wet day – Party of 50 Other ranks sent to within 1 kilometre of Demoncourt.	
	18⁵		As many men as possibly sent to baths at ACHEUX – Weather continued very bad up to the 24⁵, to last three days have been fine and very dry – R. Taylor's specialist has been enlarged – We have six signals Officer each in full strength being so small – There are also about 60 other signallers in our own battalion – The also have been trained to be qualified as company signallers – Snipers have been trained with the Barrett sight, also with other trench weapons – A special raiding party has been practising in preparation for a raid on the enemy's trenches –	
	19⁵/20⁵/26⁵			

Army Form C. 2118.

WAR DIARY
or
INTELLIGENCE SUMMARY.
(Erase heading not required.)

153

Place	Date April	Hour	Summary of Events and Information	Remarks and references to Appendices
LOUVEN COURT	20th		Lieut. C.C. FOWKES joined the Battalion.	
	21st		2/Lieut. E.M. SMITH Sherwood Foresters sent to a chemical course at 4th Army H.Q.	
			2/Lieut. C.W. HANNAH Sherwood Foresters sent to 4th Army Trench Mortar School.	
	22nd		Lieut. W. ROSS rejoined the Battalion.	
	23rd		Lieut. B.S. DAVIES and one Sergeant sent for a month's course to 4th Army Infantry School.	
	25th		Lieut. Gen. Sir Aylmer Hunter Weston K.C.B. D.S.O. visited the Battalion on the anniversary of the Gallipoli landing. All those who had landed with him were drawn up on parade (a his impression). Three Officers, the Medical Officer, the Regt. Sgt. Major and 167 other ranks were present on parade. of the RSM 6 Officers and 70 other ranks had never left the Peninsula when the Medical Officer and 12 other ranks not present who had been at the landing. There were about	
			2/Lieut. L. DAVIES 13/S. Wales Borderers. Joined the Battn from England	
			2/Lieut. S.C. MURRAY O1/S. Wales Borderers.	
			2/Lieut. E.L.D. PITTEN 13/S. Wales Borderers.	
			2/Lieut. F.H. WILLIAMS 13/S. Wales Borderers.	

Place	Date	Hour	Summary of Events and Information	Remarks and references to Appendices
LOUVENCOURT	April 27		2/Lieut. G.M. EVANS 9/Sergt W. de Bordies joined the Battalion —	
	28.		Move to MAILLY MAILLET with Divisional Reserve out took over from 1/R.D. Welsh 7 withers, who also took over from us 9 t Wille at Sailly by system — Officers reconnoitred the green line Lately Divisional Reserve in case of Attack — Message received via to R.I.P. Depot from the New Zealand Depot re arrangement of Gallipoli landing — Lieut C.C. Fowkes and 1 NCO & an by each lay not tightly — course	
	29.	2300	A Raiding Party of the Battalion attempted to carry out a raid on the enemy's trenches at the HAWTHORN REDOUBT going out from the trenches held by the Royal Fusrs. The raid failed — The party advanced to the wire five minutes too soon, and suffered heavily from our own shell fire — Captain Byrne leading the party was missing, 1 Lieut down to return by a shell, and 2/Lt. D.C. PARRY-DAVIES wounded — (Snipe raid) Total casualties 1 Officer missing, 1 wounded, 3 other ranks killed, 5 missing and 16 wounded — Scheme for raid (Appendix 1) and report thereon (Appendix 2) attached. Platoon 2 Lewis Gunners from were seen in the German wire & altn by (a hand above & 9 * from Byrne) — an Officer & other went out to search to missing men. One found wounded. They collected some equipment, and had enemy repairing wire —	Appendix 1 and 2.
	30	2000		

SECRET. *copy*   RAIDING SCHEME.   *appendix I*
april 1916

Point to be raided.:-- N.W. face of HAWTHORN REDOUBT. date 29/4/16.

Co-operation between Artillery and Infantry will be by time as follows:--

- 00.00 Raiding party ready formed up outside our wire by solitary tree.(Q.4.d.250±)
  Formation as in Diagram No.1 attached.
  Artillery bombardment commences.(for artillery scheme see forward).
- 00.30 Artillery lift off wire and front trench at point to be entered and raiding party move forward to enemy's trench as soon as wire-cutters report that a passage has been made through the enemy's wire, leaving covering parties 40 yards outside.(See diagram No.2.)
- 00.55 Raiding party retire from enemy's trench and returns to our front trench.
- 01.00 Artillery cease fire.

Detail of Raiding Party.

Officer Commanding.----- Captain Byrne. 2nd South Wales Borderers.

(1) Wire Cutting Party.-- 1.N.C.O. and 9 men armed with large wire cutters, 2 bombs per man, rifle and bayonet. A roll of white tape to connect raiders to point in wire that has been cut.

(2). Two double-blocking parties, each consisting of 1 Officer, 2 N.C.O's. and 8 men and organised as follows.:-
- 2 bayonet men.   2 bombers.   1 N.C.O.(Bomber).
- Officer.   2 bayonet men. 2 bombers.
- 1 N.C.O.(bomber).

Armed as follows :-

Bayonet men. :- Each rifle and bayonet, 12 bombs and bludgeon. (1 man with axe).

Bombers. :- Bayonet as dagger, bludgeon and 24 bombs each.

N.C.O's. :- Bayonet, bludgeon, 24 bombs and revolver.

(3). Centre Party. O.C.; 1 N.C.O. and 3 men armed as follows:- each bayonet, bludgeon and 24 bombs. N.C.O. also carries revolver and electric torch.

(4). Two search parties each consisting of:-
1.N.C.O.3 bombers, 2 police. armed as follows:-
N.C.O.:- Revolver, bayonet, bludgeon, 2 bombs and electric torch.

Contd.

   Bombers.:- 24 bombs, bayonet and bludgeon.
   Police. :- Revolver, 6 bombs each, bludgeon, bayonet, 2 pair
     handcuffs, and 8 short cords for tieing tying
     prisoners.
(5). Stretch Bearers.:- 4 men. Each equipped and armed as follows:-
     light stretcher - rifle and bayonet - 2 bombs each;
     two of these men carry out a roll of white tape and
     lay it down to mark return journey; the other two
     carry two ladders - 10 feet long.
(6) Covering Party. 1 Officer, 2 N.C.O's and 12 men divided into
     two parties;of 1 for each flank, of 1 N.C.O.and 6
     men. Armed with rifle and bayonet each man also
     carries 2 bombs.

   Total of Raiding Party.:- 4 Officers, 10 N.C.O's.and 54 men.
   Note:- 1 extra ladder and 2 drag ropes are carried by centre
     party; also 2 hand bells the latter are for giving the
     signal to return.

METHOD OF ADVANCE. Prior to time for bombardment to commence raiding
party moves out to shallow dip in front of our wire and forms up
as in Diagram 1.
00.00. Artillery bombardment commences.
00.15. Raiding party crawls forward as close to our barrage as
   possible.
00.30. Raiding party moves straight to point selected for entry
   to enemy's trench. The covering party halting 40 yards short
   of enemy's wire, faces outwards and lies down; raiding
   party moves through enemy's wire, the wire cutting party
   having previously cleared the way and reported to O.C.
   On arriving opposite enemy's trench leading men of each
   blocking party throw 2 bombs into enemy's trench; 1 bayonet
   and 1 bomber move to right and left along enemy's parapet
   bombing and the remainder of blocking parties jump into the
   trench and move outwards keeping slightly behind the men
   on the parapet. As soon as a communication trench is
   reached front half of the blocking party bombs up it; the
   and blocks it; the rear half moving on down the fire
   trench and blocking it.
   The right and left search parties follow the blocking party
   in to the trench and move along behind them bombing dugouts and securing loot and prisoners.
    The centre party remains at point of entry as a
   reserve with the O.C.and takes over prisoners and loot from
   the search party. Prisoners to be sent straight off to our
   trenches under escort from the wire cutting party.

Continued:-

Stretcher Bearers and wire cutters remain outside the trench, wire cutters improving the way out. These men will be called upon by O.C., as required.

00.55.   O.C. sounds siren and sends one man to right and one to left along the trench ringing a bell, to let all know that they must retire. The word "retire" will not be used, but some countersign will be arranged.

00.57.   Leave Enemy's trench and return. Each N.C.O. of party reporting "all clear" to O.C., as he passes.

01.00.   Artillery cease fire.

If on arriving at enemy's wire, enemy open <u>heavy rifle fire</u> and machine gun fire from the trench to be raided; the raid is to be given up and party return, otherwise the trench must be rushed. In the event of a blocking party being driven in, O.C. will send two bombers up to reinforce that blocking party and keep enemy back till he can recall parties from the other flank and will retire fighting and carrying off any prisoners he may have got hold of.

Raiding party will have all indentity marks removed, will be dressed in cord breeches and gaiters and helmets covered with black cloth. Hands and faces will be blacked and a white half diamond

　　　　　　　　　　will be sewn on chest and back.
　　　---8"---

ARTILLERY CO-OPERATION SCHEME.

The following will be bombarded similtaneously:-

<u>AREA (1).</u>   Q.17/A. 100/50.   ---   Q.17/A.85/95.
　　　　　　Q.17/B. 15/00.   ---   Q.17/B.50/00.

<u>AREA (2).</u>
　　　　　　Q.10/D.75/45.   ---   Q.10/B.80/20.
　　　　　　Q.11/C.20/80.

<u>AREA (3).</u>   Q.10.B.60/20.   ---   Pt.8863.-Q Q.5.020/20.
　　　　　　Q.5.050./10.   ---   Q.11.A.30/60.

In area (3) (the area in which the raid takes place Artillery guns and targets are allotted as follows :--

<u>9-2.Howitzers.</u>   (4 Guns).
　　　　　　<u>1st.period.:-</u>
　　　　　　00.00.- 00.30. 1 Gun point 8863.
　　　　　　1 gun Q.10b.85/80.
　　　　　　1 gun Q.5C.00/15.
　　　　　　1 gun Q.5C.30/15.

　　　　　　<u>2nd period.:-</u>   1 gun point 8863.
　　　　　　00.30.- 01.00.   1 gun Q.11A.20/25.
　　　　　　　　　　　　　1 gun Q.5.020./25.
　　　　　　　　　　　　　1 gun Q.5.030/15.

<u>6"Howitzers.(2 Guns).</u>
<u>1st Period.</u>   (Both guns are N.W.face of HAWTHORN REDOUBT.
00.00.- 00.30.   (
<u>2nd Period.</u>
00.30 - 01.00.   1 Gun Q.11.A.40/80.
　　　　　　　　1 Gun Q.5C.60/10.

<u>4-5"Howitzers.</u>   :- 2 Batteries.
<u>1st period</u>
00.00-00.30.   1 Battery N.W.face HAWTHORN REDOUBT.
　　　　　　　　1 Battery Q.4D.85/00.- Pt.8863.

<u>2nd period.</u>
00.30.-01.00.   Right Battery Q.11A.05/80.and communication trench back from Redoubt.
　　　　　　　　Left Battery. Q.4D.90/25.to Point 8863.

<u>18.lb'rs.</u> :-   (5 Batteries).

18.Pdrs. :- (5 Batteries).
1st.Period.
00.00. - 00.30.   3 Batteries concentrate on wire Q.10b.30/85.
                    (point of entry)
                    2 Batteries on wire and front trench from
                    Q.4.D.85/00.-- Q.5.C.15/75/.

2nd Period.
00.30 -- 01.00.   2 Batteries on front trench from Q.4.D.90/20.
                    to Q.5.C.15/75.
                    1 Battery on communication trench.Q.10B.30/80.
                    to 95/75.
                    1 Battery down road Q.5.C.20./30.

TRENCH MORTARS.2".:-   4 Guns.
00.00. -- 00.15.   Two guns on wire opposite point of entry.
                    2 Guns on front line trench at point of entry.
00.15.   Cease fire.

MACHINE GUNS.   2 Guns from about 4.4C.90/85.to fire on
During 2nd period   enemy's front trench from point 8883.to
i.e.00.30 - 01.00. Q.4D.95/10.
                    1 Gun to fire along "Hawthorn Ridge" towards
                    point 7332.

═══

Diagram 1.

                    Formation of Raiding Party.

                              O.(O.C.)

                    O O O O O O O O O O. Wire cutting party.
                              :
                              :
                             10'
                              :
                              :

                    O   O Officer.)
                      O   O N.C.O.) Blocking
                    O O   O O   )
                    O   )
                      O   O N.C.O.) Parties.
                    O O   O O   )
                    O O   O O   )

                         O O O O   Centre Party.
               O   O
   Covering   O O   O) Search   O
              O   O O   O O) Parties.   O
    Party.   O   O O   O)   O
              O   O Covering
              O   O
              O   O Party.
              O   O O O O.   Stretcher Bearers.   O
              O   O.   O.C.Covering Party.   O
              ═══

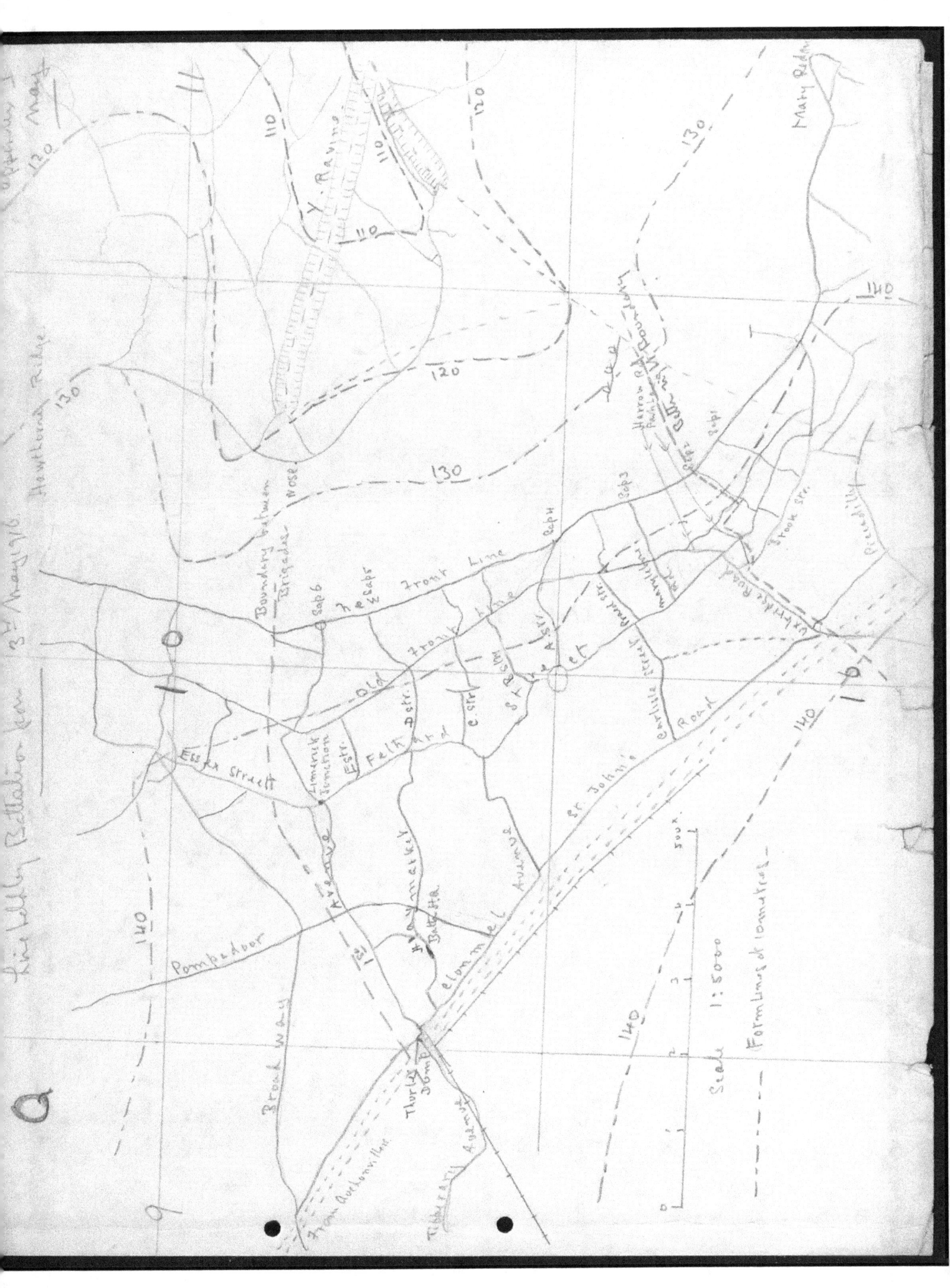

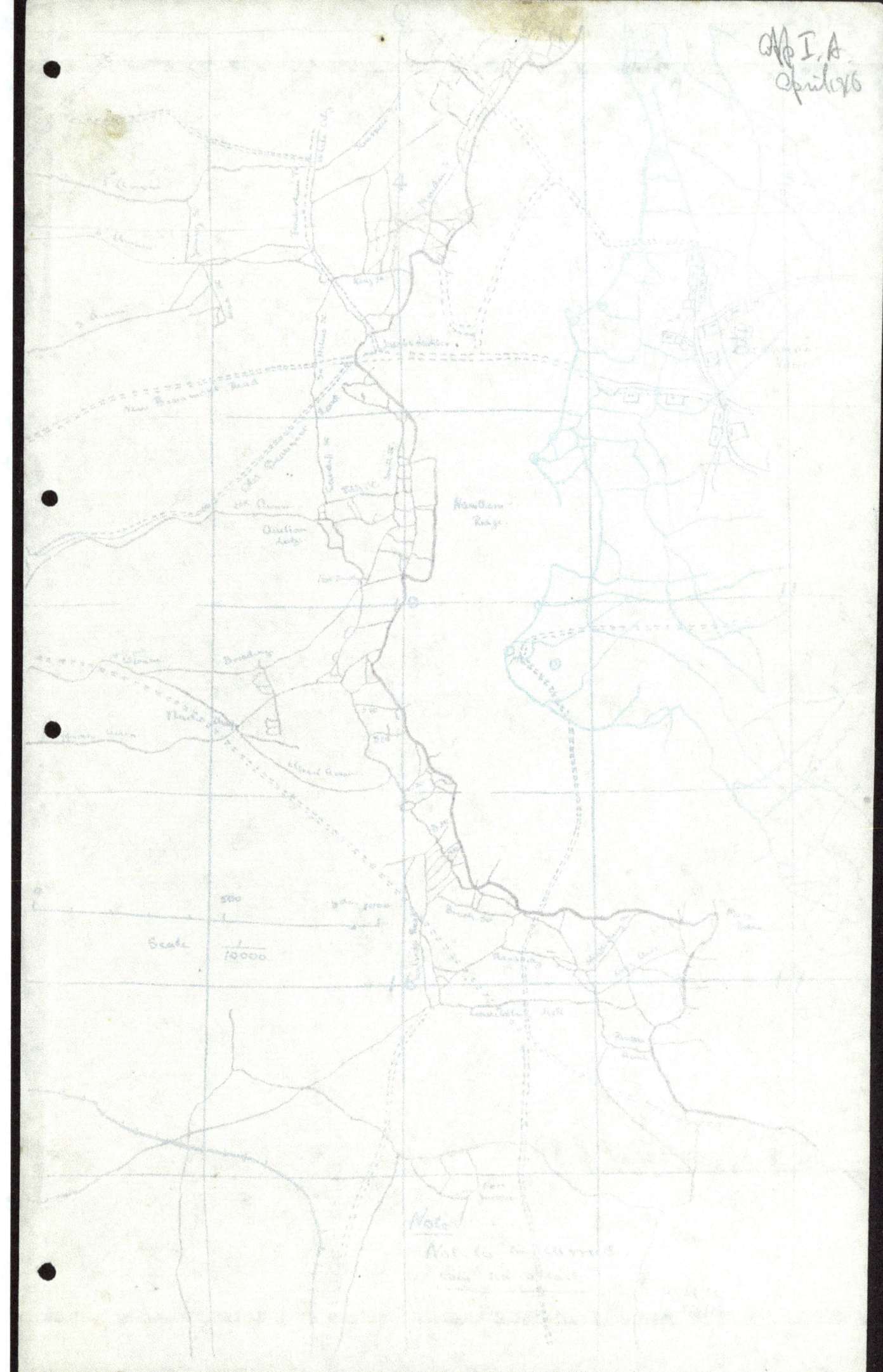

Copy.

Appendix II. April 1916

Report on Raid of night of 29th/30th April 1916.

At 11.10 p.m. the Raiding Party left our front line trench according to scheme and covered up by the artillery fire. Telephone communication from point of leaving our trench to the Bde. H.Q. was arranged.

At 11.20 p.m. our Artillery bombardment started and was replied to by the enemy's Artillery within a very few minutes with a barrage on our front line. One or two casualties occurred while waiting under the artillery fire.

At about 11.50 p.m. the raiding party moved forward a short distance, halted and then moved on again to the enemy's wire. There were several casualties during this advance and from evidence available it appears that Capt. Byrne commanding the party and 2/Lieut. Parry Davies were both hit before reaching the Enemy's wire by a shell which pitched close by them. Most of the wire cutting party were also hit and Sgt. Russell and three others commenced to cut the wire. A narrow gap was cut and the trestles pulled out. At this point several more men were hit, including the leading three men of the right blocking party who were immediately behind 2/Lt. Mayger.

The covering party had halted about 20 yards from the Enemy's wire.

2/Lieut. Mayger who had been assisting the wire cutting party and had got

(2)

well towards the German trench realised at this point that he had very few men left with him, and by the light of the Enemy Very's lights he saw about 15 to 20 men had been knocked out and were lying mostly between the Enemy's wire and the solitary tree.

2/Lieut. Edwards was a short way behind with the covering party; 2/Lieut. Mayger therefore decided it was impossible to carry on the Raid with the few men left and that they would have as much as they could do in carrying in killed and wounded.

He therefore started collecting the wounded assisted by Sergt. Russell and removing them to a point about 30 yards back.

2/Lt. Edwards and some of the covering party also came up.

All that could be found were brought back to the solitary tree.

2/Lt. Edwards, 2/Lt. Mayger and Sergt. Russell each individually searched up and down the German wire for a distance of 50 yards each way.

By this time it was 12.30 a.m. but the Artillery fire had not ceased.

Further search by 2/Lt. Edwards and Sergt. Russell was made over all the intervening ground between the tree and the German wire and all found were brought in. From the solitary tree to the front line the wounded were carried in by small parties.

(2)

2/Lieuts Edwards and Maggot coming in
with the last lot at about 12.50 am.

As far as has been ascertained at
present the casualties are as follows

Officers Missing believed killed. Capt Byrne
         Seriously wounded 2/Lt Parry Davies.

N.C.O's & men
         6 killed (includes 3 seen this morning
                  2 in German wire & 1 further N)
         16 wounded.

All casualties except those before leaving
the solitary tree were from our own Artillery
or Trench Mortars. It appears that Captain
Byrne advanced to the near edge of the
enemy's wire at about 11.55 pm; also from
the craters thereon by daylight a very large
number of shells pitched well short of the
German wire.

Three of the 6 killed mentioned above
were located this morning two on the
outer edge of the enemy's wire and one about
100 yds down the centre of the low dip
in front of the German trench, and lying
in a ditch under a bank.

(Signed) G.T Rankin Major
Comdg 1/South Wales Borderers

30/4/16

29th Division.
87th Infantry Brigade.

2nd BATTALION

SOUTH WALES BORDERERS

M A Y 1 9 1 6

WAR DIARY
or
INTELLIGENCE SUMMARY.

Army Form C. 2118.

Place	Date	Hour	Summary of Events and Information	Remarks and references to Appendices
MAILLY MAILLET	1st May	2000	Another Officers' patrol sent out which found one of the missing men dead, and brought him in. Officers reconnoitred fire line preparatory to taking over —	Appendix I Fr. May
	2nd			See Appx Wr. Dairy
	3rd	2000	moved up to firing line and relieved the 1st Newfoundland Regt. ("88" Bde in the left of the right sector of the Divisional line — This is a new line for Battalion, and accommodation for ammunition, aid post, etc. very limited, in fact no aid post at all — The cos of A,B,D from right to left, C in close support in FETHARD STREET. Boundaries night to left. See Appendix I World helmets were in use on the line Q.16. 6/1 to Q.10.97. which on taking over was an an excavated shelter the new forward line, which was being carried up from the rear — revetting — traverse etc. retirs and roofs have to be fired from AUCHONVILLERS, carrying parties have to stay in AUCHONVILLERS, carrying parties into the support at night while in poor and plentiful. 5 tanks in these separate states — Trench very old and a poor condition, especially the support line — communication and looking forward from N — The Battalion harness B Firing Lines, 6 in	

WAR DIARY or INTELLIGENCE SUMMARY

Army Form C. 2118.

Place: Trench line

Date	Hour	Summary of Events and Information	Remarks and references to Appendices
May 3rd		Front line and 2 in support. At night two guns were pushed forward to the new front line and placed there.	
4		Carried on work. No difficulty came here in front line by day, as it shows still fine — working parties — have parties from the Border Regt. working by day and night on new trench connecting THURLES DUMP with UXBRIDGE ROAD, and new cookhouse, dug out, and latrines in IVY AVENUE. Reinforcements of 76 N.C.O's and men found, 30 other ranks per draft and the remainder men (from Hospital etc.) in EGYPT. Enemy inflicted on our new trench, 19 firing at working parties — German wounded.	
5			
6	0010	Heavy firing from our by AUTHUILE WOOD Salient, X.1. Rated almost another man when machine gun fire was moderated — Enemy did answer.	
	0130.	Rain last night but not enough to dampen trenches. Trench between Saps 5 and 6 dug out to about 5'6" all day; also portion of trench between 3rd H Border Regt. working parties still continuing. 108 E superior in mutual defence, Sujet Road Ti in main avenues. Enemy artillery active to-day. Minenwerfer on the right bay, and slung heap. All day. Casualties 6 wounded (2 on duty) shapnel helmets saved the lives of 2/LT F. RICE wounded, buried 19 other ranks with him —	

WAR DIARY
INTELLIGENCE SUMMARY

Army Form C. 2118.

Place	Date	Hour	Summary of Events and Information	Remarks and references to Appendices
Firing line	May 1st		Made purchase on new line to dawn. Old & support lines — Snipers claimed are over killed — A party of the enemy were seen working in the front trench & subsequently shelled at the nose of the Salient — numerous parties in the enemy line at Q10.D 70-80. During the day the enemy repeated out-bursts of rifle & such a manner as to rouse suspicions of an intended raid. At 6.15 am to 6.15 am on front trench at Q.10.1 and Q.10.2 was reposted with H.E. Lazyville about 6" — At 8 am four minenwerfer shells fell in the vicinity of Q.10.1 and Q.10.2. Shrapnel was also fired on the line in front of Q.16.9. At 5.15 pm [?] was a shower of about 30 whizz bangs all along the line — and the minenwerfer fired on the trench at Q.16.8, Q.16.9. The immediately ? ours rifle repelled similar retaliation MARY REDAN — A raid was also to take place in the Division on our right, and a heavy barrage was opened on the area from the front trench line & lining dug outs, and [?] gun, brought on Sep 6. The enemy on retaliation was slight to commence at 11.45. Two officers Standing Patrol were sent from dusk to 11.30 pm ? s of Menin Road — Sons an enemy standing patrol of 6 men ? in front of Main German ? — [?] w sheard at Q10.D 50.70.	

WAR DIARY or INTELLIGENCE SUMMARY

Army Form C. 2118.

Place	Date	Hour	Summary of Events and Information	Remarks and references to Appendices
Firing Line	7th May	23.10	The R.I.R. [?] on our right reported two minenwerfer from enemy started a heavy bombardment of trench & listening posts with rifle & machine gun and guns. – This was in with rifle & machine gun fire till 11.45 when our guns commenced. The bombardment to be prepared – The Artillery F.O.O at Redt [?] H.Q. was able to bring to fire & one of his guns on O.11.D.52M which was the supposed position of the minenwerfer, and on this fire being opened the minenwerfer ceased. There was very little retaliation by the enemy & no shells fell anywhere in our trenches, and their rifle & machine gun fire & that of the trench mortars was apparently carried through. The artillery cease firing for two minutes at 12.06 am as pre-arranged & ceased at 12.15 am – At 1 am rifle & machine gun fire broke out from beyond the MARY railway, accompanied by heavy trench mortar bombardment. Our guns did not answer except for a very short period. At 1.29 am the trench mortars became very violent and then ceased altogether – it is not known for all this fighting were about – Casualties 2 wounded.	
	8th		Good progress made in front line. About 4.30 pm a dozen things began coming over about the front, otherwise artillery was quiet. Casualties nil and 1 wounded.	

WAR DIARY
or
INTELLIGENCE SUMMARY.

Army Form C. 2118.

159

Place	Date	Hour	Summary of Events and Information	Remarks and references to Appendices
Firing Line	May 9th		Progress made in Saps nineteen, between Saps 5 and 6 there are 4 Ray's about 6' deep & 1½' to 2' to occupy – Right ½ of 4 there are above 4 Ray's a similar ditch not unrevetted, need lot to occupy – About 40 yards of high wire entanglement between saps 4 and 3, starting at right – Forming a wire mesh fence – Our Officers Patrol went out from Sap 5 at 12.15 am last night to listen for suspected mechanical contrivance – They waited till 2 am but heard nothing. Enemy was heard working about Q.10.1. The Border Rgt. Patrols have made four forays into the entanglement and front, and are now working at sketch of old CLONMEL AVENUE. G.O.C. 29th Division came round the trenches and expressed himself as very well satisfied with the work done by the Battalion and desired that his satisfaction should be conveyed to the men – Snipers claimed a hit on a German looking over the parapet at Q.10.D.55.70 –	
	10th		One of our Q high wires put in front of new trench last night, between Saps 5 and 6 – Enemy had a large number of flares – Patrol went out at 8.30 pm from Sap 6 and sketched trench at Q.10.D.55.70, & that in rear of the same came from their trench – Enemy fired a good many Verey lights at us just to day	

Army Form C. 2118.

WAR DIARY
or
INTELLIGENCE SUMMARY.
(Erase heading not required.)

Instructions regarding War Diaries and Intelligence Summaries are contained in F. S. Regs., Part II. and the Staff Manual respectively. Title pages will be prepared in manuscript.

(160)

Place	Date May	Hour	Summary of Events and Information	Remarks and references to Appendices
Firing Line	10th (cont)		At 9 am this morning our sniper shot a man looking over enemy parapet at Q.11.C.67.50 – Enemy artillery fairly quiet to-day. 3 shrapnel near R.S.H.Q. and one large howitzer H.E. which landed in the tent near LIMERICK JUNCTION. There was a solitary shell fired about 9pm – also a great midnight two rounds fell like rattles, and at 8pm two slight explosions were heard in enemy trench about Q.10.D.80.10. A cloud of smoke & vapour was seen to rise with them & travel with the wind – The day and night kept up well after the rain – Capt. H.P. GARNETT of Welsh Regiment joined to Battn to have 1st army (W) 15 mm: month reported two hospitals in Egypt – Some new wire was observed in front & enemy trench to south & his Salient. We sketched a new trench to join to Sap to left of SA.1 Saw enemy moving slowly by the nose of the Salient – We put some more strands into the wire put out on night (W) 9/10 – Enemy was busy at the nose of the Salient late day, to smoke & dust seen rising in the salient where believed to be a cookhouse – Enemy artillery active all yesterday. Shelling our line with 77 mm field guns – Both working parties completed cookhouse + aid post, now ready for furnishing – Subsequently	
	11th		...	

1577 Wt. W10791/1773 500,000 1/15 D. D. & L. A.D.S.S./Forms/C. 2118.

WAR DIARY or INTELLIGENCE SUMMARY

Place	Date May	Hour	Summary of Events and Information	Remarks and references to Appendices
ENGLEBELMER	14		50 men in the morning and 50 in the afternoon furnishing out and draining GARION AVENUE — 10 men working with Town Commandant to 10 with R.E. in the evening — Draft of 16 men arrived —	
	15		Revd had from dawn to 10 am — Enemy main fatigue 200 men working on FETHARD STREET and ST JOHNS ROAD, 50 men from 6am to noon and 50 men from 11 noon to 6 pm. Class about 150 men on R.E. fatigue —	
			Lieut A.B. COUSSMAKER joined the Battn from 3rd Service Battn. 12=5=16. Lieut J.H. HATFORD 3rd SWB. 2nd Lieut E.G. JONES 9th SWB " " C.R. WARDLE 9th SWB } Joined the Battn. 13 = 5 = 16. " " A.E. MORGAN 1st SWB Temp.	
	16		Fine day. — Working parties on following places. TIPPERARY AVENUE — FETHARD ST — CLONMEL AVENUE. Also about 150 men on R.E. fatigue.	
	17		Working parties on TIPPERARY AVENUE — CLONMEL AVENUE — FETHARD ST — also about 150 on R.E. fatigue.	
	18		Fatigues arrived in morning. Moved also back to ACHEUX WOOD in evening. Went into huts in the WOOD.	

WAR DIARY
or
INTELLIGENCE SUMMARY
(Erase heading not required.)

Place	Date	Hour	Summary of Events and Information	Remarks and references to Appendices
ACHEUX WOOD	19th to 28th		242 men & Divisional working parties daily while in Corps Reserve – following classes were started – 1. Bombing 32 men, 8 days course, to embark 6 Headquarter Squads of 8 men each, and form a reserve squad for Coys each Coy already having two squads trained – 2. Lewis Guns all sent to Corps as part of the Coy establishment – formed to class of 32 men for a four days course – A further class of 26 men to commence on completion of first course, thus having sufficient men for 16 guns – 3. Signalling class of 8 men re-assembled under Capelli, Sergeant. 4. Bayonet Fighting. All class classes were put through a Bayonet Fighting course & no time for them – 5. Working Parties – numbers were found from each Battalion on alternate days, as far as possible – Boundary canals to be put under the Coy Bombing Officers, the working parties were trained daily under the Coy Bombing Officers. 6. Wiring. Remainder of men available were trained in wiring & consolidate – on the 24th a demonstration of obtaining wire with & Bangalore Torpedo was carried out, and a casualty rate of 38 & seconds enabled to be obtained in 25 minutes –	
	23rd		All Officers and N.C.O's available attended a practice communication between a certain	

INTELLIGENCE SUMMARY

(Erase heading not required.)

Place	Date	Hour	Summary of Events and Information	Remarks and references to Appendices
ACHEUX WOOD	May 25th		Patrol aeroplane and parties reported firing line twice. Battalion and Brigade Headquarters in advance. Communication was obtained by means of flares and signalling lamps. Headquarters now marked by a white back circle and 2 circles to Battalion and Brigade respectively. An attempt was also made to move by means of black but this was not successful.	
	26th		All officers and others ranks available attended a demonstration of a smoke bomb at LOUVENCOURT. 2nd Lieut W.H. KELLY joined the Battalion.	
	28th		80 men left on Divisional working parties. Moved to its firing line and relieved 1st Newfoundland Regt. in our old line, left subsector of right sector of Divisional front. Battn. front & trench from Q.16.c.5/6 to Q.10.b/1 (BEAUMONT, 57d.SW) AUCHONVILLERS sector. Length 540 yards. On this occasion which was carried out in the afternoon by 2 Coys at 1.10 mins interval, 1st from leaving ACHEUX at 1pm. Working parties did not arrive till 8pm. Casualties were accidentally killed whilst at ACHEUX. Heavy rain fell on the 24th, slight rain in the evening of 28th. Weather otherwise very fine. Many men suffer from colds & rheumatism. No Stores in huts & found very damp. Army Boy School FLIXECOURT — Capt H.C. GARNETT, RSM A.B. COUSSMAKER + 2 sergeants to 4th Army Boys School FLIXECOURT.	

INTELLIGENCE SUMMARY

(Erase heading not required.)

Place	Date	Hour	Summary of Events and Information	Remarks and references to Appendices
Firing line	May 29th		Corps holding line as follows. Day right, e. ents. A.Coy., B in support. FETHARD STREET. Remainder lying about T.1, 1st AVENUE, HAYMARKET, CLONMEL AVENUE, CARLISLE STREET, and UXBRIDGE ROAD. Found a large amount of work to be done in new line stated near communication trench from near e. street to new line last night. Also enfiladed large number of sandbags which were encumbering the fire steps, and did some of this. Listening patrols sent out from 2/E (strong strength) wood / each kept dumped in the enemy. I believe Q 10.d. Also the usual sounds of transport going into BEAUMONT HAMEL. Casualties. 1 man accidentally wounded.	
	30th	Work to 6am 30th	included repairs and drainage in C.T.s, deepening & improving new trench, emptying sandbags, working in FETHARD STREET, Ts in S.6.c+d. slow communication T.s. About 10 p.m. 29th Sounds of heavy mining were heard in a deep boulevard dug out in FETHARD STREET, near the foot of C. street. All work round was stopped at 11.30 p.m. & officers and M/C. were sent down to listen. Between 11.30 p.m. & 12.40 am Sounds were heard, in 6 occasions, of picks, shovels & other work. There appears to be a lot of work going on in the enemy	

WAR DIARY or INTELLIGENCE SUMMARY

Place	Date	Hour	Summary of Events and Information	Remarks and references to Appendices
Firing Line	May 30		Salient. We observed a wiring party in front of the nose at 1 am this morning with Lewis gun fire, steam & smoke was instantly seen & sounds of timber & material being chopped — also a large amount of rifle & Rain commenced to fall about 11 pm last night, & the wire was in bad state this morning — 2/Lt S.C. MURRAY, 7/Lt E.D. PITTEN & Sergeants to 2/6 DW School ACTEUX	
	31st	6 am	Two parties of some east from Bedn Regt & another were employed in draining Southern portion of FETHARD STREET and ST-JOHN'S ROAD and CARLISLE STREET. Put out a foot deal of wire last night, from 40 to 60 yards out. One belt of 7 yards width turned out from left to the left, also length of 60 yards — Another belt of new lay and an apron linked the two with old wire — first 2 left — Length about 120 yards 16 men of Bedn Regt started second belt of new cooperwire, the are built but not being long enough —	
			Today we had some Bedn partier, drainer & working in Saverster Trench. It tended quite dry by the evening — refuttin sounds of wiring heard under FETHARD STREET. —	

Wilhelm Gill
Lt-Col R Welsh Borderers

29th Division
87th Infantry Brigade.

2nd BATTALION

SOUTH WALES BORDERERS.

J U N E 1 9 1 6

Appendices attached:-   Patrol Reports.
                        Instructions fro Attack.

WAR DIARY or INTELLIGENCE SUMMARY

Army Form C. 2118.

147

Place	Date	Hour	Summary of Events and Information	Remarks and references to Appendices
Thiepval	June 1st		Quiet. There were communication trenches as now in hand between 96 and new firing line. One each at PRAED STR, E STR, and R STR. Worked on at new line. Drainage (all trenches) lands & de 25 men of Border Regt worked in St JOHN'S ROAD & CARLISLE STREET completing the drainage — Our aeroplanes are very active at present. We located a machine gun at 10am firing at them from O.10.d.70.75. German aeroplane in particularly new gun about 10.30 am. Several whizzbangs came over, he came down 2 wheel & wounded 4 men & a path working at corner of FETHARD STREET — During the day, enemy arcs observed looking our trenches O.11.c.20.30. May be Observation Post. — Casualties 4 wounded. 50 men found from Infantry Base Depot. Last night the enemy put bursts of MG fire all along W. Trenches new & old line Several shots fell in road between THURLES DUMP and AUCHONVILLERS. Interior parts of lost wing MR heard nothing. Enemy arrest Spidin Ran about. This, together with change in weather (wet morning) & wind) & the feeble looking No [illegible] may mean a relief. Work carried on as usual. Tied a living gun at Jeannetel O.11.B.30.30. 2Lt W.H. EVANS from 3Y Retn, joined Batln.	

2449 Wt. W14957/M90 750,000 1/16 J.B.C. & A. Forms/C.2118/12

WAR DIARY or INTELLIGENCE SUMMARY

Army Form C. 2118.

Place: Firing Line
Date: June 3rd
Hour:

Sent out a strong fighting patrol last night to the lines in front of Coy at Q.16.d.80.80. Strength 2 Officers 15 men – 16 Officer it seems was on ahead down towards the road bifurcation at Q.16.d.95.55. It was thought that a Hill had taken place in the German lines, and that the news of his mishap sent Patrol up this road. We hoped to capture one or two of them – Patrol neither saw nor heard anything – They kept the road important cull years, to be a sunken road about 8' to 10' deep, and never used, grass not trodden down. Also failed to find the bifurcation, all hidden in grass or growing – Machine gun fired a burst on road near THURLES again last night. We enclose 15 minutes –

87 men of the 7th Corps Cyclist Battn. have been taken hunt to the Battln. Many of them are time expired 2y Div. Cyclist Coy. turned up before going out to Shallufa, & are regular soldiers – Our strength is still very small, only 10 of the recruits having joined up to date. Strength is taken 608 –

10.0 The enemy sent us splinter proofs last night over the backs of the traverses which carried on as usual.

Enemy's artillery much quieter than usual yesterday. We put it a bombardment from 12 to 1:30 am. Our air post of a raiding scheme elsewhere. We

WAR DIARY or INTELLIGENCE SUMMARY

Army Form C. 2118.

(16a)

Place	Date	Hour	Summary of Events and Information	Remarks and references to Appendices
Trinity	4th		With draw from the front line, except for the sentry groups & Lewis Guns, & distributed the men in dugouts in the old line & retired still in case of attack. In front of fort there was very little retaliation ever, most of it going "over". ST. JOHN'S ROAD — The enemy's machine of a searchlight in No Man's Land, & kept up a fairly accurate machine fire on our parapet. Patrol day we spent some time in watching terrain. Davies states to 1st Avenue to allow of a stretcher bearing. Before to headquarters we put up 20 splints to proofs behind the terrain in front but it 21 stretchers shelters. The enemy was both seen & heard working in front. Hepner 20.7 mm shells round L3 during the morning — enemy very quiet but no W— Put it now fairs Hammered, but find very little — No walk observed. We carried a wire as usual yesterday. Enemy artillery very active to-day — Sep 6 & the mine were quite heavily shelled with 10.5 & 15 cms H.E. Whizz bangs along the line as well — 100 h O.S. 13 under t. Ly. Casualties, 1 man wounded Capt Levi arrived on night 4/5, away to our right — Enemy reply infrequently. We sent a bombardment	
	5th			

WAR DIARY or INTELLIGENCE SUMMARY

Army Form C. 2118.

Place	Date	Hour	Summary of Events and Information	Remarks and references to Appendices
Firing Line	6th		to be very futile. Watched same practice as on last occasion & showing in the hole cut for a vent after all the registration. Left 6 — At 4 pm yesterday an enemy system watches flying from somewhere at Q16b.70.80. A Lewis gun opened a hive but without effect — Started to rain last night, & continued all day. Made the trenches very bad & muddy. Spent the whole day cleaning out mud & water. At much worse than yesterday, all mud & water. Had a party of 120 6/KOSB to help. — Rained all last night, & most of this morning — Enemy field short 25 large H.E. at us yesterday afternoon of which 7 were "duds". A wooden post was seen in the Boiler yesterday afternoon from 5.15 pm to 8.25 pm — Relieved this afternoon by 1/Border Regt., & went into Divisional Reserve at	
	7th		ENGLEBELMER — We have had a new system of organisation in the firing line then came in Reserve. Each of the three coys in the line habit or platoon in support. — By day no one appears on the part his used in respect the sentries. By night the	

WAR DIARY or INTELLIGENCE SUMMARY

Army Form C. 2118.

Place	Date	Hour	Summary of Events and Information	Remarks and references to Appendices
7am the	7th		[men?] were no [troops?] The sentry groups until work was finished, when the line was manned by two platoons — The work organisation was as follows — One platoon was "duty platoon" for 24 hours — It found all sentries & patrols — The other three did 8 hours work a day — This was found a satisfactory arrangement —	
EMLEGELMER St	8th		Rain again to-day, from 5 in the evening — 230 men on fatigue — 75 men & helpers last night in living line, carrying [tools?] from dug-outs OH [?] I send dear dotting to a large number. 2/Lt. T. ROBINSON. 2/S/M R with draft of 20 men joined Batt. 9/Lt. A.E. MORGAN & 1 NCO & 20 men joined HQ course. 6 days to-day.	
	9th		Large fatigues again — 95 men out all evening W — 272 on today & tonight W — Company commanders reconnoitred the question of what to hold in event of attack —	
	10th		Another heavy day, every man on fatigue — 150 men with Rhodes Rgt. in front line and 248 on R.E. fatigue — Heavy showers of rain —	
	11th		4 men per platoon fired 5 rounds each in gas helmets. Result as usual, very good. The first three from each plat. did a 14 day course at ACHEUX firing the range — Every body else on fatigue —	

2449 Wt. W14957/M90 750,000 1/16 J.B.C. & A. Forms/C.2118/12.

WAR DIARY
or
INTELLIGENCE SUMMARY

Army Form C. 2118.

(172)

Place	Date June	Hour	Summary of Events and Information	Remarks and references to Appendices
ENGLEBELMER	12th / 13th / 14th		Heavy working parties and fatigues by day & night, every available man sent. On old days it has been possible to give specialists a little training. The weather very bad since we came out of trenches, rain every day.	
	15th		March to LOUVENCOURT in early evening - took over old billets. 260 men & Officers had to be left behind, about 1600 Rum rejoined at 7.30pm & the remainder at 6am. Then the 16th — Capt. A.A. HUGHES from 3rd Battn. joined Battalion yesterday -	
LOUVENCOURT	16th		Lieut. Col. T. GOING. D.S.O. rejoined the Battn. and took over command 2/Lieut. P.L. PRYSE from 3rd Battn. joined the Battalion — Capt. E.D. Hartley Capt. C.B. HABERSHON rejoined the Battn. —	
	17th			
	18th / 19th / 22nd		Practice every day for an attack on the German lines — Two Brigade mornings & one Divisional manœuvres in the week — Move up into front line trenches — and relieved 1/M.L.D. Regt. —	
	23rd / Today		Two coys in front line. An oh left, D on right. C by St. John's Road & warm huts. B coy ? regnls & nuredimolks 16 Lewis Guns at ENGLEBELMER — Very heavy thunderstorm burst about 2.45pm + till 11pm held water. Killed W. EVANS, E.L. JONES, L.R. WARDLE. Shot Wounded 2 Infantry battn the nursnally of Lieut D. Wilfrid Flight. It high & growing & remainder in ENGLEBELMER	

WAR DIARY or INTELLIGENCE SUMMARY

Army Form C. 2118.

Place	Date	Hour	Summary of Events and Information	Remarks and references to Appendices
Firing Line	24th June		Reported for duty — Artillery commenced cutting wire about 10 am — Something went up on first section of trenches to N. of BEAUCOURT RIDGE — It was intended to observe fire of 9.0" but the wind shifted it. I am inclined to hasten it for the night. At 10 pm our artillery ceased activity and the enemy who had been quiet all day, started an even heavier bombardment & support barrage in the front line & in the Sellpark — It was 15 am & 10.5 am hostilities ceased. Two accidentally wounded & 1 sick in wire cutting party.	
	25th May		From 2.15 am onwards we cut gaps in our own wire "during this artillery enemy very quiet. Wire cutting carried on by artillery fire up to 5 am without being fired at, and saw enemy opening in his second trench. Nicolson's Lewis gun fire was rapidly firing on men to prevent enemy repairing his wire — During the day we cleared the mud & water out of our trenches — Wire opposite our left has not failed at — We saw an enemy aeroplane shot down by our own machine over the BEAUCOURT RIDGE. Three allied aeroplanes destroyed by our aeroplanes —	

WAR DIARY or INTELLIGENCE SUMMARY

(Erase heading not required.)

Army Form C. 2118.

Place	Date	Hour	Summary of Events and Information	Remarks and references to Appendices
Third Div	25 (am)	2700	Gas for directed at POZIERES village — Gas was to have been discharged at 11 p.m. but conditions were not favourable but bombardment with flat noise rifles was carried out.	
	26. W day		Two officers patrols went out last night at 2300 to examine enemy wire Two gaps were reported passable on south face & salient, one in wire south of SUNKEN ROAD — Our Artillery was active throughout the night	
		0900	& also throughout the day — At 0900 a special heavy artillery bombardment was carried out, mainly directed on enemy front line system. This continued till 1010 hours.	
		1015	At 1015 a bombardment of great intensity was developed from 4 Div front north to within 1/2 the REDAN which appeared drawn a maximum fire between 0930 or 1030 on Gau and smoke on Glory heavies on to front line system to which enemy replied with artillery heavies on to front line system to which enemy replied with Battalion's front line front & support line were emitted from mainly H.E. mainly directed on Wire cutting — from 11 am Enemy Artillery was cutting enemy wire in front at night intern and medium trench mortars & wire round and South of Moor of Redan at 2 & of 55/10 & apparently with poor effects. BEAUMONT HAMEL appeared in a [ie] 36 Div moon W smoke gas in vicinity of THIEPVAL salient —	
		1420		

WAR DIARY or INTELLIGENCE SUMMARY

Army Form C. 2118.

Place	Date	Hour	Summary of Events and Information	Remarks and references to Appendices
Front Line	26 1916 (cont)	1600	From 1600 to 1700 enemy replied with H.E. on firing line, Supply Line and a communication trench. Heavy losses in Snowdrop & Valley of 5th Avenue & they rather on left rank. Heavy rain fell, & trenches refill knee full of water.	
		0050		
		2230 to 2330	"Silent Period." Two Officers patrols went out to examine enemy wire. One report: 100 yards S. of NOSE & Salient and no wire about 150 yards further to the right, all thin purposes. Other report from the 1st Newfoundland Regt. left Rath. seeks at Sap 3 intending to raid the South face of the Salient at Q10d 8.5/40 – They failed to get through the enemy's wire.	
		2430		
	27th X day.	0545	Our artillery increased in activity, and at 0545 another was discharged from our trenches for 10 minutes – Enemy utterly with H.E., to a lesser period. Enemy shelled Ratho front & support lines with H.E. and blew in several Bays, also two of the communication trenches. Artillery & trench mortars continued cutting enemy's wire with good effect.	
		0830	Our heavy Artillery shelled BEAUMONT HAMEL, BEAUCOURT and several villages in rear throughout the day.	

WAR DIARY or INTELLIGENCE SUMMARY

Army Form C. 2118.

(17b)

Place	Date	Hour	Summary of Events and Information	Remarks and references to Appendices
Front Line	27 June (cont)	23.30	Three raiding parties went out from Divisional front, one of the Newfoundland Regt. going out from the Battn front at Sap 3 — At the same time three Officers patrols went out, one from each of A, C, D, Coys to cut gaps in the enemy's wire — (Confer see Appendix I) Artillery fire was lifted off enemy's front trench from 2400 to 0100 Bg 243 from gaps had been cut by our patrols in enemy's wire — At this time the raiding parties came into contact with the enemy — Bomb fights started in the enemy trenches, and machine guns & rifle fire opened — The patrols were forced to lie down & return on opportunity offered — Patrols had no casualties — damage was observed on our front.	(Confer see Appendix I)
		2400	Enemy sent up flares & rockets and kept an heavy trench blast about half an hour — Rain fell most of last night, and trenches got very wet and muddy —	
	28 June	0700	Artillery bombardment increased, and from 0715 to 0725 enemy was discharged from our front trench — Enemy opened on first trench with H.E. and continued in short bursts throughout the morning — Enemy shelled ENGLEBELMER during the day, and B Coy in reserve there lost 1 Sgt killed, 6 wounded (1 officer wounded) & one shell shock —	
		7330	Patrols o/c Battn. liner to examine & cut wire — Right patrol cut	

Place	Date	Hour	Summary of Events and Information	Remarks and references to Appendices
Trenches	28. (cont)		Some more wire on line of trestles running from Q11 c 25/40 to Q11 c 60/05 - They were fired at by a machine gun from direction Q11 c 50/45, and flares were sent up from enemy's second line trench. Patrol returned safely at ca 24.55. Left patrol went out at same time and examined the wire on the front of enemy's salient — They reported the wire was well cut to passable. Practically no wire where The front trench appeared to be quite good — Patrol returned safely at 24.35	
	29. Y'tley	0100.	Raiding Party of R. Dublin Fusiliers left our trenches from vicinity of Ref. 6 after having patrols out on the interior of raiding enemy's front line of the NOSE. The raid failed owing to a light burst mortar of their second line & caused several casualties, and a machine gun opened fire on front of the enemy trench, caught them as they came back — Trenches & CTs very wet, and much knocked about no rain to day — Trenches & CTs very wet, and much knocked about by shell fire, especially the left company's area, where the enemy appear to fire at the trench mortar in C. Steel & the vicinity of the Russian Sap at Ref 6 — Wire cutting carried on during the morning — The medium trench mortar	

WAR DIARY or INTELLIGENCE SUMMARY

Army Form C. 2118.

Place	Date	Hour	Summary of Events and Information	Remarks and references to Appendices
Irish Line (cont)	29 June		settling the wind to the SOUTH of the ANCRE — They (we) were very effective at this work —	
		1600 to 1720	Our artillery carried out a heavy bombardment of the enemy's front line trenches in conjunction with 8th Division on the flanks — The enemy made very little reply —	
		1730	About 75 shells were fired by our 15" howitzers at POZIERES (Q 11 c 50/45) and did considerable damage — The enemy's artillery appears to weaken. Has filed an estimate 15 cm, 10 cm, 10 cm H.E. with an occasional shrapnel — It always falls much the same locality, and it seems as though no battling batteries to different targets all day to the line — Our casualties have been very few about 8 since we came into the line — The reserve coy at Bethlehem had more than rest — We keep most of the men in deep dug outs in the old line and FETHARD STREET — Activity in the front line by day with no sentry except in the old line — 18 pounder batteries on finishing all day by 3 pm did away any attempt at attack would be dealt with — By night the four trench guns fire the front coys to heartily prefer them than coys kept	

WAR DIARY
INTELLIGENCE SUMMARY
(Erase heading not required.)

Army Form C. 2118.

Place	Date	Hour	Summary of Events and Information	Remarks and references to Appendices
Trony Line	29 (cont)		the truth time — Along the left lane & platoon support in the old lux the rest of the men being in dug-outs all day — Artillery fire practically all night, 8 Victor guns & one 4.7 win guns kept up continuous fire on the enemy's wire to prevent him mending it. — During we have each night since 1/m night (we are in its tenth on 7 day) there has been no firing at all except the artillery, no support lines & trenches in rear. — During this the slow patrols go out to reconnoitre & cut the enemy wire.	
		2230	To-day should have been Z day, the day of attack, but all arrangements were postponed 48 hours yesterday evening — To-day is [Matter] Y.I. day — Two officers [Savage] went out, one to try & capture a [German] of hyper trench, and the other to examine the wire on the NOSE, the latter being from 50-2230 to 2330. The [first patrol] shot a German made to trying him in to effort our attempts II. The second patrol found two gaps close together on the NOSE — Enemy bombarded our wire heavily with H.E. for about 45 minutes,	O/p II
	30. 1/2 day	0800		

WAR DIARY or INTELLIGENCE SUMMARY

Army Form C. 2118.

2 S W B
180
FC 4

Place	Date	Hour	Summary of Events and Information	Remarks and references to Appendices
Firing Line	June 30 (cont)		Men in several bays in front line & FETHARD STREET — He went to the left bay near Sap 6 again — No casualties — We put up a special bombardment from 0800 to 0920, which increased in intensity about 0845 and became a very heavy shelling we have yet carried out — The Trench mortars finished all the wire S. of the NOSE to-day, I then proceeded to their bombs into the German trench, apparently with good effect — During the afternoon a battery of 4.5" Howitzers endeavoured to get in to a small redoubt in the German front line at Q 11 c 30/40, but without much success — The Infm. promised to turn heavy Howitzers on it, but at time Summary (1820) nothing had yet happened — Orders received that to-morrow 2nd July, and that the hour to assault, zero is 7.30 am — Following appendices attached :— Appendix III. Orders for the period. Similar diving bombardment & that of to-day Appendix IV. — Scheme for the attack Appendix V. Orders for 72 nig W.	III IV V

87th Bde. Appendix I.
June 1916.

Three wire-cutting patrols went out last night as follows:—

1. Right patrol left Sap 3 11.35 pm & moved straight to Q.11.c.45/20 & commenced to cut wire still in gap cut by Art: Patrol cut 3 gaps about this point; two broad gaps and one smaller one 50ˣ further North.

Patrol reports shortly after commencing work, bombing started to the North & Ey machine guns opened fire from

(a) Ey's 2nd trench about Q.11.c.75/25
(b) about pt 54 or a little West.

Patrol also reports Ey's front trench from Pt 54 to Pt 60 apparently not occupied.
Work was stopped by Ey's M.G. fire & patrol returned 1.30 am
Very lights were all sent from 2nd or

on 3rd trenches.

2. Centre patrol left our trenches at Sap 3 at 11.40 pm & moved straight to Q.11.c.00/30, examined the wire from this point to Q.11.c.20/30 & found it passable. At Q.11.c.20/30 wire bends towards SE & at this point patrol cut gap 21 ft. wide through the wire.
Patrol reports at 12.30 am bombing started close by at about Q.11.c.20/32 (there was apparently noone in the German trench to begin with).
An M.G. then opened fire from somewhere about German 2nd trench NE of pt 60 & also from near Pt 54.
Enemy sent up a red rocket from 3rd line & Ey Art. opened shortly afterwards. Very's lights were sent up from 2nd trench.

Left patrol.

Left front line 12.0 midnight & moved straight out Q10d95/p arriving 12.20 am found 2 gaps through wire 10* apart each gap 6ft wide. Before work had started about 8 flares were sent up from (German line (believes to be 1st line) & almost immediately afterwards bombing started just to the North of the nose — Machine guns & rifle fire were also reported by this patrol from Ey's 1st line. Ey sent up a Red flare & 10 minutes later Ey Art opened a barrage on our front line. Patrol returned 12.45 am. There were no casualties & work was not interfered with till the bombing started at about 12.30 am —

(Sd) G.T Raikes Major
Comdg X M Bndu

3.45 am
20/8/16

Report on Patrol. Appendix II
June 1916

I left our lines near Sap 3 at 10.20 P.M. on the 29th of June, with a party of 1 sergeant and 5 other men. We moved forward to about Q.10.b.90.20 while it was still dusk and waited in the sunken road about halfway across until it was properly dark and then crept up to enemy's wire. I left three men here to keep a look-out and the sergeant and I crept forward followed by the other two men at about 5 paces distance. I arrived on the parapet immediately over the entrance to a dug-out where there was no fire step – almost as soon as I arrived a German appeared out of the darkness about 10 yds to my left and passed immediately before me. He was about 2 yds from when he turned to go round the traverse. I fired at him with my pistol and he fell with a grunt.

Page 2.

I moved along the parapet to find a way down into the trench and heard sounds of the occupants coming out. As the rest of the party were outside the wire, I returned and the whole party moved off before the Germans could spot us. We got back to our own trench about 12 midnight.

The German appeared to be wearing a British warm but it was too dark to distinguish other details. He was not carrying a rifle. The trench was about 7 ft broad at the top and from 8-10 ft deep. The fire step appeared to be made with long strips of wood along the top and also along the side. The parapet was much knocked about by our shells but the bay did not appear to be much damaged. The dug-out I saw was in the right hand corner of the bay looking at it from my direction

Page 3.

end, was under the parapet. The entrance appeared to be larger than those of our deep dug-outs. The trench appeared to be quite dry. I went in through a good gap in the wire about 4 yds wide. The rest of the wire at this point appeared fairly strong.

J. B. Karran
  sgt
2nd South Wales Borderers
30/6/16.

Appendix III
June 1916

Orders for the Attack

1. The attack will take place on Z morning. The bombardment will last 5 days which will be denoted by the letters U. V. W. X. & Y

2. On the day before U the Battn will move up to the trenches & occupy the Battn sector as follows:—

A Coy in firing line from the left of the Bde sector up to & including B. St.

D Coy. in firing line from the right of the Bde sector to B St exclusive

C Coy. in Support occupying the deep bombardment dug outs in Reserve trench & St Johns Road.

B Coy at ENGLEBELMER.

H.Q. Bombers. 4 Squads holding the Bomb Tos in 1st AVENUE — HAYMARKET — CLONMEL AVENUE & CARLISLE St.

2 Squads at ENGLEBELMER.

Bombardment dug Outs.
The following will not be available for Coys.
1st dugout in FETHARD St. N of B St. (Bn H.Q.)
2nd " " " " " " " (Special Gas Party + RE & Signallers)

The 3rd & 4th dug outs N of B St will be allotted to D Coy.

On night Y/Z. A C & D Coys will move into the front fire trench & occupy the positions allotted to them prior to leaving the trenches last time. H.Q. Bombers will join Coys as allotted.

B Coy will move up from ENGLEBELMER and with Bn H.Q. will occupy the old fire trench from E St — Sap 4.

GAS. 3. Gas will be discharged on V/W night if wind is favourable if not on the first subsequent night suitable. A copy of Gas programme is attached.

During the discharge of Gas Coys will withdraw entirely from the front line & occupy the old fire trench & FETHARD St.

SMOKE 4 Smoke will be discharged along the front at intervals during the preliminary bombardment, but will not be commenced till after the Gas has been discharged.

Reconnoitering Wire 5 There will be no Artillery fire on the front between the hours named below.

night V/W   11.0 pm – 12 midnight
"   W/X   10.30 pm – 11.30 pm
"   X/Y   12 midnight – 1.0 am
"   Y/Z   11.30 pm – 12.30 am

Rifle Lewis Gun & Machine Gun fire on Coys front will cease during the above hours & patrols will be sent out (two each night

5. Contᵈ to examine the Enys wire. Officers going out on these patrols will be at the observation Post of the battery cutting the wire during the day. The Pᵗˢ of these posts will be notified to Coys concerned later. Reports on the wire will be submitted by the officers i/c patrols at Bⁿ H.Q. at 6.30 a.m. daily.

After the first days wire cutting the Enys wire will be kept under fire from either Machine Guns, Lewis guns or rifle fire to prevent the Eny repairing it.

There will be four guns of the M.G. Coy assisting in this, they will fire at irregular intervals & at least once every ¼ hour. These guns are situated as follows:—

<u>1 Gun</u> F Sᵗ covers nose of the Salient opposite Sap 6 & front line along S side of Salient as far as Q.11.c 00/30 & also Eny front wire from Q.11.c. 55/25. — Pᵗ 60.

<u>1 Gun</u> in Sap 2 covers Enys front line wire from nose of the Salient to Q.11.c 00/30

<u>1 Gun</u> in new firing line near PRAED Sᵗ covers Q.11.c 50/30 — Pᵗ 60.

<u>1 Gun</u> in FETHARD Sᵗ near MARYLEBONE Sᵗ covers nose of Salient & wire opposite MARY REDAN

Coy Lewis guns therefore should be laid to fire on wire in front of Eny 2ⁿᵈ trench & also if possible by D Coy on wire in front of Pᵗ 54.

<u>Art. Cooperation</u>
6. Table attached.

<u>Stokes Mortars</u> **7.** Eight Stokes mortars will be in the underground gallery leading out from 1ˢᵗ AVENUE. They will open fire 10 minutes before the assault at the rate of 25 a minute. They will cease fire at the hour of assault & three guns in possession of Red cartridges will continue for 2 minutes on Enys 2ⁿᵈ line.

<u>S.O.S.</u> **8.** SOS signal will be 5 red rockets in quick succession. 15 rockets will be carried by the Bⁿ.

<u>Flags. Screens</u> **9.** On no account are bombers flags or Art Screens to be stuck in the ground as they are liable to get left & errors may occur

<u>Assault</u> **10.** will be carried out as already arranged Coys moving out of the front trench in sufficient time to be in position to advance at the hour fixed for the assault

<u>Watches</u> **11** will be synchronised at Bⁿ H.Q. at 9.0 a.m. & 7.0 p.m. on X & Y days.

12. **Trench Traffic.** On and after Z morning WHITTINGTON, TIPPERARY & 2nd AVENUE will be used for up traffic only, GABION, BROADWAY & 3rd AVENUE for down traffic only.

13. **Prisoners** taken during the attack on the 1st system of trenches will be kept under guard from B Coy in Y RAVINE till arrangements can be made to escort them back. Prisoners coming back from other Battns should be sent straight to Bn H.Q. Officers detailing men to escort prisoners back to Y Ravine or Bn H.Q. should give the men a written authority to go back with prisoners, & men are to be warned that they are not to take prisoners to the rear without authority from an officer.

14. **Reorganisation.** After Enys first 3 trenches have been captured & while Coys are consolidating the points allotted, O.C. Coys must reorganise their platoons as opportunity occurs, bombs should be collected from the men & placed in some convenient dump. One hour after the assault commences the Bn will take over the Inniskillings area as well as our own. Points to be consolidated will be allotted to Coys as follows.

   Q 17 b 5·5/80   B Coy.
   Q 11 d 10/00   C Coy
   Q 11 c 90/40   D Coy
   Q 11 e 80/60   A Coy.

   On taking over from 1/R.I.F. ½ B Coy will proceed direct to the point allotted above & ½ B Coy will occupy the Eny 2nd trench in rear ready to relieve the front party after ½ hour. ½ C Coy will proceed direct to consolidating point allotted & commence work.
   A & D Coys will each send ½ Coy to Enys 2nd trench immediately in rear of points being consolidated, these ½ Coys will relieve the working parties in front after ½ hour.
   The Covering party will remain out till orders to retire are received from Bn H.Q. they will then act as detailed for other Coys above. H.Q. Bombers will return to Bn H.Q.

15. Bn H.Q. will be first at Q 11 c 5·5/25 & after taking over the Inniskillings area at Q. 17 a 9·5/9·5

16. **Ammunition** brought up by carrying parties after the 1st assault will be dumped in Y Ravine near Pt 6·4.   G.T. Raikes Maj for OC

22/6/16   2/Lieut Bowerman.

Gas Discharge

1. 400 cylinders of gas will be in front line trenches from Q.10.2 — Q.10.12 each emplacement holds 20 cylinders.

2. The programme of discharge will be as under on V/W or subsequent night.

   (a) Hour fixed — 0.4 ... 4 cylinders simultaneously per bay.

   (b) From 0.4 — 1.24 ... 8 cylinders per bay discharged one at a time every 10 minutes.

   (c) at 1.24 ———— 8 cylinders per bay simultaneously

3. The hour fixed will be notified shortly after 5:0 pm on the evening before discharge & no discharge will take place without direct authority of Corps.

4. ~~Just before & during discharge at "hour fixed" & at 1.24 rifle & machine gun fire will be opened to drown the noise.~~ Cancelled D.A.

= × × × × ✓ ✓ ✓

Smoke discharge

1. Smoke will be discharged at intervals of 25 yds along the front × × ×

2. Smoke will not be discharged till after the Gas has been discharged

3. Men from the Bn will be detailed to assist

4. 2400 Candles will be used on each occasion

5. Times of discharge are as follows.
   W day   10.15 am — 10.25 am
   X "   6.45 am — 6.55 am & 6.55 pm — 7.5 pm
   Y "   7.15 am — 7.25 am & 5.15 pm — 5.25 pm

6. Arrangements will be under R E Officer

Programme of Arto Bombardment & Infantry Advance

Time	Moves of Inf.	Trench Mortars	Div Art	Heavy Art
−10	—	Stokes Mortars open Hurricane bombardment.	—	—
−5	—	—	—	{ Lift to line: Q12 d 4 5/1, Q12 a 1 1/1, Q12 a 1/4, Q11 b 1/5, Q5 c 35/95, Q5 d 4/4 }
0.0	87th & 116th Bde assault 1st Objective & advance at rate of 50x per min	Stokes Mortars cease fire. Those with 1st Cartridge left to 2nd line.	Lift to Cy Support trenches or minimum of 100 yds.	—
0.2	—	Stokes Mortars cease fire.	Lift another 100x	—
0.4	—	—	Lift another 100x & continue lifting at rate of 100 yds per minute to Station Road.	0.15 Lift to 2nd Objective
0.20	87 & 116 Bdes reach Station Road.	—	Lift to 150x E of Station Road & remain till 1.00	—
1.00	Borders & KOSBs advance from Station Road again 2nd Objective rate 50x per min	—	Lift 100 yds.	—
1.2	—	—	Lift 100 yds & continue lifting at this rate till they reach Beaucourt ridge trenches where they remain till 1.20.	—
1.15	—	—	—	Lift to Beaucourt Village
1.20	Borders & KOSBs assault Beaucourt ridge	—	Lift to line R7a 6/2 to R1c 25/50 where they remain till 1.35 about to Beaucourt Village	—
1.25	—	—	—	Lift to 3rd Objective
1.30	Borders & KOSBs advance & cut wire.	—	—	Lift off Beaucourt Village
3.30	2nd Bde assault 3rd Objective	—	—	—

"Scheme for attack on German Trenches 31/6/16

Appendix IV
June 1916

Ref Trench Map 1/10,000

Position held by Bn   Q16b 55/65 — Q10c 95/85

Area allotted for Bn to attack: German 1st line system of trenches as far as STATION ROAD. South of the line Q10d 65/75 — Q11c 00/85 — Quarry at Q11D 50/80 and North of line Q11c 60/10 — S of STATION ROAD

Formation   A. C & D Coys in the first line   B Coy in Reserve
A Coy to attack between Points Q10d 65/75 & Q10d 75/45
C Coy   "   "   "   "   "   Q10d 75/45 & Q11c 30/30
D Coy   "   "   "   "   "   Q11c 30/40 & Q11c 60/10

A Coy to push through till right flank reaches Y Ravine then swing half right & advance astride Ey 2nd trench to Pt Q11c 80/60 where they consolidate

B Coy as soon as they reach Ey first trench swing half right & move between Y Ravine & Eys 1st trench then right & bomb squad on 1st trench to junction of two branches of Y Ravine. The Coy then pushes through A Coy & moves forward as covering party to E side of STATION ROAD covering Battn front. Two H.Q. Bomb Squads will be attached to C Coy to assist in clearing dug outs, Cemetery & Quarry.

D Coy advance straight through to Eys 3rd trench & consolidate Pt Q11c 85/40

H.Q Grenadiers 2 Squads attached to C Coy as above
1 Squad to A Coy to clear Eys 2nd trench
2 Squads to B Coy to assist in clearing trenches after leading Coys have moved through
1 Squad in Reserve.

B Coy. in Reserve will follow 50 yds in Rear & as leading Coys pass over Ey's trenches will send off 1 Platoon with 1 Coy & 1 HQ Bomb Squad to clear dug outs etc in 1st trench & 1 Platoon with Coy & HQ Bomb Squads to clear 2d trench.

The Battn will form up outside our trenches & 100d from German trenches as follows.

Royal Fus on flank.

Note Coy Front 150 yds.
distance between lines 50 yds.

1st R.W. Fus on flank.

A Coy. (4 Platoon, 3 Platoon, 2 Platoon, 1st Platoon)
D Coy. C Coy.
B Coy. (4 Platoon, 3 Platoon, 2 Platoon, 1 Platoon)

Each Coy will have a bomb Squad with leading & 2d line. On approaching Ey's trench Bomb squad move forward & bomb trench, trench bridge & then brought forward & leading & 2d line cross & move straight on to final objective. One bomb squad remaining at each trench to prevent Ey coming out of his dug outs till Platoon detailed from B Coy comes up to clear the trench.

Equipment Carried

(i) 1st line of sections — 170 rounds S.A.A. 2 bombs
    3 sandbags rifle bayonet & equipment less pack
    1 Trench bridge per section. 1 bangalore per section
    1 Art screen per sec'n

(ii) 2nd line of sections — as above less Art Screen

(iii) 3rd line of sections — as above as in (i) less trench
     bridge, bangalore torpedo & Art Screen. Each
     man in addition to carry a pick or shovel
     (in proportion of 1 pick 3 shovels)

(iv) 4th line of sections — as in (iii) but 25% carry
     coils of french wire & remainder 2 sandbags

(v) Reserve Coy — 170 Rds S.A.A. 2 bombs rifle bayonet &
     equipment less pack. 25% coils french wire
     remainder 2 sandbags. A Pick or shovel
     per man (1 pick – 3 shovels).

(vi) Bombers — 50 rounds S.A.A. 20 bombs 4 men per squad
     rifles. all carry bayonets. equipment less pack

(vii) Lewis Gunners — 50 rds per man, 2 per gun team
     carry rifles. equipment less pack.

(viii) Runners & Signallers 6.0 rds per man

In addition each man carries two days rations & iron ration.
All officers & 1 N.C.O. per section carry 4 flares for
denoting position to Contact Aeroplane.

30/6/16.

Cpt Rake Maj
for OC 2/5 Welsh Borderers

Appendix V
June 1916
A1430.
30/6/16

O.C. ___ Coy.   Secret

Previous arrangements for Y/2 night are cancelled and the following substituted —

1. Moves
   (a). Border Regt will arrive about 1 am and will take over Fethard Street.
   (b). B. Coy will arrive about 10.30 p.m. and will go straight to position in old fire line & issue stores for assault.
   (c). C. Coy will leave present lines at 12.15 am & move to front line.
   (d). As soon as C. Coy has passed through, A & D Coys will move to front line —
   (e). H.Q. Bomb Squads & details attached to coys for the assault will join those coys at 11 pm.
   (f). Battn H.Q. with orderlies & 2 signallers will remain in present position until 20 minutes before Zero when they will move to the Bomb T. in new BS Street. Remainder of H.Q. will join B. Coy under R.S.M. at 12.30 pm.
   (g). The following carrying party will parade under Sgt Kelly at an hour notified later & will carry ammunition for Vickers guns attached to the Battn. Sgt Kelly and 5 pioneers —
   4 servants (Ptes Carvell, Hewitt, Ryan, Tenett)
   5 Cooks — (Ptes Warner, Sullivan, Moon, Sprake, Chesterman)

(h) Remaining cooks will join their coys after tea has been sent up to-night.

2. Guards
(a) Water guards will be relieved off by water party at 5. am.
(b) The three police detailed by O.C. A Coy will report to Lieut. H. J. Leavey at 7 pm to-night.

3. Kits
(a) Great Coats & ground sheets will be retained during the night, & stacked by coys before the assault at any convenient spot in the front line. B Coy may stack in the dugout in old firing line just S. of A street.
(b) Officers kits, Mess Boxes, & all other stores will be stacked in the above dug-out. Pte Sharpe (O. Mess cook) will remain as storeman.

4. Assault stores.
All trench bridges etc. must be put over the parapet before dawn & covered up with grass so that the enemy will not see them.

5. Moving out
(a) B Coy will advance over the parapet of the old line & will not use the communication trenches.
(b) When getting over the parapet the whole of a coy will get out together from the bays in which they

are waiting, & will lie down outside the parapet. Platoons will then move off by lines to their forming up places, which must all be marked to-night. Coys must cut away to-night any wire which will interfere with the men lying down after they have got over.

6. Meals.
(a). Teas will be at the usual hour.
(b). Tea will be drawn at 10.30 pm & issued to troops before moving to new positions. Details attached to coys for the assault will get their tea from those coys.
(c). A small quantity of tea, 2 containers per coy, will be drawn at the same time and placed in position in the front line. This is for issue the following morning.
(d). The extra days ration in hand must be issued to-night. Tea, sugar, milk for to-morrow's teas will be dumped in dugout mentioned in 3(a) above, & not issued to coys at all.

8. Zero.
Zero will be at 7.30 am. Each coy will send an officer to HQ at 5.55 am to synchronise watches.

30/6/16.

J H Granville Capt.
Adjt 1/1 Wales Border

29th Division.

87th Infantry Brigade

2nd BATTALION

SOUTH WALES BORDERERS.

JULY 1916

War Diary

of

2nd Bn. South Wales Borderers

for

July 1916.

SECRET 2/631

A.G.
G.H.Q.
3rd Echelon
B.E.F.

Herewith War Diary (A.F.
C2118) for month of July 1916
Kindly acknowledge
receipt hereon.

[stamp: 2nd BATTALION, SOUTH WALES BORDERERS.]

[signature] Lieut-Colonel
Comdg. 2nd. South Wales Borderers

Instructions regarding War Diaries and Intelligence Summaries are contained in F. S. Regs., Part II. and the Staff Manual respectively. Title Pages will be prepared in manuscript.

WAR DIARY
or
INTELLIGENCE SUMMARY
(Erase heading not required.)

Army Form C. 2118.

2 S WB (180) Vol 5

? 7/29

Place	Date	Hour	Summary of Events and Information	Remarks and references to Appendices
Firing Line	1st July	~~01.00~~ 05.00	During the night Coys moved up to their positions ready for assault in Firing & Support line. Our Artillery was active all night. Morning fine but misty. Men were given hot tea at 11.0 pm last night and again at 6.0 am	
		06.30	Our Artillery commenced steady bombardment of Eys front line trenches increasing to heavy bombardment & at 07.00 Field Artillery commenced a barrage on Eys front line	
		07.20	Mine under HAWTHORN REDOUBT fired & Coys immediately commenced getting out of the trenches & through our wire. (Bn HQ moved to Bomb T in Bn at 07.10). As the leading Companies reached the outer edge of our wire machine gun fire was opened on them which rapidly increased in intensity, Enemy also opened percussion shrapnel on the advancing lines. By about 07.30 the leading companies had lost nearly all officers & about 70% of the men. A Coy reached a point about 20 yds from Eys front line just south of the nose of the salient where they were held up by MG fire & bombs from the trench. C Coy crossed the hollow by sunken road & reached a point about 60 yds from Eys wire when they were under MG fire from their right flank. D Coy reached a point about 300 yds from our wire. Position of Coys was roughly as follows:—	

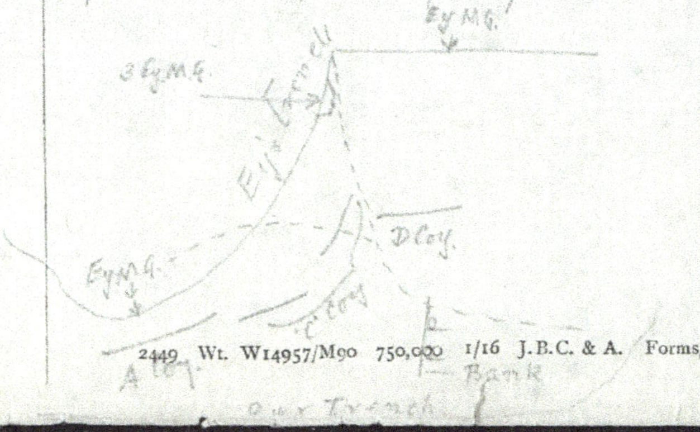

Reserve Coy B Coy left support trench at 07.30 moving over the 1st & across the fire trench by bridges. This Coy came under Ey machine gun fire while passing through our wire. They advanced steadily across the open till practically all men were hit. Capt Hughes was last seen about 60 yds from the Ey wire leading 6 or 7 men forward all these men were knocked out a few yds further on. HQ moved forward with B Coy.

According to original arrangements our Art barrage lifted off Eys front line at 07.30. Ey at once lined his parapet & MGs fired unmolested

15T

Army Form C. 2118

WAR DIARY
or
INTELLIGENCE SUMMARY
(Erase heading not required.)

(182)

Place	Date	Hour	Summary of Events and Information	Remarks and references to Appendices
Englebelmer	1st July	08.15	1/Border Regt advanced from our support trenches (FETHARD ST.) to support the B's but were enough by Machine Guns before reaching our front trench. Coy B's lost very heavily & only a few men got up near our front line & were actually reaching the front line. After the Newfoundland Regt advanced but were similarly held up by M.G. fire, a few men only managed to get along the sunken road & join up with the right of E Coy. During the remainder of the day no further attempt to advance was made, the Enemy fired heavy shrapnel over the wounded & men lying out in the open also intermittent M.G. fire. Prior to the attack it had been arranged that Coys on reaching Enemy trenches should fire Verey lights to let the Brigade know, but shortly after we advanced thirty fort of lights & for some time it was thought that we had taken the front line & were pushed on consequently our barrage was not put back on Enemy front line.	
		09.30	The 10% officers & men left behind at ENGLEBELMER arrived up to the front line & afterwards went to ST JOHN'S ROAD. The actual strength of the Batt. as it moved forward to the attack was Officers 21 O.R. 578. Casualties were as follows:—	

	Killed	Wounded	Missing	Believed killed	Missing Believed killed	Total
Officers.	2	4	5	4		15
Other Ranks.	21	160	202	—		384

Now reached the Cinema trench & it was impossible to bring the bodies in, practically all those reported missing were probably killed.

A few wounded & others managed to get back to our trenches during the day and several returned after dark.

The following are the names of officer casualties.

P.T.O.

WAR DIARY or INTELLIGENCE SUMMARY

Army Form C.2118.

163

Place	Date	Hour	Summary of Events and Information	Remarks and references to Appendices
Firing line	1st July		Killed 2nd Lieut D.F. DON 13/Sherwood Foresters attached 2/S Wales Borderers 2nd Lieut F. RICE 8/S Wales Borderers attached 2/Shrops. Borderers. Missing Capt R J McLAREN 4/Cheshire Regt attached 2/S Wales Borderers. 2nd Lieut J ROBINSON 3/S Wales Borderers 2nd Lieut G.H. BOWYER 2/S Wales Borderers 2nd Lieut T. WM. WELLS 2/S Wales Borderers 2nd Lieut J.C. MURRAY 9/S Wales Borderers aft? 2/Shrops. Borderers (believed killed) Missing Captain A.A. HUGHES 2/Shrops. Borderers " F.S. BLAKE 15/Kings Liverpool Regt attached 2/Shrops. Borderers. Lieut H.T. EVANS 2/Shrops. Borderers. 2nd Lieut J.B. KARRAN 9/S Wales Borderers attached 2/S Wales Borderers. Wounded Capt & Adjutant D.H.S. SOMERVILE 2/Shrops. Borderers Lieut C.E. FOWKES 2/Shrops. Borderers 2nd Lieut WM MASON 9/Shrops. Borderers att 2/Shrops. Borderers 2nd Lieut W.H. KELLY 2/Shrops. Borderers	
			Batt. bivouacked & spent following day in St JOHN'S ROAD. 10% officers & men knotty jerseys up.	
	2nd July	10.00	Batt. marched off via CONSTITUTION HILL & occupied the front line trenches about P.23 b 30/90 Left flank at LUVERGY St + right flank at St JEANS St. A front of about 300 yds. The B'n was connected with the Coys A & B Coys under Lieut ROSS & Col'd Corp. WATSON B'n Diapers. The 1/Border Regt on B'n left flank and 1/R.S.B. on right flank. The line held to defence	

2449 Wt. W14957/Mg0 750,000 1/16 J.B.C. & A. Forms/C.2118/12.

WAR DIARY or INTELLIGENCE SUMMARY

Army Form C. 2118

(184)

Place	Date	Hour	Summary of Events and Information	Remarks and references to Appendices
Auchonvillers	2 July	12.00	on Relief:- 3 Platoons of each Coy in Front line & 1 Platoon in Support in CONMANTRAY AVENUE LTD 4/0 in rear. 1 Coy in reserve down each Sap & H.Q. Bomb Squad in ROYAL AVENUE & JOFFRE AVENUE. B.H.Q. in step bay not about 300 yds in rear of firing line off ROYAL AVENUE. Found trenches in very bad condition & very slight communication trenches & support trench very thin, the lines of our trenches in danger etc. Enemy trenches assumed to be seen from our front line. They can be seen only from the sea of a long sap on the left flank. Throughout the afternoon there was continual fighting on the opposite side of this front from right flank where our troops occupy a portion of the 1st & 2nd German trenches.	
	3 July		Stated clearing fire trench & deepening communication trenches. Fighting still continues on right flank.	
	4 July		Enemy batting up a M.G. apparent from in front of our line was being M.G. also several bombing Pip Squeaks were encountered within our support line. During the afternoon	
		14.00	there was very heavy rain for about 3 hours, causing our trenches, which were already in very bad condition, with practically no revetments, to fall in in many places. Very little material available for repairing or strengthening trenches. The men are very wet but cheerful. Very heavy artillery fire continues on the far side	
	5 July		of the river ANCRE, where the 49th Division have been trying to extend their gains down to the river. Very little fire on our front with the exception of a little Shrapnel. Some few shells were fired into HAMEL. Work was continued throughout day on trenches and saps and also digging graves for burial of dead. During the afternoon fatigue parties were sent down to Bn. dumps for material to send up saps. 	

WAR DIARY or INTELLIGENCE SUMMARY

Army Form C.2118

Place	Date	Hour	Summary of Events and Information	Remarks and references to Appendices
Firing line	5th July (cont)		a new line of trench being dug some 300 yards to our front. During the day there was continual artillery fire on both sides to our right flank across the ANCRE and we also fired a Lewis gun against the enemy's 3rd Trench. Very little fire on our front. About 10.30 pm the 2nd Batt Monmouthshire Regt passed through our trenches and commenced work on the new Trench to our front. We found a covering party of an Officer and 12 men for them. The following Officers rejoined from 4th Army and 29th Div Schools Capt H.G. Garnett, Lieut A.B. Coulshaw — 2nd Lt. E.G. Jones, 2nd Lt. C.R. Wardle, 2nd Lt. W. M. Evans. 2nd Lt A.E. Morgan was sent to Hospital for Anti-Tetanus treatment having been slightly wounded on July 1st.	
		22.30		
	6th July		Continued during the night extending saps and working on trench. The Monmouths came in by 3 a.m. having only dug a very shallow trench, and not a continuous one. Artillery continued fairly active on our right. At night the monmouths came up again and continued work on the trench previously started. We again found a covering party.	
	7th July		About 6 a.m. smoke was discharged from the British trenches on our right across the river and also on our left in the neighbourhood of MARY REDAN, accompanied by a very heavy artillery bombardment, especially away to our right flank. Under cover of this smoke the Germans made a counter attack on the trenches held by the 49th Div. on the right of the ANCRE about Q 24 D 80.70 and retook them. We endeavoured to assist by firing on this front with our Lewis guns, but observation was difficult owing to smoke and mist. The Batt. was relieved in trenches by the KOSB's about 2.30 p.m. and moved back into support via JACOBS LADDER, MESNIL, AUCHONVILLERS	
		14.30		

extending to cover our front ROAD to a point about Q 22 C 20.30, when they occupied some vacated Artillery Dugouts

WAR DIARY or INTELLIGENCE SUMMARY

Army Form C. 2118.

(186)

Place	Date	Hour	Summary of Events and Information	Remarks and references to Appendices
Firing Line	8th July		Occupied dugouts mentioned during the day and moved back into their Reserve at ACHEUX about 5 p.m. the 87th Bde. being relieved by the 86th Bde.	
	10th July	9.30	Batt. was inspected at 11 a.m. by the Corps Commander Sir Aylmer Hunter-Weston, who congratulated the Officers and men on the way in which they advanced in the attack on July 1st. Strength on parade was 15 Officers and 217 men.	
	10th to 16th July		Batt. remained in divisional reserve in ACHEUX wood. The men were not taken on fatigues, and Coys were able to give their men some much needed training. Classes were also trained in Bombing and Lewis Guns.	
	17th July		On the 17th July the battalion moved up to the line and took over the Old Left sector from SANDY ROW on the left (Q10 B10.10) to B Street on the right (Q10 D 10.20) with B.C. and D Coys in the front line, and A Coy in support. Batt HQ was at the old place in HAYMARKET near THURLES DUMP. We had been ordered to prepare a small raiding party to go out after a discharge of gas, but as the wind was unfavourable, the raid was ordered to take place at 3 a.m. without gas.	
	18th July		While the raiding party was forming up in B street, a heavy shell fell injuring several men, and blocking the trench. By the time the men were extricated and the party reformed, the delay thus caused prevented the party getting to their starting point until too late, as the Artillery barrage arranged was nearly over, and the light increasing rapidly. Consequently the party did not go out. Work was continued by day in cleaning the trenches.	

WAR DIARY
or
INTELLIGENCE SUMMARY.
(Erase heading not required.)

Army Form C. 2118

Place	Date	Hour	Summary of Events and Information	Remarks and references to Appendices
Continued	18th July		and repairing places blown in - also collecting salvage stores. The day was wet until the late afternoon when it cleared, but trenches were very bad in places.	
	18 – 19 July		During the night the wind was North & North-East and so no gas could be discharged. Consequently we made arrangements with the Artillery to cease fire on the enemy's trenches in the neighbourhood of Q 10 D 70.40 between the hours	
		23.30	of 23.30 and 00.30. A patrol consisting of 2 Officers and 6 men (Lieut A.S Conroy also and 2nd Lt C R Wardle) left our trenches about 23.30 and got into the German wire at the above mentioned point. They heard enemy working in his trenches and also traffic on the station road behind. The patrol returned unobserved about 02.00. The enemy's artillery was fairly active during the night, shelling chiefly the communication trenches with H.E. The day was quiet with the exception of occasional activity by our Field Guns. At night the enemy's artillery were very active, shelling chiefly with H.E., our front line, LIMERICK JUNCTION and the main communication trenches. We had some wiring parties out but these had to come in losing one killed and one wounded. Some rifles and equipment of dead were brought in. These parties were evidently	
	July 19th			

Army Form C. 2118.

WAR DIARY
or
INTELLIGENCE SUMMARY.
(Erase heading not required.)

Instructions regarding War Diaries and Intelligence Summaries are contained in F. S. Regs., Part II. and the Staff Manual respectively. Title pages will be prepared in manuscript.

Place	Date	Hour	Summary of Events and Information	Remarks and references to Appendices
	July 20th	02.00	Seen by the enemy, as further attempts to go out again were always met with considerable shelling. The night was one of bright moonlight. The day was quiet with the exception of occasional artillery fire. At night we sent out a patrol of an Officer (2nd Lt Webb) and 2 men through Sap the Russian Sap at the	
	July 21st	22.45	end of 1st Avenue to examine the wire at the nose of the Salient. They observed a small enemy working party, and returned safely. During the day, artillery on both sides was very quiet except early in the afternoon. At night we again sent out a patrol of 2 Offrs and 8 men (2nd Lt Coulsmaker and 2nd Lt Robyart) accompanied by an Artillery Officer. This patrol left the trenches just to the right of our position about Q.10.D.40.10 and patrolled the German wire on the S. side of the Salient,	
		23.30	observing a large German working party in their front trench. The patrol was evidently observed, as the working party disappeared, either into dugouts, or by withdrawing. Immediately afterwards an intense barrage of artillery and minenwerfe fire was thrown partly onto the front trench of the battalion on our right (K.O.S.B) and partly out the cliff in No Mans Land. Our patrol lay still on the ridge further to the North, and were quite clear	

WAR DIARY
or
INTELLIGENCE SUMMARY.
(Erase heading not required.)

Army Form C. 2118

Place	Date	Hour	Summary of Events and Information	Remarks and references to Appendices
	July 22nd	0200	of this fire, returning to our trench untouched about 0200. Probably the enemy imagined that we were making an attack or raid on them and were evidently nervous. We were relieved about 1200 by the 1st Border	
		1400	Regt and moved back into Bde Reserve at MAILLY WOOD, leaving a party of 3 Ops and 120 men to dig in the trenches during the night.	
	July 23rd		Orders were received that the 29th Division was to be withdrawn and that we would move to BUS on the during the 24th and to AMPLIER on the 25th. We are to be relieved by the 74th Bde. A party of 3 Ops and 120 men was again sent up at night to work on a new communication trench.	
	July 24th		The battalion left MAILLY WOOD by Coys at 10 minutes interval commencing at 1030, and other Coys moving off as each relieving Coy of the 11th Lanc. Fus. arrived, and marched via BERTRANCOURT to huts in the wood about 500 yards North of BUS.	
	July 25th		The battalion left BUS about 9 a.m. marching complete with 1st Line Transport to AMPLIER a distance of about 7½ miles.	
	July 26th		We remained at At AMPLIER during the day, and orders were issued	

Army Form C. 2118.

WAR DIARY
or
INTELLIGENCE SUMMARY.
(Erase heading not required.)

Place	Date	Hour	Summary of Events and Information	Remarks and references to Appendices
	July 27th		and preparations made for entraining the next day.	
		12.30	The Battalion marched to DOULLENS (3 miles) and entrained, leaving about 12.30 and arriving at PROVEN N.W. of POPERINGHE	
		18.00	about 18.00. We detrained here and marched about 4 miles to a camp about 1½ miles W. of POPERINGHE.	
	July 28th to July 30th		We remained in camp near POPERINGHE and worked at training of recent drafts, Bombers and new Lewis gun class. The weather since our arrival here has been very fine and fairly hot. Our strength now with recent drafts is 34 Officers and 519 Other ranks exclusive of men employed away from the battalion of which there are 127.	
	July 31st	20.00	The Battalion left camp at 8 p.m. and entrained just W. of POPERINGHE, the train running up to the ASYLUM about half a mile W. of YPRES.	
		22.00	Here we were met by guides from the 2nd Sherwood Foresters, whom we relieved on the Canal Bank about half a mile N. of YPRES. The Battalion bivouaced in excellent dug-outs in the East Bank of the Canal	

J. W. H. Pollard
Lieut Colonel
Comdg 2nd South Wales Borderers

29th Division.

87th Infantry Brigade

2nd BATTALION

SOUTH WALES BORDERERS

AUGUST 1 9 1 6

2nd Battn. The South Wales Borderers

Confidential

War Diary

From 1st August 1916 to 31st August 1916

Volume — P.19 to P.30 incl.

2nd BATTALION,
SOUTH WALES
BORDERERS.

No.....................
Date...................

Army Form C. 2118.

WAR DIARY
or
INTELLIGENCE SUMMARY.
(Erase heading not required.)

Place	Date	Hour	Summary of Events and Information	Remarks and references to Appendices
	August 1st		The day was spent in sending up parties of Officers and N.C.Os to see the trenches, in the Salient, which we were to take over that night, from the 9th Norfolk Regt. The trench which we booked runs from C 22 C 68.04 to C 29 d 39.13 and the Northern Boundary of our area runs back via C 27 a 90.21 St JULIEN - Road Junction C 27 C 1.8. - Canal Bank, the southern Boundary running via C 28 d 20.15 - C 27 d 80.50. Battalion H.Q. in St JEAN. Most of the trenches are in very bad repair, and consist of a breastwork in front and a built up parados behind, as it is impossible, owing to water being very near the surface, to dig deeper than two feet. Parts of the front trench are not continuous, and it is nearly impossible to go round the whole trench system by day. There is only one communication trench which is practicable (GARDEN ST) Little or no movement on work is possible by day owing to the bad trenches, flat ground and the fact that we are near the point of the Salient and under observation from the front and both flanks. We relieved the 9th Norfolk Regt in these trenches about 11 p.m.	Ref. Map. St JULIEN 1/10000 28. N.W. 2
		2300		

Army Form C. 2118.

(192)

WAR DIARY
or
INTELLIGENCE SUMMARY.
(Erase heading not required.)

Place	Date	Hour	Summary of Events and Information	Remarks and references to Appendices
	August 2ⁿᵈ		Enemy is generally quiet on our front with the exception of considerable M.G. fire on trenches and roads by night. His artillery is very inactive. We worked during the night repairing trenches. One of our aeroplanes was seen to be shot down by the enemy's artillery about a mile to the North of ST JEAN.	
	August 3ʳᵈ	13:15	Worked during the night on repairing trenches, but the amount of work to be done is limitless. A patrol of 1 Officer (2ⁿᵈ Lt Wardle) and 6 men went out from the WIELTJE salient and reconnoitred ARGYLE Farm and the surrounding ground. The day was quiet, there being very little fire on our trenches. Work continued during the night repairing and revetting. In the morning the enemy fired some trench mortars about the end of JOHN STREET but did no damage. Work	
	August 4ᵗʰ	01:00		
		08:00		
		21:30	Continued at night on the trenches and the enemy's M. Guns were much quieter, probably due to night firing done by our M. Guns and artillery retaliation. About 8 to 9 am enemy trench mortar was very active again about the end of JOHN ST until we obtained retaliation from	
	August 5ᵗʰ	08:30		

Place	Date	Hour	Summary of Events and Information	Remarks and references to Appendices
August 5th Contd.		0900	The whole of the left group divisional Artillery, when the T.M. ceased firing. Serious damage to the trench was done in JOHN ST but no casualties. Enemy artillery was also slightly more active during the day, and	
		1700	hostile aeroplanes were active late in the afternoon and evening. Work continued in the trenches at night.	
August 6th		0330	Early in the morning a small enemy patrol encountered one of our posts in the WIELTJE salient. They fired a few shots and threw some bombs, wounding one man. They then hastily retired. During the day enemy was much quieter. Firing very few shells on the trenches. Our aeroplanes were very active in the evening and some new kind of bomb or shell was seen in the air which burst and dropped numerous lights which sank right down to the ground leaving heavy trails of smoke in the air. These presented an extraordinary appearance and seemed to be some form of incendiary bomb, but whether they were shells fired by the enemy or bombs dropped by our aeroplanes it is difficult to say. At night	

WAR DIARY or **INTELLIGENCE SUMMARY.**

Army Form C. 2118.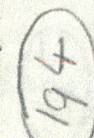

Place	Date	Hour	Summary of Events and Information	Remarks and references to Appendices
Aug 6th contd.		22:30	The Batt'n was to be relieved by the 1st Border Regt, and moved back into Bde Reserve on the Canal Bank.	
Aug 7th			Remained on the Canal Bank, sending up a working party of 200 men to the trenches at night. (This is to be a nightly party while in Reserve.)	
Aug 8th			In the morning the "Gas Alert" was received from the Brigade, the wind having turned nearly "due East". In the afternoon orders were received that we were to be relieved by the 1st R. Dublin Fus. and that we were to move back into Div. Reserve at Camp O (A 30 d & 7).	
		22:00	Just before the arrival of the Dublins, we heard the gas alarm sounded from the front by means of "Strombos Horns", and also red S.O.S. rockets were seen to go up. Shortly afterwards the Dublins arrived, and we were ordered by Brigade to Stand to and not move off until further orders.	
		22:45	After waiting some time we got warning that there was gas in YPRES and it was moving in a North Westerly direction; consequently the order was given to put on Helmets, which had already been placed on the	

WAR DIARY
or
INTELLIGENCE SUMMARY.
(Erase heading not required.)

Army Form C. 2118.

(195)

Place	Date	Hour	Summary of Events and Information	Remarks and references to Appendices
	Aug 8th Contd	23.45	heads rolled up. After an hour's wait however there was no sign of gas on our part of the Canal Bank, and the order was given to move off to the spot where we entrained for a point near the reserve camp (the ASYLUM West of YPRES).	
	Aug 9th	00.15	The Battalion moved off, having removed Gas Helmets and reached O Camp, the detachment from LA BRIQUE post following later as it took some time to relieve. It transpired that gas was discharged on each side of our sector i.e. the Right subsector of our Brigade where the 1st Inniskilling Fus suffered considerable casualties from it and the 4th Division on our left, but our sector escaped entirely. The Gas apparently travelled back for some distance and was felt to a slight extent in our Camp (O) previous to our arrival.	
	August 9th to 14th	03.30	The battalion remained in O Camp, and a thorough programme of training was commenced, for Officers and men, and special classes for Specialists started. On the 14th Aug we were ordered to march to a road just North of POPERINGHE, where we waited halted by	

WAR DIARY
or
INTELLIGENCE SUMMARY.
(Erase heading not required.)

Army Form C. 2118.
(96)

Place	Date	Hour	Summary of Events and Information	Remarks and references to Appendices
	Aug 14th contd		the side of the road, until the King passed in a motor. The battalion was called to attention (by Coys) let the King did not stop. We then marched back to Camp.	
	Aug 15th – Aug 16th		Training was continued, and during the night the Gas Alert was given and shortly afterwards the Gas Alarm was sent round. The battalion was roused and stood to with helmets out, but there was no sign of gas, and in about half an hour the order was received to stand down as there was no gas on our front. Apparently this was a false alarm.	
	Aug 17th Aug 18th		Remained in Camp and training programme was continued. The Battalion moved up at night and relieved the 16th Bn Middlesex Regt on the Canal Bank in the same position as mentioned before. The weather in the last 3 days has broken up considerably, and there has been a considerable amount of rain.	
	Aug 19th	21.00	The Battalion moved up and relieved the Dublin Fus in the left subsector i.e. the same trenches which were occupied before. The enemy, generally, were very quiet and the relief was not interfered with	

WAR DIARY
or
INTELLIGENCE SUMMARY.

(Erase heading not required.)

Army Form C. 2118.

197

Place	Date	Hour	Summary of Events and Information	Remarks and references to Appendices
Aug 19th Contd	Aug 20th		The 1st Border Regt. relieved us on the Canal Bank. During the day the enemy was fairly quiet, but fired some shells on our lines and in our neighbourhood during the afternoon. Our artillery was active in the afternoon. Enemy machine guns were very active at night and interfered considerably with our working parties.	
	Aug 21st	0100	In the early morning a patrol of 3 Officers and 11 men went out in front of WIELTJE but nothing was seen of the enemy, Though he was heard working on his trenches.	
		1500	In the afternoon a heavy bombardment of the enemy's trenches on our front was carried out, owing to suspected installment of gas cylinders there. We withdrew most of our men from the front line during this bombardment, leaving posts and Lewis Guns. The enemy retaliated a little, and we had 3 killed and 4 wounded. We men returned	
		1900	to their trenches when the bombardment finished. At night the wind died down and slight puffs came from all quarters. Gas alarm horns	
		2200	were heard and the battalion stood to, but no sign of gas was seen, and the wind gradually rising from the west again, work was continued	

WAR DIARY
or
INTELLIGENCE SUMMARY.
(Erase heading not required.)

Army Form C. 2118.

Place	Date	Hour	Summary of Events and Information	Remarks and references to Appendices
	Aug 22. 1916		The early morning was quiet except for periodical fire from our guns to stop the enemy repairing his trenches. In spite of this he was heard working hard especially about 7 a.m. The enemy's artillery was rather more active during the day, and in the early afternoon he shelled ST JEAN village with High Velocity 5.2" gun and 77 mm gun and possibly also with 4.2 howitzers. We obtained retaliation from our heavy artillery on to the locality of his guns, and the fire stopped. Continual work is being done at night on the trenches, and where possible by day also, and although an immense amount of labour and material are used, there is very little apparent result to show for it, especially to those who do not see the actual work done. There are many cases of battalions being told that they are not doing sufficient work, but in reality far more labour is being expended than ever before, and these remarks are due to the impossibility of any individual forming a correct estimate of the work done, unless he is continually on the spot.	
		0700		
		1400		
	Aug 23.		A quiet day on the whole, and although "Gas Alert" had been received on the previous day, the wind was approximately	

WAR DIARY or INTELLIGENCE SUMMARY

Army Form C. 2118.

Place	Date	Hour	Summary of Events and Information	Remarks and references to Appendices
	Aug 23 (contd)		South, and there was very little danger of a gas attack; but the "Alert" was kept on in case of a change of wind. In the morning St JEAN again received a few shells, apparently 4.2 Howitzer, and the house, behind which Batt H.Q is situated, was struck, but no damage done.	
	Aug 24th 1916		The night was exceptionally quiet, there being practically no Artillery or machine gun fire by either side, and the Germans there not heard working so much on their front trenches. We have been sending a patrol out nightly, but beyond hearing the Germans working, and occasionally seeing an enemy listening post, which always retired, no results have been obtained. Information was received last night that the following Officers had been awarded the decorations shown against their names, for gallantry on July 1st 1916. Major G.T. Raikes — D.S.O. Capt A.J. Blake RAMC — Mil Cross 2 Lt C F Dutton — " " " 2 Lt F J.L Magger — " " " 2 Lt W H Kelly — " " "	

WAR DIARY
or
INTELLIGENCE SUMMARY.
(Erase heading not required.)

Army Form C. 2118.

201

Place	Date	Hour	Summary of Events and Information	Remarks and references to Appendices
	29th Aug 916 Contd.	22.00	10 p.m. the alarm was heard Sounding on the Strombos Horns, just as relief was taking place. There appeared to be no sign of gas, however, and after standing to for about half an hour, the ordinary routine was continued. The night turned very wet again and the wind changed to S.W.	
	30th Aug.		A very bad day, blowing a gale from the west, and later veering to N.W. accompanied by deluges of rain. We had to find numerous working parties for the front trenches by day and night, chiefly for draining the trenches.	
		20.00	In the evening, the rain ceased, but the wind remained strong, drying towards morning.	
	31st Aug.		A very fine day, and the men were able to dry their clothing. The usual working parties were found.	

1.9.16

Tony McDonell
Comg 8th South Wales Borderers

29th Division.

87th Infantry Brigade.

--- ---

2nd BATTALION

SOUTH WALES BORDERERS

SEPTEMBER 1 9 1 6

CONFIDENTIAL.

WAR DIARY OF

2ND. BATTALION THE SOUTH WALES BORDERERS.

FOR SEPTEMBER 1916.

VOLUME 20.

Army Form C. 2118.

WAR DIARY
or
INTELLIGENCE SUMMARY.
(Erase heading not required.)

(202)

Place	Date	Hour	Summary of Events and Information	Remarks and references to Appendices
	1st Sept 1916		Remained in Canal Bank in Reserve, and worked on trenches mostly by night, but small parties were sent up by day also.	
	2nd Sept		During the day the wind veered to South and later showed a trace of East, and "Gas Alert" was received. During the night	
	3rd Sept	12 00	three separate "Gas Alarms" were received and Strombos Horns were heard, chiefly from the South. Owing to the direction of the wind (S to SSE) it seemed very unlikely that any gas could be discharged on our section of the salient, and no trace of gas was seen or heard of, though possibly there may have been some at the most Southern point of the Salient. These numerous false gas alarms are very apt to make men casual and careless with regard to gas, and may lead to a disaster when gas really arrives. Great aeroplane activity on both sides in the morning.	
	4th Sept to 6th Sept	10 00	The usual work carried on chiefly by night up in the trenches, which owing to further rain are in a very wet state again. Any piece of trench which has not been thoroughly revetted, at once commences to fall in	

WAR DIARY
or
INTELLIGENCE SUMMARY.
(Erase heading not required.)

Army Form C. 2118.
(203)

Place	Date	Hour	Summary of Events and Information	Remarks and references to Appendices
	6th Sept cont		and has to be re-dug. For the last two nights work has been almost entirely concentrated on wiring BIDA and ADMIRAL'S ROAD trench with a double row of hoop wire with an apron each side. In the morning the wind changed to NNE and "Gas Alert" was received.	
	7th Sept		No gas alarms occurred during the night, though the wind remained between NNE and NE.	
	8th Sept	2300	The Battalion was relieved on the Canal Bank by the 1st Dublin Fusiliers, and moved back into Divisional Reserve at O Camp as before. One Platoon however was left as a guard at the Div. Artillery H.Q. at the REIGERSBURG Chateau (G.6.c).	
	9th Sept		The Battalion remained in O Camp during this period and carried	
	12th Sept		out as Special Training Programme.* Gas alert was taken off, having been continually on for over a week. A new type of Gas Respirator has now been issued (the Small Box Respirator) and this should give practically complete protection against the heaviest concentration of Phosgene. Daily practice is carried out with this.	* Appendix I

WAR DIARY
INTELLIGENCE SUMMARY

Army Form C. 2118.

204

Place	Date	Hour	Summary of Events and Information	Remarks and references to Appendices
	14th Sept	23.00	The platoon at the REIGERSBURG Chateau was relieved by the 1st Inniskilling Fusiliers, and returned to O Camp.	
	15th Sept 16th Sept & 17th Sept 18th Sept		A special scheme was carried out by the signallers, with contact Aeroplanes. Training Programme was continued. Classes for specialists being closed on this date. A Regimental tour was carried out near Camp. A very wet day, but the camp is now fairly well drained, and paths of trench boards laid along all main lines of traffic throughout the camp. Consequently the mud is not troublesome. At night we moved up to the ASYLUM by tram and relieved the Dublin Fusiliers on the Canal Bank.	
	19th Sept		Remained on the Canal Bank by day, and at night moved up	
	20th Sept	21.00	to the trenches, relieving the 16th Middlesex Regt in the left subsector. The trenches were found to be in fairly good condition, considering the recent rain. The draining work done during the last month has had a very marked effect. The usual work is being carried on, where	
	21st Sept		possible by day, but mostly at night. During the afternoon a German	

WAR DIARY
or
INTELLIGENCE SUMMARY.
(Erase heading not required.)

Army Form C. 2118.

(205)

Place	Date	Hour	Summary of Events and Information	Remarks and references to Appendices
	21st Sept Ctd.		Observation balloon on our right front was seen to be brought down in flames by one of our aeroplanes. The remaining German balloons (3) were up immediately. Came down. Our air Supremacy is very marked, a German 'plane being rarely seen, and then only at a great height.	
	22nd Sept.		Nightly patrols have been sent out during the present tour, generally consisting of about 2 Officers and 8 men. They have obtained some useful information, but have not had the fortune to obtain any identification. A.G. Our aeroplanes were very active during the day, and although ideal for observation, the German balloons did not dare go up. The enemy has been extraordinarily quiet during our present tour in the trenches. There has been very little artillery, and no trench mortar fire. His machine guns are fairly active at night. There can be little doubt that he has not many guns in this neighbourhood and he also appears to suffer from a shortage of ammunition. Our artillery, both heavy and divisional, is usually fairly active,	

WAR DIARY
or
INTELLIGENCE SUMMARY.
(Erase heading not required.)

Place	Date	Hour	Summary of Events and Information	Remarks and references to Appendices
	22nd Sept Contd.		and the conditions of the war are completely reversed, to those under which we suffered in the early stages of 1915 (i.e. being under continual artillery fire without being able to reply.)	
	23rd Sept.	21.00	A strong patrol of 2 Officers and 12 men was sent out last night with orders to make every effort to bring in a German, dead or alive, in order to obtain identifications. The patrol was out	
		to 03.30	for 6½ hours and thoroughly searched "No man's land" for a distance of about 500 yards. They remained for some time in the ruins of ARGYLL Farm and WHITE Cottage, but no sign of the enemy was seen.	
	24th Sept.		Another patrol went out during the night with no better success. They found, however, the Sap at C.22.d.85.42 on the ST JULIEN Road, occupied by a few of the enemy. They threw some bombs into the sap, and the enemy replied with one bomb, and rifle fire; the patrol, however, returned without casualties. The enemy's fire action still remains very quiet, except for	

WAR DIARY or INTELLIGENCE SUMMARY

Army Form C. 2118.

267

Place	Date	Hour	Summary of Events and Information	Remarks and references to Appendices
	Sept 24th Contd		the usual machine gun fire at night. Our aeroplanes are also continually active, but very few enemy machines are seen, nor does he often dare to send up observation balloons.	
	Sept 25th	21.00	We were relieved in the trenches last night by the 1st Border Regt as usual, and moved back into reserve to our old dugouts on the Canal Bank. The weather for the past 3 days has greatly improved, there being bright sunshine but unfortunately an Easterly breeze, necessitating a continual "Wind Dangerous" precautions. We left a washing party drawn from every available man from 2 Coys, to work at night in the trenches & sent up working parties by day as well.	
	Sept 26th to 28th		Remained on the Canal bank, and some small parties by day. The weather has continued very fine, with an occasional shower but the wind has also remained Easterly. The enemy continues very quiet, scarcely a shell coming near the Canal, though our artillery is usually fairly active.	

Army Form C. 2118.

WAR DIARY
or
INTELLIGENCE SUMMARY.
(Erase heading not required.)

Instructions regarding War Diaries and Intelligence Summaries are contained in F. S. Regs., Part II. and the Staff Manual respectively. Title pages will be prepared in manuscript.

Place	Date	Hour	Summary of Events and Information	Remarks and references to Appendices
	Sept 29th	1900	The Battalion moved up and relieved the 1st Border Regt in the left sub-sector of the trenches as usual.	
	Sept 30th		The enemy's artillery was rather more active than usual in the morning. Several shells from a 4.2 howitzer were fired into ST JEAN unfortunately killing a Sergeant of the A.S.C. who had been attached to the Batt for a month, to qualify for a commission.	
		2100	At night, after half an hour's intense bombardment of the enemy's trenches by our artillery, a raiding party from the 1st Border Regt, consisting of about 2 Officers and 32 other ranks, entered the German lines at C 29 a. 30. 95. The bombardment had been most effective, and the party returned in about 10 minutes with 12 German prisoners, suffering only 2 casualties themselves. The enemy did not appear to offer any resistance. His retaliation was also weak, and we suffered no casualties. There was also an almost complete cessation of the usual machine gun fire.	

1/10/16

Ernest H Colonel
Comdg 1 South Wales Borderers

2nd Batn. The South Wales Borderers.　　　　Appendix I.

Daily Programme of Work whilst Battn. is in Divisional Reserve.

For all Ranks. (Including Officers, Headqr. men and Specialists.)

1. 7am. to 7.30am.	Physical Drill	Under Coy Commanders
2. 9am. to 9.30am.	Squad + Coy Drill	Under Adjutant
3. 2pm. to 3pm.	Gas Drill	Under Coy. Commdrs. & special Bn. N.C.O.'s

Note. Gas Helmet drill should be practised under all conditions, and every man should be able to get his Gas Helmet on in 10 seconds, and be ready to open fire within 30 seconds.

Officers. (with the exception of Coy. Commanders, Officers in charge of special classes and officers required by Coy. for training N.C.O.'s and men in various duties.)

1. 10am. to 1pm.	Instruction in the following subjects:- Revetting, Wiring and drainage; Lewis Gun; Bombing; Bayonet Fighting; Trench Standing Orders	Under arrangements and supervision of the 2nd in Command with the assistance of Specialist Officers.

Companies' Training.

1. 10am. to 12.30pm.	Instruction in the following subjects:- Bayonet Fighting; Elementary Bombing; Wiring, Revetting and Draining.	Under Company Commanders and selected Officers

Note. Each Coy. to practice patrols and wiring by night, on at least one occasion during the Battn's tour in Reserve.

2. 3pm. to 4pm.	Squad Drill for backward men and awkward squad	Under selected N.C.O.'s with supervision of R.S.M.

Special Classes.

1. 10am. to 12.30pm.	Raiding party of 2 Officers and 35 Other Ranks.	Under 2/Lt. H. Webb and 2/Lt. Wm Evans

Note. This party will train and practise on a definitely selected point on enemy's line, which should be marked out with tape.
Full details to be worked out and practised on at least 3 nights whilst in Reserve.

2. 10am. to 12.30pm	Advanced Bombing Class of 4 N.C.O.'s and 28 men.	Under Bn. Bombing Officer, and selected N.C.O.'s

Daily Programme of Work. Contd. (2)

3.	10 am. to 12:30 pm.	Lewis Gun Class of 1 Officer, 2 N.C.O.s and 24 men.	Under Battn. Lewis Gun Officer and selected N.C.O.
4.	10 am. to 12:30 pm.	Snipers training	Under Battn. Sniping Officer
5.	10 am. to 12:30 pm.	Class of 22 men to be trained as Pioneers	Under Pioneer Sergt. and present Pioneers

Note:
In addition to the above the following Specialists will be trained away from the Battalion:—

(a) A Divisional Bombing Course for 2 Officers and 25 O.R. Rarity, commencing 9th Sept. Details will be issued later.

(b) Gas Course, under Divl. Gas Officer. Details issued later.

(c) Combined Patrol Scheme with M.G. Squadron R.F. Corps. Officer M.G. Teams and all available signallers to attend. Details issued later.

A Regimental Tour will take place while the Battalion is in Reserve, at a time and date to be notified later.

Morris, Lieut-Colonel
Commanding 1/16th Battn.

Sept 1st 1916.

29th Division.
87th Infantry Brigade.

2nd BATTALION

SOUTH WALES BORDERERS.

OCTOBER 1 9 1 6

CONFIDENTIAL.

WAR DIARY

OF

2nd. BATTALION THE SOUTH WALES BORDERERS,

October 1916

PP. 209 to 220

VOLUME 22.

WAR DIARY
or
INTELLIGENCE SUMMARY.
(Erase heading not required.)

Army Form C. 2118.

2 SWB (209) Vol 8

Place	Date	Hour	Summary of Events and Information	Remarks and references to Appendices
	1st Oct.	0850	In the morning we saw an enemy observation balloon brought down by one of our aeroplanes. The aeroplane dived straight on to the balloon from the clouds and passed very close it, then turning and making a second attack. Nothing appeared to happen for about ten seconds, and then some smoke appeared, and immediately afterwards, a large sheet of flame shot up from the balloon, which fell and disappeared from view still burning. Just before the balloon fell, two men were seen to jump from it and descend by parachute, but they were apparently caught up and engulfed by the flaming balloon. The same afternoon, a Belgian balloon was apparently brought down in a similar way to our North. The enemy continues quiet and has made no subsequent retaliation for the raid last night.	
	2nd Oct.	0930	In the morning the enemy fired a few trench mortar shells on B.9. Our artillery retaliated very heavily with 6 inch howitzers, as well as Divisional Artillery. The enemy has been much less active for the last two nights with his machine guns. In the	

Army Form C. 2118.

WAR DIARY
or
INTELLIGENCE SUMMARY.
(Erase heading not required.)

210

Place	Date	Hour	Summary of Events and Information	Remarks and references to Appendices
	2nd Oct contd.	2030	Evening an advance party of the Liverpool Scottish, 166th Bde., who are to relieve us on the night of 4th-5th Oct consisting of 4 Officers and 8 N.C.Os., arrived.	
	3rd Oct.		Enemy very quiet. The usual work carried on in the trenches.	
	4th Oct.		The weather has been much worse during the last two days, there being generally a steady rain during the day and clearing up at night.	
		20.00	At night the battalion was relieved by the 10th Liverpool Scottish, and	
		21.30	marching back to the ASYLUM, entrained for L Camp, west of	
		24.00	POPERINGHE, where they arrived about midnight. One Coy was too late to catch the train, and arrived about an hour later, having travelled by a subsequent train.	
	5th Oct		The battalion remained in L Camp and was inspected in the	
		12.00	morning by the Corps commander, Lieut-General Sir Aylmer Hunter Weston. The Battalion was formed up on three sides of a square, the men who had been at the Original Landing at Gallipoli being formed up together on one flank. The General spoke to each	Total numbers 4 Officers 125 O.R.

WAR DIARY
or
INTELLIGENCE SUMMARY

Army Form C. 2118

Place	Date	Hour	Summary of Events and Information	Remarks and references to Appendices
	5th Oct Cont		of this party individually, and addressed the battalion, congratulating them on past achievements, and wishing them luck for the future.	
	6th Oct.		We remained in L Camp, making preparations for a move on the following morning, en route for the SOMME battle front again.	
	7th Oct.	01.30	The battalion left L Camp in the early morning, and marched	
		04.00	to HOPOUTRE siding, just South of POPERINGHE, where they entrained and travelled via HAZEBROUCK, STOMER, CALAIS, BOULOGNE, and AMIENS to LONGEAU which is about 1½ miles South of AMIENS	
		16.30	arriving in the afternoon. Detraining here, they marched to CARDONNETTE, about N.E. of AMIENS, a distance of 6½ miles,	
		19.45	arriving after dark. The battalion was billeted here, the billets however not being of the best, and the men somewhat crowded.	
	8th Oct		Remained in our billets, every attempt being made to proceed with the training of Bombers, but facilities for this were very	
	9th Oct		limited as the battalion is continually on the move, and it is impossible to obtain any dummy material. A scheme was carried	

WAR DIARY or INTELLIGENCE SUMMARY

Place	Date	Hour	Summary of Events and Information	Remarks and references to Appendices
9th Oct Contd			out for a few Officers and N.C.Os at the Aerodrome near by, in connection with Contact Aeroplanes.	
	10th Oct	14.00	The battalion left CARDONNETTE and marched via ALLONVILLE QUERRIEUX and cross roads at D.17 a.1.1. to BUIRE on the river ANCRE. a distance of between 12 and 13 miles, arriving after dark and going into billets, which were considerably better than those at CARDONNETTE. Most of the march was along the main BAPAUME Road, which was very congested by traffic, and very dusty. The battalion has had very little marching recently, and consequently this represented a very considerable effort, but very few men fell out, and the march was accomplished creditably.	Ref Map 1/20,000 Sheet 62 d. N.E.
11th Oct			The Battalion remained in BUIRE and continued training etc	
12th Oct			Practice for an attack was carried out, though not on any specified portion of the line.	

WAR DIARY
or
INTELLIGENCE SUMMARY.
(Erase heading not required.)

Army Form C. 2118.

(213)

Place	Date	Hour	Summary of Events and Information	Remarks and references to Appendices
	13th Oct	13.30	The Battalion marched from BUIRE to a Camp South West of FRICOURT a distance of about five miles. As the Somme battle front is approached, the congestion of traffic on the roads becomes worse and horse. The battalion had to march for most of the way on extremely bad tracks by the side of the main roads. The Camp is extremely bad, consisting of rough Tarpaulin huts and tents, and Officers and men are very crowded. The Camp was also found to be extremely dirty.	
	14th & 18th Oct		The Battalion remained in the Camp and training was carried on with practice was also continued for an attack on two objectives, such as we may be required to carry out. The weather has turned considerably colder, and there has been a good deal of rain.	
	19th Oct	10.30	Orders were received in the early morning to move at 10:30 a.m. to BERNAFAY Wood camp about S.22d We moved off to as ordered, but our progress was terribly slow owing to the tremendous congestion of traffic on the roads, and we did not reach our camp till late afternoon, although	
		16.00		

Army Form C. 2118.

WAR DIARY
or
INTELLIGENCE SUMMARY.
(Erase heading not required.)

(214)

Place	Date	Hour	Summary of Events and Information	Remarks and references to Appendices
	19th Oct		the distance was only 4 miles. When we arrived in the camp, which only consisted of 3 or 4 tents and a number of small bivouac shelters, we were informed that we had to move up to the trenches that night. It had been raining hard all day, but cleared in the evening.	
		17.30	Our transport did not reach us till dusk, and after getting the men	
		20.15	a meal and dumping all packs and blankets, we moved off after dark. The Batt followed the road through LONGUEVAL to 88th Bde HQ at about S.12.b. Where we were met by guides from the 1st Hants Regt. The latter part of the road was very deep mud and the men became very exhausted getting through it. We then left the road and followed along a very long and muddy Communication trench to the Batt HQ of the 4th Worcester Regt in a Sunken ~~Hestep~~ road S.W. of GUEUDECOURT. The Coys were then led up to the	
	20th Oct	01.00	front line by guides, the line to be occupied being GREASE Trench from N.21.d.3.7 to N.20.d.6.9. The guides however were not too sure of their way and there was heavy shelling of the Communication trenches and GUEUDECOURT Wood, which were very congested owing to the relief	

WAR DIARY
or
INTELLIGENCE SUMMARY.
(Erase heading not required.)

Army Form C. 2118.

(215)

Place	Date	Hour	Summary of Events and Information	Remarks and references to Appendices
	20th Oct contd		of the Hunts Regt taking place at the same time. We suffered considerable casualties and the long becoming mixed, relief was not complete before	
		0530	dawn, only a proportion of men having reached the front line. During the morning nothing further could be done until the situation had been cleared up. Later it was found the whole of a half of A & half of B had completed relief. At dusk the remainder of relief was carried out & Brigade & Hants Regt to left their Trenches.	
	21st Oct	2230	A party of the K.O.S.B.s carrying up our rations were fired on and the party forced to get rid of 2nd Beasts days was sent to find where rations were left and brought by mistake into the next Brigade & was carried to dead body in the enemy. Rations eventually brought up by our own men. The night 20/21st & 21/22nd were very cold. The men had arrived wet in the Trenches & as there was no cover there was no chance of getting dry. The result of this was that a very large number of the men got trench feet some of them being very bad cases. During the two days the 18th was in the front line, the Enemy kept up a	

Army Form C. 2118.

WAR DIARY
or
INTELLIGENCE SUMMARY.
(Erase heading not required.)

(216)

Place	Date	Hour	Summary of Events and Information	Remarks and references to Appendices
GUEUDECOURT	21/10/16		More or less continuous shelling on GUEUDECOURT + communication trench to the West of it. Our front line trench was little shelled by enemy but our own artillery was continually short.	
		19.30	1/4 O.S. Borderers relieved us in the front line & B^a retired to support line.	
	22/10/16		The last Coy arriving back at 4.0 a.m. The following were the casualties during the two days in the front line	

Killed
Capt B.J. DAVIES   20-10-16
2/Lt D.R. BATTY   20-10-16   2/Lieut C.J. WILTON 21-10-16
                                                                    Killed
2/Lt A.C. WEBB   20-10-16 ⎫
Lieut A.B. COUSSMAKER 21-10-16 ⎬ Wounded   Died of wounds –
2/Lt W.F. DAVIES   21-10-16 ⎪   2/Lieut R.D. BEARDSHAW 21-10-16
2/Lt W. RHYS JONES 21-10-16 ⎪   2/Lieut E.T.S. BRICKNELL 22-10-16
2/Lt C.P. OWENS 21-10-16 (at duty) ⎭

NCOs + men.
Killed 20.   Wounded 58.   Missing 45.

WAR DIARY
or
INTELLIGENCE SUMMARY.
(Erase heading not required.)

Army Form C. 2118.

(217)

Place	Date	Hour	Summary of Events and Information	Remarks and references to Appendices
	22/10/16		On leaving the trenches the following were sent to hospital nearly all suffering from trench feet:- Lieut M. THOMAS. - Lieut W. J. RHOADES - 2Lt P. J. MULVEY - 2/Lt J.E. HARRIS N.C.O's - men - 64.	
	23/10/16		We remained in the support trench 600 yards S.W. of GUEUDECOURT and during the day 75 men were sent to hospital, mostly suffering from trench feet. All men had been given dry socks and whale oil on leaving the trenches, and every endeavour made to check the sickness. Each man was also issued with a leather jerkin.	
	24/10/16		Remained in support trench and 25 further men admitted to hospital. Rain fell for nearly the whole day.	
	25/10/16		Remained in support trench, and 78 men admitted to hospital. The strength at present with the battalion is 19 Officers 393 other ranks, the number in trenches being 16 Officers and 330 other ranks. The Battalion moved up to	
		1800	the trenches again at night, but did not hold quite the same line. Only half the previous front trench was held i.e. the right half	

of GREASE Trench in front of GUEUDECOURT, a front of about 350 yards. This was held by two Companies (A and C), the remaining two being respectively in support in the Sunken road, west of GUEUDECOURT, and in reserve in GOAT trench near Batt. H.Q. The relief was accomplished during the night without mishap. Head Quarters Bombers and Lewis Gunners were attached to Coys, owing to casualties in these specialists.

26th Oct

A normal day with the exception of heavy shelling by the enemy in the afternoon, due apparently to nervousness of an attack by us. Orders were prepared for an attack by us on the 28th inst Oct

02.00 which had been previously postponed from today. In the early morning a patrol under Lieut. J.H. Harford went out to discover if the enemy had any wire out on our front. The patrol was unfortunately caught by the enemy's fire and Lieut. Harford was killed. During the night also, both Capt. B.J.R. Kelly and 2-Lt W.M Evans reported sick and were sent to hospital.

WAR DIARY
or
INTELLIGENCE SUMMARY.
(Erase heading not required.)

Army Form C. 2118.

Place	Date	Hour	Summary of Events and Information	Remarks and references to Appendices
	27th Oct		During the day orders came through that our attack had again been postponed, and that we were to be relieved at night by the 4th Worcester Regt. The relief was carried out without mishap and the battalion moved back into Brigade reserve in SWITCH and GAP trenches about half a mile in front of DELVILLE wood. The weather had been very bad during the day and our new trenches were in a terribly muddy condition, and there was practically no shelter from rain or cold for Officers or men.	
	28th Oct		The Battalion remained in Bde reserve and some material having been obtained, some shelters were improvised for the men. The day was fine with occasional showers, and cold.	
	29th Oct		The Battalion remained during the day in Bde reserve and during the afternoon our trenches were heavily shelled but no damage was done to our men. 2nd Lt H.P. Robjent reported sick and was sent to hospital, and each day a number of men were sent away sick. At night the Battalion was relieved by the 7th Australian Infantry Regt	

WAR DIARY
or
INTELLIGENCE SUMMARY.

Army Form C. 2118.

Place	Date	Hour	Summary of Events and Information	Remarks and references to Appendices
	30 Oct contd.		and moved back into a camp at POMMIER Redoubt about half way between MAMETZ and MONTAUBAN. The main road is now terribly broken up and muddy, and our camp was no better than a sea of mud, though the men had tents.	
	30 Oct	10.30	The Battalion moved back into wooden huts about a mile west of FRICOURT. The transport took all day and most of the night to arrive however, owing to the congestion of the roads. The day was very wet, with a gale of wind blowing, but the huts provided very good shelter. A number of men rejoined from hospital and rest camps.	
	31st Oct.		Remained at camp near FRICOURT and spent the time reorganizing, cleaning up, and checking casualties. Baths were obtained for the men at VIVIER MILL. Strength with battalion including transport, Medical Officer and Chaplain 15 Officers 416 Other ranks	

CD Mahershon Capt for Lt Col
Cmdg 2 SW Borderers

Fricourt Camp. 1/11/16

29th Division.
87th Infantry Brigade.

2nd BATTALION

SOUTH WALES BORDERERS

NOVEMBER 1 9 1 6

CONFIDENTIAL.

WAR DIARY of the

2nd BATTALION THE SOUTH WALES BORDERERS,

From 1st November 1916 to 31st November 1916

VOL. ~~23~~

Pages 221 to

Army Form C. 2118.

WAR DIARY
or
~~INTELLIGENCE~~ SUMMARY.
(Erase heading not required.)

Place	Date	Hour	Summary of Events and Information	Remarks and references to Appendices
FRICOURT	1915 1st Nov		The Battalion remained in Camp, and some attempts were made to clear paths through the mud round about the huts. The weather however continues bad, and fresh mud is continually formed over everything. Classes in Lewis Guns and Bombing were started, but no material is available and there is no suitable training ground.	
	2nd Nov		The Battalion received orders in the morning to entrain at	
	3rd Nov		ALBERT at 2 p.m. for AIRAISNES. (about 24 Kilometres from ABBEVILLE) All transport including officers chargers has been sent. The day before to CORBIE. Here it will remain until the Battalion returns to the line which is expected to be by the 12th or 13th inst. Battalion entrained at 12.15 p.m. and marched to ALBERT Station. Owing to congestion of traffic our train did not leave till nearly 4 p.m. and instead of arriving at AIRAISNES at about 6 p.m. did not reach our destination till midnight. Fortunately the weather was not hard and so done and all were settled in billets an hour late. Quite the best billets the battalion has had yet.	

Army Form C. 2118.

WAR DIARY
or
INTELLIGENCE SUMMARY.
(Erase heading not required.)

Place	Date	Hour	Summary of Events and Information	Remarks and references to Appendices
AIR AISNES	1916 Nov 4th		Company inspections were carried out, and intends to equipment and clothing rendered. The latter is in a very bad state due to bad weather conditions to which the men have been subjected. Captain Aspinall of Halverhas proceeded to England on ten days leave.	
	Nov 5th		Sunday. Installation parade to Divine Service in the Cinema at 9.30 a.m. Canon Hill Ried (who has been attached to Battalion since arrival in France) conducted the service. Esprobes parade followed at 11 a.m. A good deal of ammo drive is needed.	
	Nov 6th		Sgt Majors parade from 9 to 10 a.m. followed by Coy officers parade 10.30 to 12.30 for practice in attack with barrage. Wire cutters by flags. One Company at Musketry in Bombing range. Training carried out in the afternoon in Bombing Signalling and Lewis Gun drills. Also Communication drill for NCOs. The same arrangements, that includes have been arranged for tomorrow. One Company in the morning and one to two afternoons. There are several Officers and NCOs to have So	

T2131. Wt. W708—776. 500000. 4/15. Sir J. C. & S.

WAR DIARY
or
INTELLIGENCE SUMMARY.
(Erase heading not required.)

Army Form C. 2118.

(223)

Place	Date	Hour	Summary of Events and Information	Remarks and references to Appendices
AIRAISNES	1916			
	Nov 8		If a complete change of clothing could be issued at the same time Ordnance is apparently unable to supply the demands on it at present. The troops are now in a very bad condition.	
	Nov 9		Training carried out as on the two previous days. Capt H.O. Garrett proceeded on ten days leave to England. Although there is a marked improvement in the appearance of the men, the same drill is such quantity considering the short time the battalion has been out of the trenches & considerate amount of rain have fallen during the last ten days. It has suffered to interfere with the training.	
	Nov 10		Captain P.R.M. Munday took over the duties of acting Adjutant. The Battalion is employed with the 1st K.O.S.B. furnished the attack of the camp & picquet during the night. In the afternoon the Brigade Signal Officer & Stats.	
	Nov 11		The Battalion as well as the 1st K.O.S.B. were inspected in the	

Army Form C. 2118.

WAR DIARY
or
INTELLIGENCE SUMMARY.
(Erase heading not required.)

224

Place	Date	Hour	Summary of Events and Information	Remarks and references to Appendices
AIRAINES	Nov. 11		Jackson & Major General H.B. de Lisle. The general commented on the excellence of the landing of arms by the Battalion, after its inspection. Lieutenant Hollins R.A.M.C. and Lt. Jones R.I. Reg. were each decorated with the Military Medal. Troops both battalions. R.S.M. ran an stretcher bearers and carried their wounds by conspicuous gallantry and skill and will the Battalion was today GREASE TRENCH & point J, GOEUDECOURT. Battalion did a counter attack of the large front. A good crowd of the 87th Field Amb. when they got in the evening.	
	Nov. 12		There was a slight genial this morning near the Chaplain. Inspector of Small Arms was held during the day. During the morning as attack was practised when the suggestion made by the Divisional Commander Signallers, Bahy and Lewis gun classes were held in the afternoon. Orders were received for the Battalion to move French retrn. late to the Citadel Camp in the afternoon. Rev. Chaplain Rev. Evan Reid left the battalion & proceed to Scotland as a Chaplain of the Force of young with H.M. army.	
	Nov. 13			

Army Form C. 2118.

225

WAR DIARY
or
INTELLIGENCE SUMMARY.
(Erase heading not required.)

Instructions regarding War Diaries and Intelligence Summaries are contained in F.S. Regs., Part II. and the Staff Manual respectively. Title pages will be prepared in manuscript.

Place	Date	Hour	Summary of Events and Information	Remarks and references to Appendices
AIRAINES	Nov. 14		The Battn. proceeded by French motor buses to CITADEL CAMP via SRICOURT. The motors took the regiment up from the BOIRE. For there a very tiring march. The cost was extremely muddy. Major Parks rejoined from leave.	
CITADEL CAMP	Nov. 15		The Battn. moved at 10 a.m. to CARNOY in the support, took the land occupied by 2nd Batt. the Middlesex Regt. near the duckwalks. Going to our own line. Regiment was not moving. Essentially after recovering about the H.P.L. the regiment was put into bivouacs near BRIQUETERIE. It must have been very cold, but inclement day. We had accommodation and the night was bitter, cold. There were about 80 % frost. Very little food was obtainable for the men.	
LES BOEUFS	Nov. 16		The Battn. moved up into the support trenches behind LES BOEUFS named JOHN BULL – OK – HOGS BACK trenches. Arrived early in the afternoon and the relief was effected by daylight. At Col J. Going went to Hospital Sick. Major G. T. Raikes thereon assumed command. Trenches in very bad condition; still very thaw; a nasty daybreak. The night was very cold. All out to° of frost and a strong East wide (blowing). The day was beautiful, fine and the men and all ran laid Fraser staff clerks made themselves much easier. Men were employed in improving the trenches, &c.	
	Nov. 17			

T2134. Wt. W708–776. 500000. 4/15. Str J. C. & S.

WAR DIARY
or
INTELLIGENCE SUMMARY

Army Form C. 2118.

226

Place	Date	Hour	Summary of Events and Information	Remarks and references to Appendices
LES BOEUFS	17	am	enemy shelling our trenches for GINCHY; a long way. The enemy shelled our trenches intermittently and reports of casualties. The wind had veered [...] the night and rain continued to fall throughout	
	18		[illegible] noted in the day [...] A new [...] was started [...] when the DUCK WALK finished. [...] from FLERS-MORVAL ROAD. Digging was fairly easy. [...] the trench had 2' which had been [...] had had the GP TRENCH. The enemy did not do much shelling today. & to every large carrying party had the details to take up material. Rifles, rations, RSA, wire at. Also led light to carry, and no foot had seen to dig & had rides.	
	19		Again red led rations [...] trenches [...] full of water and the now has been extremely wet. GOC Division came [...] in the army to what the men had of defence. Later the memory of Price Johnson + Brig Gen Gartner, they visited the Batt Hqs. The commander had ten cathedras on the alarms. The 1st KOSB, whom we were on centre of either GOR BUST [...] for the next two as well as WATERLOG essex. Received orders to go up the front line for one day for men.	

Army Form C. 2118.

WAR DIARY
or
INTELLIGENCE SUMMARY.
(Erase heading not required.)

Instructions regarding War Diaries and Intelligence Summaries are contained in F. S. Regs., Part II. and the Staff Manual respectively. Title pages will be prepared in manuscript.

Place	Date	Hour	Summary of Events and Information	Remarks and references to Appendices
LES BOEUFS	Nov. 20		Day bright and clear. Had still 160 bad and 40 casualty marshal stats logged. The Batt. moved up to front line trenches. The move delayed by relief counterattack.	
	21		Throughout the day all quiet, a few casualties, two caused by our own guns. Situation is a bad one for our unit as lot of shrapnel. Relief did not take place and the Batt. not back into support.	
	22		The Batt.'s own Lewis which was returned early reached arrived. Communication trenches very deep made the Pioneer Batt. front Reserve caries of shallow depth. Died 7.10 a.m. the enemy opened a heavy bombardment a different nature & on left flank Gases discovered. It lasted about half an hour; our guns replied with great vigour. Troops held out "north" had this kept.	
	23		Brigdr. Morris aid clnl. 5° of Irish. The Batt. was relieved by 1st Essex Fusiliers and lus. branch back to CARNOY CAMP. Relief was completed and Coys here 9 to 10.20 p.m. A good deal of aerial activity on both sides. The German planes came right on to the supposed lines.	
CARNOY	24		This day was occupied in clearing up and the men resting; the camp is in mud, and needs a deal of draining.	

WAR DIARY or INTELLIGENCE SUMMARY

Army Form C. 2118.

228

Place	Date	Hour	Summary of Events and Information	Remarks and references to Appendices
CARNOY	Nov 25		Bathe men allotted to the Bath at MEAVITE. Boys sent for who had to take all the hot baths MSos. Linen has been prepared. Sent all clean under clothing which has truly lacked.	
	26		Church service.	
CUREMONT	27		Bath paraded up to the Radw Line of BILLEMONT and were accompanied & dug out - camp to nearly. The Bn's aeroplane brought down near GINCHY. Two officers arrived. 2nd Lieut. Lowe and 2nd Lt. Dante.	
	28		Day spent in cleaning & arriving the camp. 250 men of a R.E. fatigue party cut dugouts and smoke pipes. A draft of 7 officers arrived. 2nd Lt. J.S. Reid – 2nd Lt. Morgan – 2nd Lt. S.H. Irvin – 2nd Lt. R. Phillips – 2nd Lt. A.T. Lewis – 2nd Lt. H. Davis – 2nd Lt. Salaud. The Battn. moved up ? to the front line trenches in front of LES BOEUFS	
LES BOEUFS	29		relieving 1m 1st Border Regt. Very cold weather with frost.	
	30		Misty day and cold about 10° of frost. Guns on the ground sent. To the last build shelling all day. ½ to twice. Battn. lost one man abt 200 yds of front from 125th French Reg't of Infantry. On trench is really butter trench not as in the trenches rather the fire steps.	

G.T. Parker Major
Comdg 2/L [illegible]

29th Division.

87th Infantry Brigade

2nd BATTALION

SOUTH WALES BORDERES

DECEMBER 1 9 1 6

CONFIDENTIAL.

WAR DIARY

OF

2ND. BATTALION THE SOUTH WALES BORDERERS,

From 1/12/16 - 31/12/16

VOLUME 25

Nos. 228 to 231.

CONFIDENTIAL.

WAR DIARY
or
INTELLIGENCE SUMMARY.
(Erase heading not required.)

Army Form C. 2118.

Place	Date	Hour	Summary of Events and Information	Remarks and references to Appendices
LES BOEUFS	Sep 1st		Cold and frosty and left trenches. Intermittent hostile shelling all day and slow shelling in the front line. Front line was clearing trenches and digging forward new T.'s. About 3.30 p.m. the enemy commenced a very heavy hostile barrage which lasted two mins. most of the shells went over the front line. Our artillery replied vigorously. The 1st Essex Regt. took over some 200 yds of front line trench on the left.	
	2nd		Hard frost again and thick mist. Some shelling but during the morning it died down and for the rest of the day all was fairly quiet. The Germans were reported to be leaving this night. The 16th Middlesex lost one officer & one N.C.O. & 14 other ranks wounded owing to their gas going wrong. The Batt. went to GUILLEMONT all to be by 9.30 p.m.	
GUILLEMONT	3rd		The Batt. moved from GUILLEMONT b.m. 22 Camp CARNOY. L.t P. ROSS rejoining H.Q. The Batt. was in b 5.30 p.m. in hutments here improved a little.	
CARNOY	4th		Batt. overhauled in huts and employed in refitting and changing clothing.	
	5th		The Batt. was attached the 5th Division at MÉAULTE. A party of 200 men went to GUILLEMONT for carrying fatigues under Capt Garrett.	
	6th		Very cold east wind & all Batt. on fatigues. Road in the camp began to be corduroyed etc.	

INTELLIGENCE SUMMARY

(Erase heading not required.)

Place	Date	Hour	Summary of Events and Information	Remarks and references to Appendices
CARNOY	Dec. 7		Batt. on fatigue up at GUILLEMONT; parts returned in the afternoon. Col Cellier, Capt Yglesia & Capt Barton from 1st Batt came over from the MAMETZ huts. 1st Batt relieving the East Surreys west of GUEUDECOURT	
	8		Rain today: parties detailed to dig strong points behind front line	
	9		Battalion moved by rail to VILLE. 1st Batt K.R.R.C. took over its camp. Parade at 12.30. Left the Plateau station. Arrived at Edgehill station at 5.45 p.m.	
VILLE	10		y. Billets at VILLE	
"	11		Advance party sent forward to prepare billets at our next village. Batt moved by road to Corbie (via) relieved by 1st Bat Rifle Brigade. arrived CORBIE 4 p.m.	
CORBIE	12		Batt moved by train to HANGEST; from there ? marches to RIENCOURT where it was billeted. Very bad day. Snow, sleet and rain.	
RIENCOURT	13	y	TRaining carried out as per programme attached.	
	16			
LE QUESNOY	17		The Battalion moved at 10 a.m. by road to LE QUESNOY. a distance of 3½ miles. Training carried out as per programme attached	

INTELLIGENCE SUMMARY.

(Erase heading not required.)

Place	Date	Hour	Summary of Events and Information	Remarks and references to Appendices
LE QUES.	18"		Training and improvement of Billets continued.	
NOY			The following officers arrived on joining 2nd bn 24-12-16. 2nd Lieut. Shaw. 25-12-16. 2nd Lieut. Weeks 26-12-16. 2nd Lieut. Keele 29-12-16.	
			2nd Harris rejoined from Hospital 29-12-16. 2nd Jones went sick on 17-12-16.	
			Capt. H. Garrett was promoted Temporary Major 28th December 1916. 2nd Ovens and 2nd Reman were promoted Temporary Captains to date	
	31st		22-11-16 & 24-11-16 respectively.	

H Harvey Major
Comdg 2 Swale Borderers

8/29

Vol XI

Confidential

War Diary of
2nd South Wales Borderers.

Volume I

January 1917

Army Form C. 2118.

WAR DIARY
or
INTELLIGENCE SUMMARY.
(Erase heading not required.)

Instructions regarding War Diaries and Intelligence Summaries are contained in F.S. Regs., Part II. and the Staff Manual respectively. Title pages will be prepared in manuscript.

Place	Date	Hour	Summary of Events and Information	Remarks and references to Appendices
	1917			
LE QUESNOY	Jan 11		The rest at LE QUESNOY; Training carried on as per programme.	
			On January 10th an unfortunate accident occurred. 2nd Lt Waddle was throwing bombs when one burst prematurely, shattering his right hand and wounding him in the leg.	
			The following Officers joined: 2nd Lieut Parr, 2nd Lieut E. Green 10-1-17; 2nd Lt F.E. Walton 10-1-17.	
BEESLE	Jan 12		The Batt moved by train to BEESLE, 12 going up into the forward area. Arrived at the village at 9 p.m.	Casualties 2nd Lt Smith E.A. French (sick)
CARNOY	Jan 13		The Batt marched to CARNOY CAMP a distance of about 12 miles. The roads were good until towards the end. The (camp was to some extent occupied before. The dugouts were exceedingly bad, the entrance being 3 ft deep in mud. We took fifteen hours to dig out during our absence.	
GUILLEMONT	Jan 14		Moved up to B.C. Nissen huts at GUILLEMONT. Journey was cold and some of the men fell out of hunger. Frost during the night.	
MORVAL	Jan 15		Batt moved up into the right Batt. Left sector relieving 11/7 B Battn Dorset Regt. The relief is very bad; FLANK AVENUE completed before the Division left. Further hostile has ceased.	

Army Form C. 2118.

WAR DIARY
or
INTELLIGENCE SUMMARY.
(Erase heading not required.)

Instructions regarding War Diaries and Intelligence Summaries are contained in F. S. Regs., Part II. and the Staff Manual respectively. Title pages will be prepared in manuscript.

Place	Date	Hour	Summary of Events and Information	Remarks and references to Appendices
	1917.			
MORVAL	Jan 15.		Is still ½ the top of British. 300 yds of N front line has been ducked boarded. Practically no shelling and the relief was completed by 4 p.m. Delay was caused owing to the bad going. The front line is extremely bad and only consists of small posts holding it. There is no wire in front & there are no communication trenches. Day very bright.	
MORVAL	Jan 16		There was a frost of 10°, which made the ground quite firm. The day was very cold and trusty. No trains during the day. Shelling very mild and considerably less than when the Batt: was last holding the front line. "B" Coy and ½ "D" Coy in front line; "C" Coy and ½ "D" in support "A" Coy in reserve.	
	Jan 17		Hard frost and guns 3 inches deep. Difficult of pushing men in crumps. Some sniping carried on in the front line and on the enemy at least was hit. The Batt: was relieved by 1st Border Regt and the relief was completed by 10 p.m. which was quick considering the bad going.	
CARNOY	Jan 18		Hard frost and some snow storms. Six men dispatched with trench fut. Lt M. Thymer also went to hospital today.	
	Jan 19		Inspection of Kit and training carried out. Snow still on the ground and little way	

T2134. Wt. W708—776. 500000. 4/15. Sir J. C. & S.

Army Form C. 2118.

WAR DIARY
or
INTELLIGENCE SUMMARY.
(Erase heading not required.)

Place	Date	Hour	Summary of Events and Information	Remarks and references to Appendices
	1917.			
CARNOY	Jan 20		Battalion marched to Bodis class 6. Improvement of cant carried at	
	21st		Somme i YMCA hut: Snow still on the ground and frost ha ever night. Col W.E. Matthews joined	
LES BOEUFS	22nd		Battalion next day. Just worked in new att. strict post (not Permanent) Still at Carnoy.	2/Lt A Jauch (sick)
			is to be to be used ———————— to transform into trenches with wooden tops up between	
			1st Batt Border Regt in LES BOEUFS Sector. find hard and made the track walk	
			very slippery. Relief completed by 9.30 p.m. The night passed quietly. 'A' and 'C' Coy	
			in front line - 'D' Coy Suffolk - 'B' Coy in reserve.	
	23rd		Very hard frost about 15°. night spent in digging front line and carrying stores	
			bombs and fuel up to front line. Bright sun earlier but day was misty. 5 German	
			aeroplanes over early about 10 a.m. Ours appeared later. Machine guns open	
			fire at dusk.	
	24th		Frost came on last night: patrol sent out reported Germans wire to have been	
			badly damaged by artillery fire, heavy artillery has been plenty in German trenches	
			East. Two days with evident good results. Trench Boards carried up to front.	
			Line: very difficult job owing to slippery state of ground and track. Several	
			German aeroplanes over the trenches today and a good deal of a.a. aircraft shooting.	

WAR DIARY
or
INTELLIGENCE SUMMARY.
(Erase heading not required.)

Army Form C. 2118.

Place	Date	Hour	Summary of Events and Information	Remarks and references to Appendices
LES BŒUFS	Jan 24		Our aeroplanes over our lines and afternoon. MORVAL was being shelled intermittently with 5.9" howitzers. Mist in the distance again today and difficult to observe. Batts. relieved by 1st Newfoundland Regt. relief carried out up to 11 p.m.	
GUILLEMONT	Jan 25		Batts here very cold of the Wiggers types. had frost and snow continuous	
	26		Corps employed in practising for in the morning and dressing trench die up for the mopping up parties who are letting part in the attack. Inspection had be premier day for brown to CARNOY to get ready little push in the assault. At 4 p.m. the Batt. moved to new line had 1st of 7th Village. The mopping up parties joined the 1st Border Regt. and 1st R Irish Fusiliers in GUILLEMONT at 8 p.m. when these Batts. passed through to later of their positions for the attack up. Batts. spent the night till 2 a.m. here.	
MORVAL	27	5.30 a.m.	The Barrage commenced and the assaulting Batts. went over Mopping Up parties went forward. It first objective was easily gained with practically no casualties. The Boches evacuated the Trenches and took shelter in 6 officers and 395 men prisoners. During the day there were heavy hostile shell of the whole forward area from forward their BOLE DUMP. At 9.30 a.m. a hostile aeroplane was brought down by on anti aircraft gun.	Our Casualties:- Capt. W. Matthew 2/Lt Hilton 2 Lt Eyles (wounded)

Army Form C. 2118.

WAR DIARY
or
INTELLIGENCE SUMMARY.
(Erase heading not required.)

Instructions regarding War Diaries and Intelligence Summaries are contained in F. S. Regs., Part II. and the Staff Manual respectively. Title pages will be prepared in manuscript.

Place	Date	Hour	Summary of Events and Information	Remarks and references to Appendices
MORVAL	Jan 21		At 2 p.m. the Germans were reported to be massing for a counter attack behind LE TRANSLOY. No attack was made. Up to dawn the Batt. moved up one Lewis gun from 1st Newfoundland Regt. Relay was complete by 10.30 p.m. 2nd section and Lewis gun left wounded. Capt Matthew was also wounded at several times. Casualties	
LES BOEUFS	Jan 28		Stand for at night and cold. Saw him Hostile Shelling continued all over the forward area in the afternoon. BENNET TR. was systematically bombarded but with the result of only two casualties. Hostile aeroplane was brought down at 2:30 p.m. near GUEUDECOURT. Coys. were distributed as follows: D'Coy. FALLIT R. : 'B' Coy. BENNET TR. : 'C' Coy. in support of WINTER STREET and AUTUMN TR. : 'A' Coy. in Reserve at COW TR. During the night 'B' Coy. took over a bit of the new A. captured line and 'C' Coy. moved into the front line. A Coy. came up into support. Batt. very weak ab. 295 all told	2 Men wounded slight Casualties 2nd Lt. R. Rowland wounded
	Jan 29		Held Shelling continued all day but the afternoon. Half moved. Aeroplanes F/15 and 16 casualties including 2 Lt. Garland(?) half wounded German flew low over the front line audibly regaining the mornings. The hpe Batt was relieved by 1st Essex Regt. Relief complete by 10.30 p.m. Coys. were shelled going out of the line by the Duck Walk.	

Army Form C. 2118.

WAR DIARY
or
INTELLIGENCE SUMMARY.
(Erase heading not required.)

Instructions regarding War Diaries and Intelligence Summaries are contained in F.S. Regs., Part II. and the Staff Manual respectively. Title pages will be prepared in manuscript.

Place	Date	Hour	Summary of Events and Information	Remarks and references to Appendices
EDLLEFONT	30/7		Bath. Spent the night here. Still cold and frosty. Difficulty in starting water cart & trucking of hipes. 1st Newfoundland Regt relieve the Batt at 2.30 A.M.	
CARNOY	July 31st		from where it proceeded to CARNOY. Frost less severe but there still in the ground. Day spent in refitting and ineffictive and re-organising Coys.	
Add Note	27th		The 1/Inniskilling Fus. & 1/Bord Regt carried out the attack on 27th, the position of Enemys line attacked was from T5.6.8/10 to N.36.D.2/2. - Immediately two attacks on the right & Bord. Regt to left. 4 officers and 16 parties of 1 N.C.O. & 8 men each were found from 2/Scottish Borderers for mopping up the German front trench 2 officers & 8 parties went with each attacking Batts. These parties advanced with the first wave & each party was 50" from the next; on arrival at enemys trench the leader of each party placed a flag on the parapet & commenced clearing the trench on his left. There was little resistance except on the extreme left where 2nd Webber was wounded. These mopping up parties remained in the captured positions for 2 days & during this period suffered about 35 casualties. The following casualties occurred in the Bns between 27th & 29th Jan. inclusive, mopping up parties	

Army Form C. 2118.

WAR DIARY
or
INTELLIGENCE SUMMARY.
(Erase heading not required.)

Instructions regarding War Diaries and Intelligence Summaries are contained in F.S. Regs., Part II. and the Staff Manual respectively. Title pages will be prepared in manuscript.

Place	Date	Hour	Summary of Events and Information	Remarks and references to Appendices
Additional WD Cont[d]			Killed wounded missing	
			Officers - 5 -	
			O.R. 13 66 5	
			Four men of the mopping up parties received too unsuitable metals for work done on 27th.	
			31/7/17	
			A Paras M.C.	
			O.C. 2 Strafo Borderers	

Confidential.

87/29

2nd South Wales Borderers.

War Diary

February 1917.

Army Form C. 2118.

WAR DIARY
or
INTELLIGENCE SUMMARY.
(Erase heading not required.)

Instructions regarding War Diaries and Intelligence Summaries are contained in F. S. Regs., Part II. and the Staff Manual respectively. Title pages will be prepared in manuscript.

Place	Date	Hour	Summary of Events and Information	Remarks and references to Appendices
Carnoy	1/2/17		Frost still severe. Enemies carried out inspections of dirt & feet, otherwise the battalion rested.	
Carnoy	2/2/17		No change in the situation. Battalion rested.	
Carnoy to Guillemont	2/2/17		The Battalion moved up to Guillemont and took over the trenches from the 1st K.O.S.B. We arrived just at night.	
Guillemont to Trenches	3/2/17	4.30 a.m.	The battalion left Guillemont for the line for a 3 days tour. A and D Coys occupied the old German strong points, B and C Coys occupied the front line German trench which had been taken on the 27th Jan. The battalion took over from the Border Regt.	
	4/2/16		During the day the artillery shelled our trenches vigorously, it was impossible to communicate with the men by day. By night anything was possible, but Capt Kennedy was wounded and the Sandys Thomas killed, told by enfilade antimony work on a new strong point.	
	5/2/17		Our trenches were again heavily shelled by day, during the day work outside the trench was impossible, and at night every to chances of enemy and his man at was found difficult to put out wire or carry on work digging. The ground too was exceptionally hard.	

Army Form C. 2118.

WAR DIARY
or
INTELLIGENCE SUMMARY.
(Erase heading not required.)

Instructions regarding War Diaries and Intelligence Summaries are contained in F. S. Regs., Part II. and the Staff Manual respectively. Title pages will be prepared in manuscript.

Place	Date	Hour	Summary of Events and Information	Remarks and references to Appendices
In the line	6/2/17		Battalion was relieved in the evening by the R. Inniskillings and returned to Carnoy camp	
Carnoy to Méaulte	7/2/17		We left Carnoy before noon and marched into billets at Méaulte for rest.	
	8/2/17		Company commanders held inspection, otherwise a 'rest' day	
	9/2/17		Training under S.O. Commanders. Weather still freezing	
	10/2/17		The regiment seems to be harassed by fatigues. Company training was therefore difficult	
	11/2/17		Being Sunday, Church Parades were held. No change in weather.	
	12/2/17		A gentle thaw set in after more than 3 weeks hard frost. During bomb throwing practice an unfortunate accident occurred which resulted in 2 officers and 6 men being wounded. 2nd Lts Wood & 2nd R.S. Lyons	
	13/2/17		The thaw continues. Two new officers 2nd Lt Partridge & 2nd Lt Nightingale joined the Battalion. On account of fatigues companies are reduced to about 10 men on parade.	
	14/2/17		Frost at night continues; by day it thaws gradually. Companies look up to training purposes on account of small numbers.	

WAR DIARY
or
INTELLIGENCE SUMMARY.
(Erase heading not required.)

Army Form C. 2118.

Place	Date	Hour	Summary of Events and Information	Remarks and references to Appendices
Meaulte	15/2/17		Snow continues, but only gently. Companies carry on with training under difficulties owing to shortage of men. Frost entirely disappears, and the mud begins to thaw itself again.	
	16/2/17		A fatigue party of 100 men of the regiment were working at the ammunition dump. When it was bombed from enemy aeroplanes. No casualties were suffered by us.	
	17/2/17		Training continued under O.C. Coys. Arrangements for moving up into the line made.	
MALTZ HORN	18/2/17		The battalion left MEAULTE at 11.30 a.m. and marched via MAMETZ to MALTZ HORN CAMP. They arrived at 3.30 p.m. It was very going on account of mud and traffic. Two companies B & D had been detailed to move to BOIS D'ORE but had to return to MALTZHORN	
	19/2/17		The battalion moved up into the line (SAILLY-SAILLISEL), relieving the 9th Northumberland Fus. MALTZ HORN at 4.30 p.m. Relief was not completed until 11.45 p.m. [Condition of front line very muddy - chiefly held by posts.]	

Army Form C. 2118.

WAR DIARY
or
INTELLIGENCE SUMMARY.
(Erase heading not required.)

Instructions regarding War Diaries and Intelligence Summaries are contained in F.S. Regs., Part II. and the Staff Manual respectively. Title pages will be prepared in manuscript.

Place	Date	Hour	Summary of Events and Information	Remarks and references to Appendices
	20/2/17		Rather an uneventful day in the trenches. The first line companies fell back into support trenches during daytime, because of our artillery bombardment of our own guns.	
	21/2/17		The battalion was relieved by the 1st Royal Dublin Fusiliers, and had to return direct from trenches to BRONFAY a distance of over 10 miles. The men were dead beat. Fortunately a tram was arranged for to carry the men from TRONES WOOD to the PLATEAU.	
BRONFAY	22/2/17		The battalion rested. Company commanders carrying out their usual inspections.	
	23/2/17		The training was carried on under 6" bombs, in barracks rooms, the weather being wet, and no outside accommodation available near the camp on the account of the mud.	
HARDE- COURT.	24/2/17		Sudden orders came to move up to HARDECOURT. The battalion arrived there (in war camp) at about 4 p.m and spent the night there.	
SAILLY SAILLISEL	25/2/17		At 11.30 a.m. we left HARDECOURT for the line, not borrowsthe battalion halted for trench feet treatment, & the enemy as moved up only the	

Army Form C. 2118.

WAR DIARY
or
INTELLIGENCE SUMMARY.
(Erase heading not required.)

2 S W B 5/

Place	Date	Hour	Summary of Events and Information	Remarks and references to Appendices
	Note		[Lt. Col. Ricks left the battalion to attend a Senior Officers Course. Major Gunter assumed command in his absence]	
	26/2/17		SAILLY sector and took over from the 16th Middlesex Regt. Orders from Brigade were received to patrol the enemy's front line to find if it was found unoccupied to hold it. 2nd Lt J.L.C. Morgan with 10 men went out & entered enemy's trenches, not knowing what had happened to his immediate right left he returned to our lines. He himself had encountered none of the enemy. At 12 noon he took out the same party to the same trench & enemy turned & escaped it. In the afternoon he was reinforced by a Lewis Gun team, these unfortunately was caught by machine gun & in was killed and 2 wounded. At night from our own line aimed (through the line) "Lt J.L.C. Morgan & his party suffered no casualties, just before midnight 2nd Lts A.S. Davies M.C. and Lt Cooke took out patrols with a view of occupying every hand on Morgan's immediate night but all all places too easy and was found to be held. The day had been fine & the ground was drying rapidly.	

Army Form C. 2118.

WAR DIARY
or
INTELLIGENCE SUMMARY.
(Erase heading not required.)

Place	Date	Hour	Summary of Events and Information	Remarks and references to Appendices
BOULEAUX AREA	27/1/17		2Lt Morgan withdrew his men from enemy lines at 6am in order not to interfere with the artillery bombardment on our part to destroy enemy wire and trench prior to an attack by the 8th Brigade. In the morning we were relieved by the 1st Royal Dublin Fusiliers who were going over the top at dawn next morning. We moved into the BOULEAUX AREA	
BRONFAY	28/1/17		The Battalion went back to BRONFAY leaving a 100 men and 3 officers at Brigade Hd Quarters as a carrying party. (they returned next day)	

28/1/17

W.J. Kennedy Major
Commdg 2/South Wales Borderers

Vol 13

Confidential.

War Diary
of
2nd South Wales Borderers.
for
Month of March 1917.

WAR DIARY
or
INTELLIGENCE SUMMARY.
(Erase heading not required.)

Army Form C. 2118.

Place	Date	Hour	Summary of Events and Information	Remarks and references to Appendices
BOULEAUX AREA	27/2/17		2/Lt Morgan with three men from every Coy at 6 a.m. in order not to interfere with the artillery bombardment, on our front to do the Engineers wire to trenches prior to an attack by the 86th Brigade. In the evening we were relieved by the 1st R.D.F. who are going over the top but down not making. We moved into the BOULEAUX AREA.	
BRONFAY	28/2/17		The battalion went back to BRONFAY being a 100 men and 3 officers at Brigade Hd Qrs as a carrying party. (They returned next day)	
	1/3/17		A fatigue party of 130 men was supplied to a rejement to the Brigade, the Cpl not one single man for duty of any kind.	
MEAULTE	2/3/17		We left BRONFAY and marched to MEAULTE into billets.	
BONNAY	3/3/17		At 10 A.M. the battalion marched from MEAULTE to BONNAY into rest billets.	
	4/4/17		Being Sunday there was no parade.	
	5/4/17		Training under the Company Commanders, who being free of snow. did the general very anxdly to which without out of door work.	

T2134. Wt. W708-776. 500000. 4/15. Sir J. C. & S.

Army Form C. 2118.

WAR DIARY
or
INTELLIGENCE SUMMARY.
(Erase heading not required.)

Instructions regarding War Diaries and Intelligence Summaries are contained in F.S. Regs., Part II. and the Staff Manual respectively. Title pages will be prepared in manuscript.

Place	Date	Hour	Summary of Events and Information	Remarks and references to Appendices
BONNAY	6/3/17		In the morning the battalion paraded for a route march. Companies were at the disposal of their respective commanders in the afternoon.	
	7/3/17		C.O.s conference under Divisional Commander at Ville. Lt. Col. Raikes returned to the battalion from Course of Instruction.	
	8/3/17		There was a heavy fall of snow in the morning but a thaw set in at once and did not interfere with training. Training under O.C. Coys was carried on. Transport lines inspected by the G.O.C. 87th Brigade, he expressed his satisfaction.	
	9/3/17		G.O.C. 29th Division paid an informal visit to the battalion to see them at their training.	
	10/3/17		The C.O. attended a Brigade conference for Commanding Officers.	
	11/3/17		The first real spring day. Church Parade was held in the open in conjunction with 1/Lt., 87th Field Ambulance.	

WAR DIARY
or
INTELLIGENCE SUMMARY.
(Erase heading not required.)

Army Form C. 2118.

Place	Date	Hour	Summary of Events and Information	Remarks and references to Appendices
BONNAY	17/9/17		Entrenched training in open warfare begins. A regimental scheme for officers was held under the C.O in the afternoon; the G.O.C 87th Brigade also attended.	
	18/9/17		Battalion was reinforced by Capt F.G. Dickinson and one subaltern officer. The regimental Screen team beat the 87 Field Amb. by 3 goals to nil.	
			Below is the composition of the Battalion at this time.	
			Commanding Officer Lt. Col. G. T. Raikes D.S.O.	Strength of Batth. (approx)
			Second in Command Major H.G. Garnett, M.C.	Officers 30
			Adjutant Lieut. H.W. Weeks.	O.R. 500
			Quartermaster Lieut. E.K. Lawson	
			Medical Officer Capt. Blake M.C.	
			Chaplain F. Swallow	
			O.C. A Coy " R.A. Hill	
			" B " " W.H.M. Gibson	
			" C " " F.G. Dickinson	
			" D " " C. Owens	

C⁰ Lt Col. H. Morgan; B. L. Shaw; V. Jones; J.H. Davies; C.L. Woolridge; W.C. Began.

Army Form C. 2118.

WAR DIARY
or
INTELLIGENCE SUMMARY.
(Erase heading not required.)

Instructions regarding War Diaries and Intelligence Summaries are contained in F.S. Regs., Part II. and the Staff Manual respectively. Title pages will be prepared in manuscript.

Place	Date	Hour	Summary of Events and Information	Remarks and references to Appendices
LE QUESNOY	19/3/17 – 29/3/17		Battn moved from BONNAY to Le Quesnoy. Billets good.	
	22/3/17		2/Lt A.P. Ashmore left for hospital with trench fever.	
	30/3/17		2/Lt H.V. Clarke, 2/Lt A.E. Crowder, 2/Lt J.C. Phillips joined the Battalion, with a draft of 75 O.R. The whole month was devoted to intensive training in open warfare, beginning with platoon training and company training at BONNAY, the battalion on moving to Le Quesnoy, continued this training with battalion schemes and field days; finally the Bn took part in Brigade and Divisional one day manoeuvres.	
VIGNACOURT	29/3/17		The regiment left LE QUESNOY & marched with remainder of the Brigade to VIGNACOURT into billets for one night; the next day, 30 it inst, we continued the march & went into billets at MONTRELET.	
MONTRELET	30/3/17 to 31/3/17		Here we stayed the following days and conducted training under Coy arrangements.	

G.T. Parker? Lt Col
Comdg 2/West Yorks Reserve?

T.2134. Wt. W708—776. 500000. 4/15. Sir J.C. & S.

Confidential

War Diary

of

2nd South Wales Borderers

Month of

April 1917

Volume N° 26

M Peck
Lt. Colonel
Commdg 2nd South Wales Borderers

WAR DIARY
or
INTELLIGENCE SUMMARY.
(Erase heading not required.)

Army Form C. 2118.

Place	Date	Hour	Summary of Events and Information	Remarks and references to Appendices
OCCOCHES	1/4/17		The Brigade continued its march, we reached OCCOCHES having come from MONTRELET. 2 Battalion (?) in the meet part was put into huts.	
LUCHEUX	2/4/17 to 6/4/17		We left OCCOCHES and marched to LUCHEUX the following day, and we again hut up in huts. The rest of these few days were that and the work had for many long. We halted here for 3 days and company Commanders went their own officers for nearly Commanders. Whilst at LUCHEUX the battalion was again strengthened with a draft of 56 O.R.	
ETREE-WAMIN SOMBRIN	5/4/17 to 7/4/17		On the 5th we marched to SOMBRIN ETREE-WAMIN, and from there we continued the march on the 7th inst. to SOMBRIN, where we stayed for one night, the following day the 8 inst we reached MONCHIET; here	
MONCHIET	8/4/17 to 12/4/17		training was carried on under Company Commanders so far as was possible on the small area of ground available. On the 12th we marched from MONCHIET to ARRAS. At ARRAS the transport was left behind, four Officers and 40 other ranks remained behind	

WAR DIARY
or
INTELLIGENCE SUMMARY.
(Erase heading not required.)

Army Form C. 2118.

Place	Date	Hour	Summary of Events and Information	Remarks and references to Appendices
MONCHY				
In the line	12th		also the Battalions left ARRAS at dusk for the line, 87th Brigade	[On the 13th
			was put in reserve. The Battalion took over from the 5th BERKSHIRE	sent a draft
			REGT. about 2 miles west of MONCHY-LE-(PREUX). Bank. On the following	of M.O.R.
			day the 13th that we moved into the front line just south of MONCHY	arrived for
			and took over from the 12th WEST YORKSHIRE REGT. There were two	us at ARRAS]
			companies in the front line and companies in support. On the 14th	
			the two supporting companies moved up to extend our line to	
			the left. These two companies took over from the 4th WORCESTERSHIRE	
			REGT. thereupon.	
	15th		On the 15th the shelter which contained D Coy's Headquarters was blown	
			in, burying Capt. E.P. Owens, 2/Lt. A.D. Lowe, R.T. Lewis and	
			J.H. Davies. Capt. Owens was killed, and 2/Lt Lewis and Davies were	
			dug out alive. 2/Lt. Lowe carried on and took over	
			temporary command of "C" Coy. 2/Lt. E.C.R. Gullan going from "C"	
			to take over command of D Coy.	

WAR DIARY
or
INTELLIGENCE SUMMARY.
(Erase heading not required.)

Army Form C. 2118.

Place	Date	Hour	Summary of Events and Information	Remarks and references to Appendices
	16th		Mr A.J. Lewis was taken out of the line to hospital, his back being slightly injured as the result of being buried.	
	17th		On the night of the 17th the Battalion was taken out of the front line, and put in the reserve trenches (BROWN LINE) near FEUCHY CHAPEL X ROADS. Here the Battalion stayed two days, and were relieved by the 64th Camerons. This tour in the trenches cost the Battalion about 60 casualties and the weather conditions were for the most part bad. The chief work accomplished was the digging of a front line preparatory to a big attack.	
ARRAS.	19th		On the night of the 19th the Battalion returned to ARRAS, pretty well exhausted, and were put into billets. On the following day Battalion had to change billets, and were put into the SCHRAMM BARRACKS, where there was not much accommodation. Here we stayed until the 22nd. On the evening of this date we moved into the front line trenches just E of MONCHY-LE-PREUX	

Army Form C. 2118.

WAR DIARY
or
INTELLIGENCE SUMMARY.
(Erase heading not required.)

Instructions regarding War Diaries and Intelligence Summaries are contained in F. S. Regs., Part II. and the Staff Manual respectively. Title pages will be prepared in manuscript.

Place	Date	Hour	Summary of Events and Information	Remarks and references to Appendices
MONCHY LE PREUX.	23rd		At 4.45 on the morning of the 23rd the Battalion went over the top and successfully captured the first line German trench. A and B. Companies constructed strong points about 300 yards beyond the captured German positions. The covering barrage for the attack fell very short, and caused a number of casualties to our own men. After the attack and during the consolidation hostile sniping was very active. On this day the following Officers were killed:- Capt. P. L. Hill, 2/Lt R. Phillips, 2/Lt R. L. Shaw & 2/Lt W. B. Nightingale died of wounds; 2/Lt D. J. Hopkins and J. E. Harries were wounded and missing, and believed died of wounds. Lieut Morgan Thomas 2/Lt W. C. Beynon and 2/Lt H. J. C. Clarke were wounded. About mid-day the enemy counter attacked but were easily dispersed. In the early hours of the morning of the 24th we were relieved by the 1st Battalion Lancashire Fusiliers, and went back to the reserve trenches. In the evening we were relieved	Account of operations on 23rd attached Appendix I

T2134. Wt. W708-776. 500000. 4/15. Sir J. C. & S.

Place	Date	Hour	Summary of Events and Information	Remarks and references to Appendices
	25th		again by the 2nd Royal Scots and went back into Barracks at ARRAS. The following morning the battalion was conveyed by motor buses to a hutment camp at DUISANS. Here we stayed	
	26th		one night and the following day marched to LATTRE ST. QUENTIN and went into billets. On the 27th the Battalion marched to ST.	
	27th		AMAND (a distance of about 11 miles) where we remained until the 1st of May. On the 28th the Battalion was reinforced by a draft of 220 men	
	1.5.		& Officers, 2/Lt. H.H. Evans 2/Lt D.C. Phillips 2/Lt L.G. Morgan 2/Lt A.E. Crowder also rejoined the Battalion on this date from the XVIII Corps Depot.	

W Parker
Lt. Col.
Commndg 2/South Wales Borderers.

Army Form C. 2118.

WAR DIARY
or
INTELLIGENCE SUMMARY.
(Erase heading not required.)

Instructions regarding War Diaries and Intelligence Summaries are contained in F.S. Regs, Part II. and the Staff Manual respectively. Title pages will be prepared in manuscript.

Place	Date	Hour	Summary of Events and Information	Remarks and references to Appendices
Casualties	13th to 17th		Additional to Diary for APRIL 1917.	
			Inclusive Officers 2 Other Ranks 80	
In attack on	23rd			
			Killed. Wounded Missing Total.	
			Officers 4 2 3 9.	
			Other Ranks. 26 159 43 228	
	30th		Strength of Battn. Officers 20 (includes MO & Chaplain) Other Ranks 602.	Appendix V
			Company Commanders A Coy Lieut Hon C A French	Nominal Roll of Officers
			B Coy. Capt. W. H M Pinion (temp at School of Instruction)	
			C Coy. Capt. F G Dickinson	
			D Coy. 2 Lieut C M Gibbon	

4/5/17

G N Parker Lt Colonel
Comdg 2 Bn South Wales Borderers

Confidential

War Diary

of

2nd Battn. South Wales Borderers

from 1-5-17 to 31-5-17

Volume No 27   R.J. Hecky

Lt Colonel
Commdg. 2nd South Wales Borderers

Army Form C. 2118.

WAR DIARY
or
INTELLIGENCE SUMMARY.
(Erase heading not required.)

MAY, 1917.

Instructions regarding War Diaries and Intelligence Summaries are contained in F. S. Regs., Part II. and the Staff Manual respectively. Title pages will be prepared in manuscript.

Place	Date	Hour	Summary of Events and Information	Remarks and references to Appendices
ST AMAND	1/5/17	6.15	Marched to WANQUETIN (11½ miles). Major A.L.WRENFORD joined, attached to Battn for duty as 2ᵈ in Command.	
WANQUETIN	2/5/17	18.15	Marched to ARRAS. Men issued with extra ammunition, bombs, flares, Tolite etc preparatory to moving up to line.	
ARRAS.	3/5/17	7.0am	Marched to OBSERVATION RIDGE & occupied trenches about 1000ˣ N of T1220Y.	
			At 3.45ᵃᵐ there was general attack on front of 3ʳᵈ Army.	
OBSERVATION RIDGE ARRAS.	4/5/17	11.30 am	Marched to ARRAS.	
	5/5/17		On hillets. Training of gun classes continued. Billets cleared of accumulated refuse.	
	6/5/17 7/5/17	11.30	Desultory shelling of Arras at intervals. 7/5/17 Marched to DUISANS.	
DUISANS	7/5/17		Following reinforcements arrived from XVIII Corps Deft.	
			Officer 3 Other Ranks 90. Trained, all with France service in France.	
	8ᵈ		Very wet, training under Coy Commanders in Barrack rooms.	
	9ᵗʰ		Major Wrenford returned to 1ˢᵗ R.Lunck Fus.	2/Lt Newman 2/Lt Nethercliff W.Wilkins
	10ᵈ		Grid to Trench attack, digging of strong points, Lung Lewis gun on the more and close order drill were practised. Weather very warm.	
	11ᵗʰ		Capt. B. J. Davies 2/Lt Dryoll and C. O. R. joined.	

Army Form C. 2118.

WAR DIARY
or
INTELLIGENCE SUMMARY.
(Erase heading not required.)

Instructions regarding War Diaries and Intelligence Summaries are contained in F. S. Regs., Part II. and the Staff Manual respectively. Title pages will be prepared in manuscript.

Place	Date	Hour	Summary of Events and Information	Remarks and references to Appendices
DUISANS.	11/5/17 to 13/5/17		Capt. B.J. Davis took over Command of D Coy 11/5/17 – Brigade Sports 12/5/17 – Marched to ARRAS. 6.0 p.m. 13/5/17	
ARRAS.	14/5/17	21.00	Marched up to MONCHY LE PREUX + took over MONCHY defence trenches from 7" K.S.L.I. Brigade dispositions as follows: Firing line – KOSB on left. Inniskilling Fus on Right. 2/SWB's in Support (with 1 Coy attached of KOSB). 1/Border Regt in Reserve at BROWN Line.	
MONCHY LE PREUX.	15/5/17		Dispositions "C" Coy (att? 1/KOSB) in front line SNAFFLE Tr. – A Coy ORCHARD Tr. – B + D Coys EAST Trench. See appendix I	APPENDIX I Dispositions + detail of trenches.
	15/5/17 to 18/5/17		Work carried out on trenches, shelters, latrines etc. C.T. from EAST Tr. – SNAFFLE commenced. Wire + trip bridles carried to front line + new trench grenade dumps formed behind SNAFFLE Tr.	
	18/5/17		Night 17/18 "D" Coy relieved "C" Coy. A Coy moved from ORCHARD Tr. to CHAIN Tr. Between 15" + 19" Monchy defences were shelled intermittently also MONCHY a few casualties occurred mostly whilst carrying parties at night.	
	19/5/17		An attack on enemy's trenches opposite the B" front took place at 21.00	

T2134. Wt. W708–776. 500000. 4/15. Sir J. C. & S.

Army Form C. 2118.

WAR DIARY
or
INTELLIGENCE SUMMARY.
(Erase heading not required.)

Instructions regarding War Diaries and Intelligence Summaries are contained in F.S. Regs., Part II. and the Staff Manual respectively. Title pages will be prepared in manuscript.

Place	Date	Hour	Summary of Events and Information	Remarks and references to Appendices
MONCHY LE PREUX.	19/5/17	2100	Attack carried out by 1/Border Regt on left & 1/R9 Inns on right. D'Coy 2/SLTB was attached to the 1/Border Regt & attacked on left flank. Instructions to Coys and plan showing dispositions before & after attack are attached. At Zero A, B & C Coys moved as directed. 'D'Coy* went over the parapet promptly at Zero but both Machine Guns opened immediately & casualties occurred in the first yard or two, nevertheless the Coy moved on on reaching about 100x from the jumping off trench casualties became very heavy & Capt Davies was killed. Most of the casualties were being caused by an enfilade M.G. apparently by Capt Cecil. Sgt White rushed forward through a hail of bullets in a gallant attempt to get to the gun & put it out of action. He was cloudy followed by Capt Norrel. They were both killed when only a few yards from the gun. After this the attack checked, the enemy's MGs were apparently firing through our barrage all the time, & rendered the objective longer Than circumstances were impossible. Only 1 Officer & 36 O.R. got back unwounded after dark.	APPENDIX II *APPENDIX III Report on Operation by 2/Lt Morgan.

Casualties

	Killed	Wounded	Missing	Total
Officers	2	1	–	3
Other Ranks	6	26	44	76

Army Form C. 2118.

WAR DIARY
or
INTELLIGENCE SUMMARY.
(Erase heading not required.)

Place	Date	Hour	Summary of Events and Information	Remarks and references to Appendices
MONCHY LE PREUX.	19/3/17		The following were named Officer Casualties.	
			CAPTAIN B.J. DAVIES Killed	
			2ⁿᵈ LIEUT V. JONES Killed	
			2ⁿᵈ LIEUT NEWMAN Wounded (with C Coy)	
	20/3/17 night		The Battⁿ was relieved & returned to ARRAS. Tk. 1/Royal Fusiliers taking over Monchy defences. 16ᵗʰ Muffs and 1/Lanc Fus taking Tr. front line in Rifle & left respectively. Relief completed by daylight.	
ARRAS.	21/3/17 to		Training in trench to trench attack with barrage, silent attack by night and bombing was carried out, also range practices. On the 29ᵗʰ inst 7/Lt. S. W.S. Cooke was accidentally hit whilst instructing men to	
BROWN LINE	29ᵗʰ	9.0 pm	fire rifle grenades.	
			Marched to BROWN LINE.	
MONCHY	30ᵈ	7.30 pm	Took over MONCHY defences. A Coy in ORCHARD TR.; B Coy in rear trench 150x W of EAST TR.; C Coy in EAST TR.; D Coy in BROWN LINE.	
	31ˢᵗ		Took over the front line trenches from 1ˢᵗ R.D.F. A Coy (on left) SNAFFLE TR.; C Coy (in centre) and B Coy (on right) in TWIN TR. D Coy in support in Sharpnel Trench.	

WAR DIARY
or
INTELLIGENCE SUMMARY.
(Erase heading not required.)

Army Form C. 2118.

Place	Date	Hour	Summary of Events and Information	Remarks and references to Appendices
	May 31.		Strength of Battn:- Officers 2 O (include M.O + Chaplain) Other ranks 502 Company Commanders A Coy Lieut. Hon. E. A. French B " Capt. W. H. M. Pierson C " Capt. F. G. Dickinson D " Lieut. W. Rose G T Raikes Lieut. Col Comdg 2nd Nob Borders	

2/6/17

Confidential

War Diary

of

2nd Battn. The South Wales Borderers

VOLUME 28

from June 1st 1917.   to June 30th 1917.

G P Raikes   Lt Colonel
Commdg. 2nd South Wales Borderers

Army Form C. 2118.

WAR DIARY
or
INTELLIGENCE SUMMARY.
(Erase heading not required.)

JUNE.

Place	Date	Hour	Summary of Events and Information	Remarks and references to Appendices
MONCHY	1/6/17		Trenches in very bad condition after rain, 250 x gap existed between our right and the Battalion (1st KOSB) on our right. To counteract this B Coy dug a strong point to protect the exposed flank and built a bombing post. By night a Lewis gun post was manned (this post was at about the middle of the gap)	
	2/6/17		Weather fine, trenches got dryer. Relieved by the 2nd Bn 1st Royal Scots Fusiliers returned to ARRAS.	
ARRAS	3/6/17		Rest day. Lt Col Raike on leave, Major Wreford (1st R.I.F.) assumed command.	
	4/6/17		Transport moved to BERNEVILLE (making for CANDAS).	
CANDAS	5/6/17		Companies under O.C. Coys for inspections etc. Entrained to CANDAS.	
	6/6/17		Lt A.P. Shore returned from BASE and brought draft 63 O.R. Training under O.C. Coys.	
	7/6/17		4 officers and 40 O.R. arrived as reinforcements from base left St POL. (Lieuts. W.F. Page, R.M. Hayden, Lts G.F. Gibson, R.R. Rees) Training - Drill, Assault training, musketry.	

T2134. Wt. W708—776. 500000. 4/15. Sir J. C. & S.

Army Form C. 2118.

WAR DIARY
or
INTELLIGENCE SUMMARY.
(Erase heading not required.)

Instructions regarding War Diaries and Intelligence Summaries are contained in F.S. Regs., Part II. and the Staff Manual respectively. Title pages will be prepared in manuscript.

Place	Date	Hour	Summary of Events and Information	Remarks and references to Appendices
CANDAS	8/6/17		Company training. Summary. Baths at disposal of command.	
	9/6/17		Commanding Officers (drill) parade. Company inspections.	
	10/6/17		(Sunday) No Parades.	
	11/6/17		Battalion moved to AUTHEUX training area. At B Coy did the trench to trench attack. B & C Coys dug strong posts. Reinforcements arrived: 3 officers: 2/Lt J.G James, J.N.V. Thomas, E. Lewis. Training under O.C. Companies.	
	12/6/17		Fine & Movement in AUTHEUX area.	
	13/6/17		Training by A & B Coys & by C & D Coys. B/O.O.R. Lough 124 other ranks arrived.	
	14/6/17		Lt Col Ruds D.S.O. returned from leave U.K.; Major Humfrey returned to 1st Bn Royal Inniskilling Fusiliers.	
	15 "		Training under O.C. Coys.	
	16 "		General Horse Show near GORGES. 2nd Stage for horses & lorries. G.S. Limbered wagon and water cart with 16 horses (Shewed Prize 10.45am?)	

Army Form C. 2118.

WAR DIARY
or
INTELLIGENCE SUMMARY.
(Erase heading not required.)

Instructions regarding War Diaries and Intelligence Summaries are contained in F.S. Regs., Part II. and the Staff Manual respectively. Title pages will be prepared in manuscript.

Place	Date	Hour	Summary of Events and Information	Remarks and references to Appendices
CANDAS	18/6/17		Marched to AUTHEUX at 6.0 a.m. following [Marched to have at h (Rifle grenades), Lewis gun (Regulation), Wood fighting and bayonet Lieut G.D.O. Lloyd appointed, and took over acting Adjutant to the battalion. Companies formed under their own arrangements - Ranges-Bombing.	
	19/6/17		Battalion training at AUTHEUX. Hard aft 4.30 a.m. Training 4 Companies in morning. Battalion Exploitation scheme in afternoon. Very wet all day. Companies trained under then own arrangements. 6 O.R. arrived for Bass.	
CANDAS.	26/6/17		Roving parties were specially trained. Entrained at DOULLENS 10.30 p.m. 26th.	
POPERINGHE	27/6/17 to 28/6/17		Battn. detrained at HOPOUTRE and marched to bivouac in a wood some seven miles North near CROMBEKE. Battalion moved to bivouac in a wood 40/9/10 N.9 BRIELEN. Very wet.	
BRIELEN	29/6/17 to 30/6/17		Remained in wood. Small fatigue right of 29th/30th - Heavy shelling of battalion near battalion during daytime, one casualty. Two battalions of Brigade - Borders + R.I. Fusiliers are in front line - we are support to the right battalion the R.I. Fusiliers. Strength of battalion 34 officers 831 other Ranks. (Chaplain + doctor not included).	

Coy Commanders. A Lieut. W.G. Page
B Capt. H.M. Pierson
C Capt. J.G. Rosa Dickenson
D Capt. W. Ross.

B.T.Raker
Lieut Colonel
Comdg 2nd S. Wales Borderers.

CONFIDENTIAL.

2nd BATTALION,
SOUTH WALES
BORDERERS.

War Diary

of

2nd Battn. South Wales Borderers.

From :- July 1st 1917.   To :- July 31st 1917.

Volume 29.

Army Form C. 2118.

WAR DIARY
or
INTELLIGENCE SUMMARY.
(Erase heading not required.)

JULY. 1914.

Instructions regarding War Diaries and Intelligence Summaries are contained in F. S. Regs., Part II. and the Staff Manual respectively. Title pages will be prepared in manuscript.

Place	Date	Hour	Summary of Events and Information	Remarks and references to Appendices
BRIELEN	1-7-17 2-7-17		Remained in rest. a large number of fatigues in front line.	
			Sea Canal with the ZWAAN/HOF Sector. 2Lt D. McKIE & 2Lt J.B. STERNDALE-BENNET joined.	
ZWAANHOF SECTOR	2-7-14 to 8-7-14		Relieved 1.R.T. fusiliers. K.S.S.B. on our left and 39th Division on our right. - Two companies up, one for line, one support. D & C Coys. A&B Coys. Reserve on Canal bank. MAJOR B.H.S.	
			GARNETT rejoined from Aldershot. Night. 1-9 OR arrived from Base Depot all rejoined.	
do	3-7-14		Fairly quiet day. Canal Bank shelled intermittently. Heavy fatigues day & night to make new front line. Raids carried on by Gordons on our right & Guards on our left during night.	
do	4-7-14		Fairly quiet day. Canal Bank again shelled. One trench gun was knocked out by shell fire and two gunners killed. The Guards & Gordons again raided enemy trenches. Enemy appeared to have been silenced. Work in front line carried on. Hydraulic shield started at midnight.	
do	5-7-14 1.5 a.m.		Enemy patrol met our patrol just as it left our trench. 2Lt DAVIES and three men being wounded, one man missing. 2Lt DAVIES died of wounds. Day fairly quiet. Enemy shelled as usual. Artillery very active about 6.0 p.m. Relief of A & B Companies from 1st Newcastle Regiment arrived 10 a.s p.m. C&D Coys banners on front line. Slight casualties.	
do	6-7-14 1.3 a.m.		Raid carried out by K.O.S. Borderers who were unable to reach objective owing to fire. C & D Coys relieved & platoon returned to CANAL BANK. Same Coys was relieved later and	

Army Form C. 2118.

WAR DIARY
or
INTELLIGENCE SUMMARY.   JULY 1917
(Erase heading not required.)

Instructions regarding War Diaries and Intelligence Summaries are contained in F.S. Regs., Part II. and the Staff Manual respectively. Title pages will be prepared in manuscript.

Place	Date	Hour	Summary of Events and Information	Remarks and references to Appendices
CROMBEKE	7.7.17		Marched back to camp in CROMBEKE wood arriving about 4.30 a.m.	
			Battalion remained in wood doing Joint Training. Pachesham attacked & trained fighters.	
	12.7.17	8ᵗʰ	A draft of 42 arrived from the Base. Nearly fine out for a second time - 11ᵗʰ another	
			draft of 23 arrived, all transfers from 65ᵗʰ T.R. Battⁿ — 12ᵗʰ The Battⁿ moved to camp	
			about 1500 yds S.W. of WOESTEN. A large number of fatigues all day.	
WOESTEN	13.4.17		Battalion resumed in wood. CAPTAIN G.A.N. ROBERTSON arrived and took over	
			Acting Adjutant & the Battalion. Thirteen OR ranks arrived as casuals coming over	
	14.7.17		A large number of fatigues transferring wet stuff etc. 1 wght 14/1/2 the officer A Gussan	
			and 50 OR dispatched to permanent fatigue with Heavy Artillery. - 15ᵗʰ Working Parties	
			as before - 16ᵗʰ Working parties again. Commanding Officer & Coy commander went into Guards line	
			training trench area. 18ᵗʰ quiet day. working parties reduced considerable. 2/Lt F.J.L. MAYGER	
			rejoined from Base. 19ᵗʰ Working parties as usual. A draft of 28 OR arrived from the	
	20.4.17		Base. 20ᵗʰ Battalion moves to camp in P.2 area near CROMBEKE.	
CROMBEKE	21.4.17		2/Lt J.L. MORGAN struck off strength from today on transfer to RFC. Al. W.F. PAGE appointed	
			Acting Captain whilst commanding a company. Training carried on under lay	
			arrangement —. 2/Lt M.J.A. MORGAN admitted to hospital on 24ᵗʰ	

Army Form C. 2118.

WAR DIARY
or
INTELLIGENCE SUMMARY.
(Erase heading not required.)

Instructions regarding War Diaries and Intelligence Summaries are contained in F. S. Regs., Part II. and the Staff Manual respectively. Title pages will be prepared in manuscript.

Place	Date	Hour	Summary of Events and Information	Remarks and references to Appendices
CROMBEKE	27/7/17		Training continued. Special attention to attack in pillcoming operations. 27.7.17 Capt F.G. DICKINSON	
			Hospital; march to HERZEELE for Brigade field day. 28.7.17 Battalion complimented by	
			Brig. Commander on previous attack. Marched back to CROMBEKE. 29.7.17 to C.O. MAYDON to	
			hospital. 30.7.17 by 10 march to FOREST CAMP arriving 2 am 31.7.17. 2nd Lieut H. Williams and escort	Appendix I
FOREST CAMP	31.7.7	3.50am	Officers opened 20" drum rum Grenadg XIV Corps; All Corps objectives attained on line of STEENBEEK Butts (WIAP 75 Corps Reinforcing Camp.)	
(NOORDEN)			moved at 7.30 am and were working at 11 am making road from point 300 yards S.W.of St.JULIEN (a point at BOSSINGHE complete.	
			along CARIBOO AVENUE thence SE to CACTUS JUNCTION along it about 1700 x ft. road completed	
			by 4 pm relieved by 1st R. INNISKILLINGS. "D" Coy 1 officer 27th D. MCKIE and 5 O.R casualties esterday, 3	
			NCO's (incl - 1 man killed).	
				Captain Commanding
				Acg. Capt. W.F. PAGE
			Strength of Batt on July 31st	B - Capt. W.H.M. PIERSON
			33 officers 829 other ranks	C - 2nd Lt. E.A. GIBSON
			Nominal roll of officers attached Appendix II	D - Capt. W. ROSS

5/8/17

Confidential.

War Diary

of

2nd Battn The South Wales Borderers

From 1/8/17   To 31/8/17

VOLUME

No 30

[signature]
Lt Colonel
Commdg 2nd South Wales Borderers

Army Form C. 2118.

WAR DIARY
or
INTELLIGENCE SUMMARY.
(Erase heading not required.)

AUGUST 1917.

Instructions regarding War Diaries and Intelligence Summaries are contained in F. S. Regs., Part II. and the Staff Manual respectively. Title pages will be prepared in manuscript.

Place	Date	Hour	Summary of Events and Information	Remarks and references to Appendices
FOREST CAMP Nr WOESTEN	2/8/17		2 Lieut J STERNDALE BENNETT & 2nd Lieut T E JOYCE to Hospital. 3/17 2/Lt T C JORDAN	
	2/8/17 to 3/8/17		joined on promotion from 1st Bn. — moved to PICCADILLY Camp near CROMBEKE	
			continued rain since 31st	
PICCADILLY CAMP	4/8/17		Carried out training for offensive. 7/8 2nd Lieut G M HAYDON returned from Hospital +	
	7/8/17		to Recce commenced. "C" Coy - moved to Camps No 1 & 2 in Forest Area	
CAMPS No 1 & 2	8/8/17	10·0 am	Moved to Dublin Camp (1 mile). Weather fine since 6/8/17	
DUBLIN CAMP	9/8/17		Practised forming up for attack by day & by night. also flewing out under the barrage.	
	10/8/17	2·0 pm	To Camp at B.7.C. ETON CAMP (Victorian WOESTAN & ELVERDINGHE) 2 mile nearer front than	
			before. Conference with French Officers of 2nd Regiment who are attacking on our left. Points for liaison	
			arranged & details of forming up.	
ETON CAMP	11/8/17		2/Lt J S BENNETT returned from Hospital. Practised formation & advance for offensive. little	
			Shelling by night, on the whole with satisfactory results. Rec Operation orders from Bde. Issued battle	
			Stores.	
	14/8/17	6·0 pm	moved up to left support position. Bn relieved in depth. Bn H.Q at SAVLES Farm	
			relieved 1/Kos B. quiet relief. Took up rations & water for 15th & 16th	
			On night 14/15th 2nd Lieut J HAYCOCKE 2/Lt KNAPPER & 2/Lt RENWICK with 2 men each	

Army Form C. 2118.

WAR DIARY
or
INTELLIGENCE SUMMARY.   AUGUST 1917.
(Erase heading not required.)

Instructions regarding War Diaries and Intelligence Summaries are contained in F. S. Regs., Part II. and the Staff Manual respectively. Title pages will be prepared in manuscript.

Place	Date	Hour	Summary of Events and Information	Remarks and references to Appendices
LEFT SUPPORT SAULES FARM	15/8/17		Reconnoitred along STEEN BEEK & see ground for forming up. Very satisfactory report. STEENBEEK impassable but 7 good bridges have been put up by R.E. As result of reports it was decided to form the whole Bn. up on the far side for the attack.	
		8.30 pm	The Bn. moved forward to form up at A. B. C. D. 1 Platoon from A & B ahead as covering party. The Bn. formed up very satisfactorily without hitch or more on the tape previously laid. Bn. HQ moved forward to SENTIER Fm. 1st Stand Rodder joined 10%. Major H.G. Garnett taking over command for the attack. The following Officers took part in the attack.	
			A Coy. B Coy. C Coy. D Coy.	
			Capt French Capt Pusan Lieut Hayter Capt Rees	
			2/Lt Crater 2/Lt Maggee 2/Lt Gittoes 2/Lt Retherford	
			2/Lt Barnett 2/Lt Rees 2/Lt Phillips 2/Lt Garen	
			2/Lt Jordan 2/Lt Lewis 2/Lt Grenen 2/Lt James	
			Bn. HQ. Major H.G. Garnett, Co. hurt French	
			Capt. G.A.N. Robertson, Adj'. 2/Lt Crater	
			Lieut G.W. Holyoake, Int. 2/Lt Barnett	
			2/Lt S.F. Hearder, Sig. 2/Lt Jordan	B: Order Appendix I.
SENTIER Fm	16/8/17	4.45 am	At Zero 4.45 am the barrage opened an Bn. advanced to the attack. See Bn. Instructions for attack Appendix I + Account of Operations Appendix II	Account of Operation Appendix II

Army Form C. 2118.

WAR DIARY
or
INTELLIGENCE SUMMARY.   AUGUST 1917
(Erase heading not required.)

Instructions regarding War Diaries and Intelligence Summaries are contained in F. S. Regs., Part II, and the Staff Manual respectively. Title pages will be prepared in manuscript.

Place	Date	Hour	Summary of Events and Information	Remarks and references to Appendices
SENTIERI	16/8/17	5.40am	Message received from A Coy. 1st Objective, the 3rd Objective was taken at 10.0 am. The Troops on left were held up & recalled their barrage. By 10.0 am the whole of the 2nd & final Objective was captured by French & ourselves also on the right the 3rd Objective on the whole Divisional Front. The 70th Div. on right & 29th Div. also took their final Objective with few exceptions. The Bn captured 53 Prisoners, 2 damaged 5-9 Hows. 1.77mm Gun, 2 Machine Guns and one 240mm Trench Mortar. Casualties Officers:- Captain G.A.M. ROBERTSON } Killed Lieut D.C. PHILLIPS } Killed a/Captain W ROSS. 2nd Lieut N.V. EVANS } Killed a/Capt G.M. HAYDON Lieut Hon E.A. FRENCH } died of wounds 2nd Lieut J.S. REID attd T.M.B }	Appendix III Map & Objectives
			Other Ranks. Killed Wounded Missing Total	
			2nd Lt 2 27 2nd Lt 7 127 9 163	
	17/8/17	2.0am	Bn relieved by 1st R Innis Fus in front line & 16th Northumber in Support Line	

Army Form C. 2118.

WAR DIARY
or
INTELLIGENCE SUMMARY.
(Erase heading not required.)

AUGUST 1917

Instructions regarding War Diaries and Intelligence
Summaries are contained in F. S. Regs., Part II.
and the Staff Manual respectively. Title pages
will be prepared in manuscript.

Place	Date	Hour	Summary of Events and Information	Remarks and references to Appendices
ADDINGLY Camp	17/8/17		A returned to ADDINGLY Camp (near to ETON Camp) arriving 7.30 a.m.	
			2nd Lieut F.J.L. Mayger MGR now Commanded of D Coy	
			2nd Lieut E.M. Gibbs " " " C Coy.	
			Lieut G.D. Olley's LGR Open Musketd	
			Bn went to the baths in evening.	
— do —	18/8/17		Reorganised Companies in 2 Platoons. Inspection of all arms & equipment at	
	19/8/17		Continued inspection returning. 20th Moved up to DULWICH CAMP & relieved 1. R D Fusiliers	
DULWICH CAMP ELVERDINGHE WIDIJNDREF	20/8/17 22/4/17 23rd		2nd Batt. tracked on dead Track II — 22nd worked, down on road forward to trenches. Left	
			front Battalion — B. on left 201st French Regiment, Right BORDER REGT — A & D Coys in	
			front line, C & B Coys in Support. Night patrols out. 12 Moves very quiet. By night	
			patrols were pushed across BROENBEKE into NEY WOOD & NEY COPSE. No enemy	
			encountered. 1st HOLYOAKE to Hospital.	
	24th		Quiet day in trenches. Coys worked on their lines and put up wire. By night Lt	
			PARK pushed further forward. Now 8 posts in on the edge of BROENBEKE.	
	25th		Day quiet — PoS consolidated. No PoW taken. No 8 Post taken over by FRENCH 201st Regt	
			relieved by 1st St. Batt.	

WAR DIARY or INTELLIGENCE SUMMARY

Army Form C. 2118.

Place	Date	Hour	Summary of Events and Information	Remarks and references to Appendices
WIDJENDREFT L.S.y			Morning quiet. 1.55 pm attack took place on right. A LARGE MARCH made in three Lines Combatant. Ribbleton on our Line - never but overcame ditto Late.	
	2nd	5.30	Enemy counter attack further East, Lines of our Lines - Few casualties. Relieved by 2nd Battn SCOTS GUARDS (2 Coys.) 1 Coy relieved A + B Coys and 1 Coy C. D. Relief somewhat delayed by foot over BROEMBEKE.	
DULWICH CAMP 28			Battn moved on relief to DULWICH CAMP.	
			and arriving new PLUMSTEAD CAMP about 6.30 pm.	
PLUMSTEAD CAMP 29			Battn cleaned + inspected. Draft of 120 other ranks and the following officers joined Battn:- Lieut. F. J. Whitehouse 2/Lt G. J. Briggs M.M. – Occ Dickinson.	
	30th		P.T. and R.S.M. Parade. Coy inspections. 14 Military Medals awarded Battn. Lieut. C. MUMFORD joined from 6th Battn.	
	31st		Coy training. A/RAF.M. HAYGER awarded bar to M.C. 2/Lt W. H. PIERSON and 2/Lt F. GIBBON the M.C.	

A. F. GIBBON
Lt. Col.

Army Form C. 2118.

WAR DIARY
or
INTELLIGENCE SUMMARY.
(Erase heading not required.)

Instructions regarding War Diaries and Intelligence Summaries are contained in F. S. Regs., Part II, and the Staff Manual respectively. Title pages will be prepared in manuscript.

Place	Date	Hour	Summary of Events and Information	Remarks and references to Appendices
PROVEN/2 CAMP	31-8-17		Officers 31-8-17	
			Lt Colonel G.L. Parker DSO Commanding	
			Major H.J. Garrett 2nd in Command	
			Lieut Geo Hoyt Adjutant	
			Capt. W.H. Page Comdg "A" Coy	
			" W.M. Pearson " " "B" "	
			" F.L. Madges " " "C" "	
			Lt. Ewo Gibbon " " "D" "	
			Strength of Battalion	
			Officers Other Rks	
			25 730	

R. Parker
Lt. Colonel
Commdg. South Wales Borderers

Account of Operations 16th Aug 1917.

1. Boundaries and objectives are shown on attached map.
The steenbeek was impassable except by the bridges of which there were 7 in the B'n area.

2. The Steenbeek was well reconnoitred on the night of 14th/15th & it was decided to form up for attack on the far side using the 2 central bridges. At dusk on 15th 1 platoon was sent forward to occupy our forward post on the far side of the Steenbeek & in the right half of the B'n area. On the B'n front this was the only post we held across the Steenbeek. A strong patrol was also pushed out on the left across the Steenbeek. The B'n formed up under cover of the above, two companies in single rank in front and two companies in single rank behind, the rear two companies being 20 yds across the Steenbeek. At dusk on 15th a tape was laid from near Fourche Farm forward & across the Steen-beek by the bridge opposite Scottish Farm and a forming up tape along the line for the front Companies. The forming up took place without incident.

3. Liaison with the French was maintained by

a company of the 2⁰ Bⁿ 208ᵗʰ French
Infantry Regiment which formed up behind
our left flank. ½ the Company behind B
Coy + ½ behind D Coy.

4. Coys were allotted to objectives as follows
   1ˢᵗ Objective A Coy on the right
                     B Coy on the left.
   2ⁿᵈ Objective C Coy on the right
                     D Coy on the left.

Stokes Gun detachment followed in the
centre to the first objective where it took up
position to cover Mont ~~~~~ and Gnomve
Farm.

1 Section Vickers Guns accompanied B Coy
+ later moved on to the furthest Objective.

5. Shortly before Zero the Enemy started
shelling the Steenbeek + the near side of
it. the rear Companies therefore moved
forward a little.

At Zero the whole moved forward close
under the barrage. the ground was
very marshy + in many places men
sank in over the knee.

A + B Coys moved under the barrage
to the 1ˢᵗ objective. only a few Germans
were found in dug outs behind the
right Company. A gap had occurred
between these two Companies owing
to some flooded ground in the
centre. Touch was maintained with

the K.1.S.B. on the right but the French
on the left had got held up partly by misuse
& partly by some concrete dugouts at
Champaubert Farm.
The ground was very muddy & cut up
& it was very difficult to recognise the
position on the ground. the leading
Companies went beyond their Objective
& did not halt till the barrage stopped
for the 35 minutes. While halted here
machine guns opened from the flank
(Champaubert Farm) this held up
the two Companies going through
to 2nd Objective. The enemy also opened
fire from two strong points one on
either side of Moulinvail Farm. This
caused a delay & the barrage went
right ahead.
The officer cmdg. D.Co (left Co. for
2nd Objective) was informed by the French
that they were putting down a second
barrage on Champaubert Farm &
shortly afterwards the Enemy ceased
firing from there. The two Companies
then advanced straight on to
the 2nd Objective without opposition.
The French came up about ½ hour
later.
Patrols were sent out to the Broa-

Broembeek. There was apparently no opposition beyond them except for a few men firing from Nay Wood and a machine gun and a few snipers opposite the French. Strong points were dug on both objectives & a Lewis Gun was pushed out to a hedge about 150 yds from the Broembeek.

6. About 4.0 pm Germans were seen coming up in small parties on the other side of the Broembeek. They formed up in two lines & advanced to the far bank. There was also a lot of movement in the woods & farms behind.
Fire was opened on the enemy & the S.O.S. was put up. A large number of the enemy were hit by rifle & L.G. fire & the Art put down a very heavy barrage. Most of the enemy appeared to be knocked out & a few were seen running back into the woods behind.

7. In the 2nd objective touch was obtained quickly on both flanks. There was a tendency throughout to advance too much to the left possibly owing to the fact that

the French were not up
8. Montmirail strong points were held by 25 men (prisoners) and two machine guns. There were also some prisoners taken from dug outs by Crassons and U15 central.

18/3/17

G T Raikes 2 Lieut
Comdg 2/ Shales Bricau

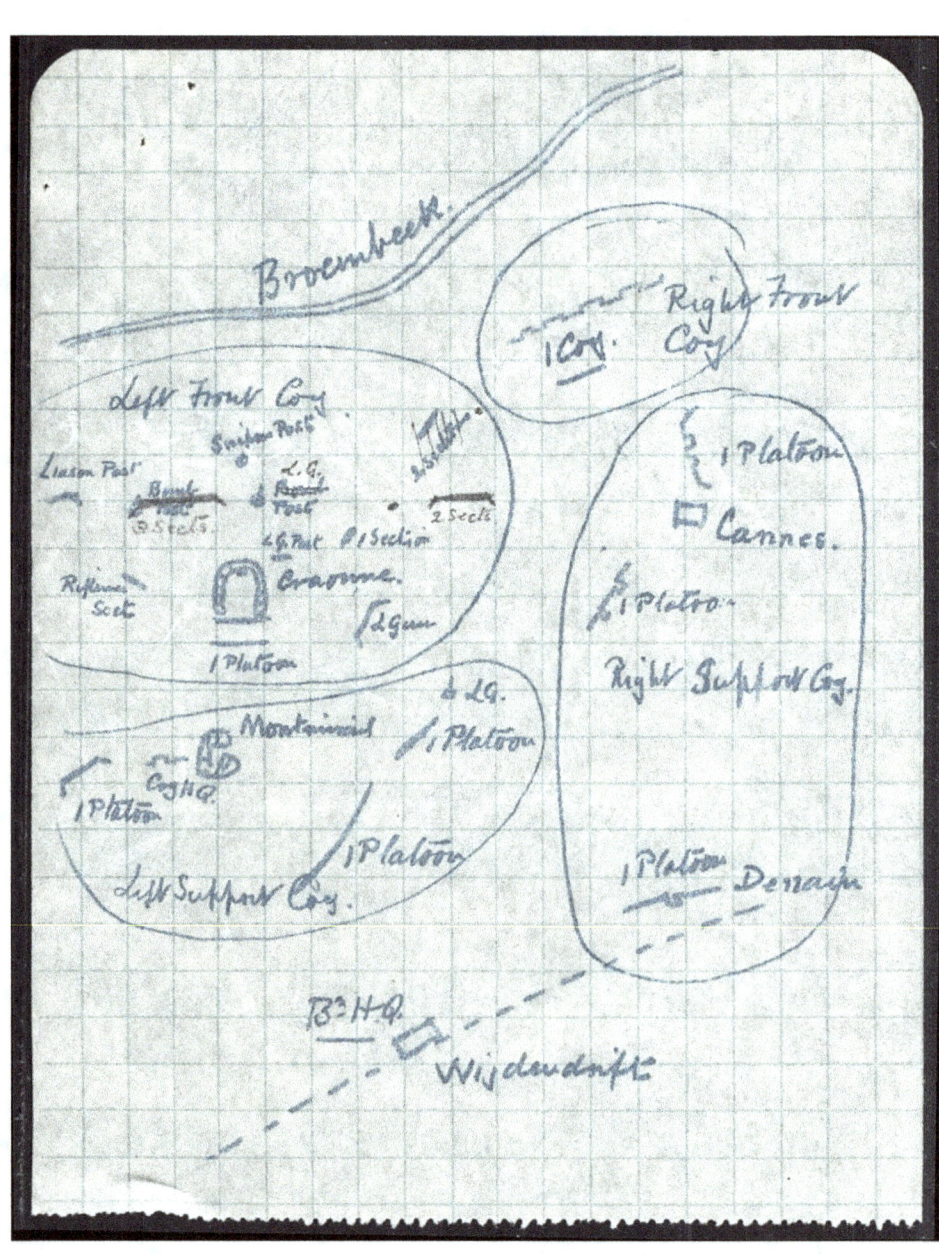

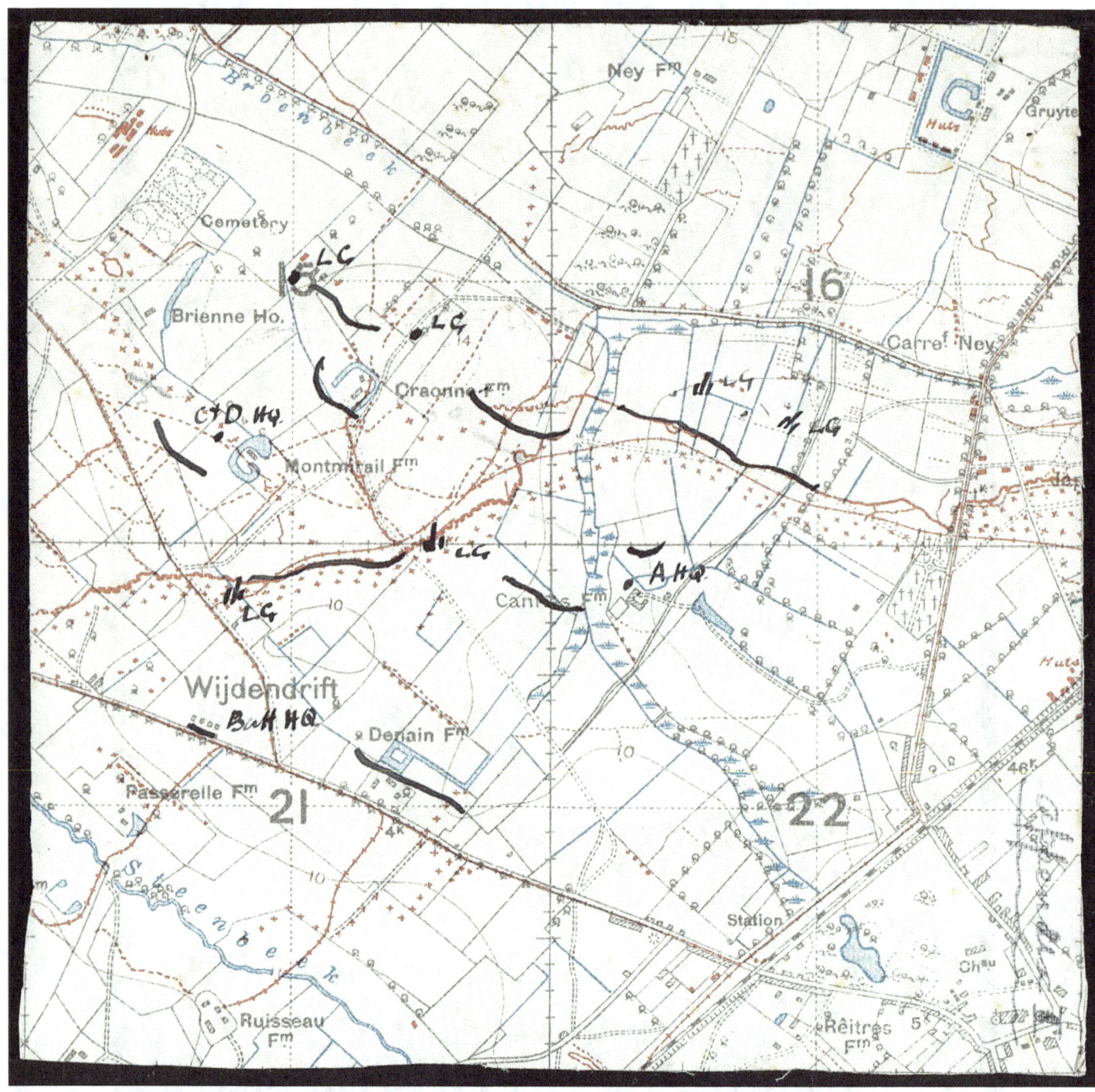

Vol 19

Confidential

2nd BATTALION,
SOUTH WALES
BORDERERS.

29†

War Diary

of

2nd Battn. The South Wales Borderers

From 1/9/17   To 30/9/17

[signature]
Lt Colonel
Commanding 2nd South Wales Borderers

WAR DIARY
or
INTELLIGENCE SUMMARY.
(Erase heading not required.)

Army Form C. 2118.

SEPTEMBER 1914.

Place	Date	Hour	Summary of Events and Information	Remarks and references to Appendices
PLUNSTEAD CAMP PROVEN.	1st		Coys. do training and drill etc. Lt. G.D.O. Hoye leaves Battn. to report Details	
			office for appointment to Indian Army. Lt. C. MUMFORD takes over duty of Adjutant.	
	2nd		Coys do training.	
	3rd		Inspection of the 89th Brigade by the Divisional Commander. Presentation of	
			decorations for attack of 16th August	
			Three Officers and men of Battn. decorated as under:-	
			A/Capt. F.J.L Morgan } Bar to Military Cross	
			——— 101471 Pierson } Military Cross	
			——— Lt. Gibbons } Military Cross	
			9 other ranks - Military Medal.	
	4th		4th Coy training - Others Musketry training Vickers & Lewis attack & T.E.T. supervised	
	5th			
	5,6 & 7th		Ceremonial Parade, Specialist training, Platoon Training (capture or	
				Practise for the capture of enemy strong point. (strong points.)
	8th		Battn. moves to training area. HERZEELE. and carries	
	9,10 & 11th		out attack practices Lt.Col.LLOYD rejoined with Ambulance Draught	
	12th		Battn. returns to Plumstead Camp from Training Area.	

WAR DIARY or INTELLIGENCE SUMMARY

Army Form C. 2118.

Place	Date	Hour	Summary of Events and Information	Remarks and references to Appendices
PLUMSTEAD CAMP PRADELLES	13th to 17th		Company's continue Training. 2/Lt W.S. Williams to hosp. Lt. CEEK Hospital	
	18th		Brigade parade and Inspection by Gen'l BARLETT. MAJ. H.G. GARNETT, CAPT. H.N. PIERSON, SGT. H.L. MASON, and PTE. TSKIFT presented with LE CROIX DE GUERRE.	
	19th		Company Training	
	20th	0800	Battalion moved to DE HIPPE CAMP FOREST AREA — 8 miles.	
DE HIPPE CAMP	21st to 22nd		Companies do Training, Work on Tracks and Camp improvements.	
RUGBY CAMP	23rd		Battalion moved to RUGBY CAMP. 2 miles.	
	29th		All arms felt moved preparatory to moving up to front line. — 1745 Marched off to relieve Northumberland Reg't in left sub-sector of Div. front. Lewis Guns & Ammn were to be taken up by lorries to Wulverghem Rd. B Coys moved up via Track 12 and Bridge St. — Quick relief completed by 2130. B + C Coys in front line on right & left respectively. A & D Coys in support. Sketch of disposition attached Appendices I — 165th French Regiment on our left. 1/Royal Inniskilling Fus on right.	App I Disposition
Front Line	30th		Nothing/So Quiet; hostile Arty active from 0500 – 06:30 One shell	

Army Form C. 2118.

WAR DIARY
or
INTELLIGENCE SUMMARY.
(Erase heading not required.)

Instructions regarding War Diaries and Intelligence Summaries are contained in F. S. Regs., Part II. and the Staff Manual respectively. Title pages will be prepared in manuscript.

Place	Date	Hour	Summary of Events and Information	Remarks and references to Appendices
Front LINE	30-		Snipers in A Coy Support Notten killing 1 OR & wounding 3- Other ranks.= Fire positions completed for each post during the night. Patrol under 2nd Lieut Bennet "C" Coy reconnoitred the Broembeek, reported no enemy movement, Broembeek fordable, but cut up by shellholes + swampy on the left.	
	Oct 30-		Killed 2nd Lieut F.G. JOYCE. The following officers were in command of Companies in the line. A Coy Capt W.J. Page C Coy 2nd Lieut ADN LOWE B Coy 2nd Lieut H.H. Evans D Coy Capt W Davies	
	30-		Strength of Battⁿ 30-9-17. Officers 21 Other Ranks 718	

G.T. Parker Lieut Colonel
Comdg 2/4th Bn Borderers

Appendix II.

2nd BATTALION,
SOUTH WALES
BORDERERS.

Roll of Officers with Battn on ...

Rank and Name		Remarks
Lt. Colonel	G.L. Raikes DSO	
Capt	C. Mumford MC	
"	J.F. Page	
"	F.J.L. Maygor MC	
"	W. Davies	
Lieut	G.D.O. Lloyd	
"	F.J. Whitehouse	
2/Lieut	J.B. Stoyndale-Bennett	
"	H.H. Evans	
"	C.L. Woolveridge	
"	A. DeO. Lowe MC	
"	J.C.C. Dickinson	
"	S.W. Angell	
"	G.P. Gibson	
"	S.F.S. Hearnes	
"	J.R. Williams	
"	C.E. Crowder	
"	H.R. Nethercleft	
Lieut & A.Mr.	E.K. Laman	
Capt.	A.J. Blake MC	
"	Rev A.R. Swallow	

In the Field
Sept. 30th 1917

G.L. Raikes
Lt Colonel
Commdg 2/ South Wales Borderers

Confidential

War Diary

of

2nd Battn. South Wales Borderers

From 1/10/17   To 31/10/17

Confidential

87 Brigade

Herewith Battalion War Diary for month of ~~October~~ for transmission through the proper channels.

H.J. Parnell Major
Comdg 2/S Wales Borderers

2/11/17

Army Form C. 2118.

WAR DIARY
or
INTELLIGENCE SUMMARY.
(Erase heading not required.)

OCTOBER 1917

(1)

Place	Date	Hour	Summary of Events and Information	Remarks and references to Appendices
FRONTLINE	1st		Hostile Artillery active at dusk on 30th and again from 5.0 a.m. – 6.30 a.m. on 1st Oct. During the night about 250 yds of wire were carried up & put up on the left Coy front – 150 yds of communication trench dug on right Coy front. Day quiet.	
"	2nd		Hostile Art again active at dawn – During the night wiring was completed along left Coy front except for 20 yds on right Coy front. Communication trench on right Coy Front completed about 300 yds altogether. 2 Patrols went out one from D Coy under 2/Lt Netherclift on left Coy front & one from A Coy under Capt Jackson on the right Coy front. BOK patrols descended along the Broembeck. Broembeck is reported to be from 7 to 12 ft broad with high banks except on the extreme left where ground is boggy & broken with shell holes. Enemy posts located on far bank opposite right front also in MAY WOOD & WEY COP S6. Relieved by 1/Border Regt, relief complete by 9.0 p.m. moved back to CHARTER HOUSE Camp. taking over from 1/Border Regt. about 1½ miles W of BOESINGHE. Relief quiet. 5/70 1 B. remained at	

Army Form C. 2118.

WAR DIARY
or
INTELLIGENCE SUMMARY.
(Erase heading not required.)

Instructions regarding War Diaries and Intelligence Summaries are contained in F. S. Regs., Part II. and the Staff Manual respectively. Title pages will be prepared in manuscript.

(2)

Place	Date	Hour	Summary of Events and Information	Remarks and references to Appendices
			Bedford Camp which Bn was in the line. Total casualties whilst in the line.	
			Killed	
			O.H. 1	
			O.R. 2 13	
			Tents & Shelters only but comfortable	
			Rested.	
CHARTER HOUSE CAMP	2nd to 5th	17.30	Moved up & took over front line (reinforced on L.wing) relieving 1 Coy 1/Munster B. – 1/7th R Lothian Fusiliers. 1 Coy 1st Brecons and 1 Coy 1/Royal Fusiliers. 3 Companies in front line from U17c.05/20 to U18d.30/50. One Coy in close support. Total front 1800 yds from U17c.05/20 to U18d.30/50. The Officer time each Coy was sent on in advance to reconnoitre position of Companies of these Bns. 2 Lieut A.D.W. LOWE M.C. was killed and Lieut G.P. GIBSON wounded. Relief was very difficult owing to the country being unknown & guides bad. Shell fire was more or less continuous throughout the night all round Charterhouse Division & there were several casualties. Relief was completed by 3.0 a.m. 6th inst. Dispositions of Companies attached Appendix I. 1 Company 1/R Innishkilling	Appendix I Dispositions of Companies

Army Form C. 2118.

WAR DIARY
or
INTELLIGENCE SUMMARY.
(Erase heading not required.)

October 1917.

Place	Date	Hour	Summary of Events and Information	Remarks and references to Appendices
FRONT LINE	6/10/17		Furicke was attacked to the 73rd & Kept in Reserve in vicinity of LANGEMARCK. Hostile Shelling was fairly heavy till 6.30 a.m. after that till about 11.30 a.m. the whole area was very quiet. Remainder of the day hostile shelling was intermittent.	
"	7/10/17		During the night of 6/7: Four patrols were sent out from the Front Companies along the Broenbeek. - The Broenbeek reported impassable except with bridges. Capt Smith D.Coy & Lieut Beverley A.Coy both did very good patrols. - Rations & water for r/f W Front Company had to be carried about 3000 yds over very bad country, Ration did not get up to Bn. firing of the Transport animals were killed by shellfire which carried up rations to the ration dump.	
"	8/10/17		Relieved by 4th Worcester Regt on the left sector and 1/James Fusiliers on the r/f W sector. Relief very late completed about 3.0 a.m. Enemy intermittent shelling during the night.	

Casualties during tour 5/10/17 – 7/10/17.

	Killed	Wounded	Missing	Total
Officers	1.	1		2
O.R.	5	37	5	47

WAR DIARY
INTELLIGENCE SUMMARY.
(Erase heading not required.)

Army Form C. 2118.

October 1917.

Place	Date	Hour	Summary of Events and Information	Remarks and references to Appendices
	8/10/17		Moved to WHITE MILL Camp ELVERDINGHE about 6 miles. Good Camp all Nissen Huts.	
WHITE MILL Camp.	9/10/17	9.0 am	Entrained at ELVERDINGHE detrained at PROVEN & moved into Poodle Camp. a bad camp & very muddy. Transport moved by Road.	
POODLE CAMP	10th to 14th Oct 1917.		Rain every day, mud very bad. No training possible. On 11th Oct. Lt Col. G.T. Raikes DSO proceeded on leave, command of Battn was assumed by Major H.L. Fawcett Herbert 1/ Border Regt. Lt. Col 12th Oct. Capt D.H.C. Somerville M.C. returned Battn. from England and resumed duties of Adjutant, Capt E.C. Mumford M.C. taking over command of C. Coy. Regimental Hospital 27 NCOs men. Draft arrived 27 NCO men. Following Officers also joined the Battn - 2 Lieut D.R. WINDSOR from 3rd Battn. posted to C. Coy. " A. H CRUMMACK " " " B " Lieut. e.H. DAVIES } A.S.C. " " D " " F.N.W. COOPER } attached to Battn " " C " 2/Lt H.C. CAIN " " D "	

Army Form C. 2118.

WAR DIARY
or
INTELLIGENCE SUMMARY.
(Erase heading not required.)

October 1917

Place	Date	Hour	Summary of Events and Information	Remarks and references to Appendices
POODLE CAMP	15th	8.45am	Batta marched out of Camp and entrained at HOPOUTRE siding at 11am. Train left at 1am for BAUMETZ siding in the VI Corps area, arrived 2.30am and went into billets in BELLACOURT. Billets very fair, wine beds in about half, but shortage of seats.	
BELLACOURT	17th		Lieut C.D.O. LLOYD went into Hospital. Capt W.F. PAGE returned from Hospital.	
	17th to 21st		Coy Training, Baths, again to billets. 2/Lt CL WOOLVER.DEE. Sh. on leave U.K. 18th Oct.	Appendix II. Training Programme
	21st to 28th		Programme of work attached. Rain stopped work on Tuesday. Three Companies ??? all Thursday; Friday filling in trenches & pulling ? wire to make Bicycle Puncle ground — Brigade General Practice held on Saturday. Battn ? routine, woollen gloves, waterproof caps issued. Two Officers proceeded on 14 days Paris leave, and 2 to CATAMIERS. 2/Lt. A.E. CROWDER proceeded as Adjutant 29 Divnl Depôt Battn. Revd G.T. BAGGALY proceeded on P.T. & R.F. course Third Army School. Lieut E.G.W. COOKE rejoined from leave.	
	23rd			

Army Form C. 2118.

WAR DIARY
or
INTELLIGENCE SUMMARY.
(Erase heading not required.)

Instructions regarding War Diaries and Intelligence Summaries are contained in F. S. Regs., Part II. and the Staff Manual respectively. Title pages will be prepared in manuscript.

(6) October 1917

Place	Date	Hour	Summary of Events and Information	Remarks and references to Appendices
	O.U.			
BELLACOURT	25th		2/Lt N.C.O. & men returned from Hospital. Three newsmen joined Battn.	
	26th		2nd Lt Mr E K LAMAR proceeded on leave to U.K.	
	28th		2 Lt. C. LEWIS proceeded to 37 TMB for duty.	
	31st		2 Lt H K NETHERCLEFT proceeded on leave to U.K.	

H.P. Kennett Major
Comdg 2/Wales Borderers

Appendix I A.1. War Diary Oct 1917

Message Pad.

Your Message must be such as will enable the Addressee to know what the Situation is with You and your Neighbours.

NEGATIVE INFORMATION IS ALSO VALUABLE.

Strike out and alter sentences as necessary.

TO..

1. Am advancing to..
2. Am putting out (Have put out) protective parties.
3. Am sending out. Have sent out and am keeping out patrols to keep touch with the enemy.
4. Am (Have) consolidating (ed).
5. Our line now runs...
6. I require (give article or articles and No. required):

Send the above to...

7. Troops on my right are (give situation)

8. Troops on my left are (give situation)

9. My strength now is...
10. Am being shelled from......................................
11. Am held up by M.G., T.M., rifle, artillery fire from..........................
12. Am now ready to...
13. Enemy line runs...
14. Enemy (strength)......................at...........................
    doing..
15. Have captured ....
16. Enemy prisoners belong to.................................
17. Enemy counter-attack forming up at....................
18. Other remarks—

Time   a.m. (p.m.)   Name...
Date.................................   Rank..
Place...............................   Platoon................ Company...............
(Map Ref. or mark on back of map).   Battalion...................................

5TH FIELD SURVEY Co R.E. 1(176.)

Training Programme for week ending 26/10/17

Appendix II

Coy	Monday	Tues	Wednesday	Thurs	Friday	Sat
A	Range	As for B Coy on Monday	8.45 P.T. & B.F. 9.45 Specialists Coy Training 11.30 C.O. Ceremonial Parade	—	8.45 P.T. & B.F. 9.45 Close order drill & musketry 10.45 Specialist & Coy Training to 12.45 attack & raid practice	Rifle Models
B	8.45 P.T. & B.F. 9.45 Saluting, Platoon arms drill. Ceremonial 10.45 Specialist & Coy Training to 12.45 attack & raid practice	Range -	8.45 P.T. & B.F. 9.45 Specialists Coy Training 11.30 C.O. Ceremonial Parade	Rifle Models	8.45 P.T. & B.F. 9.45 Close order drill. Musketry 10.45 Specialist & Coy Training to 11.45 attack & raid practice	
C	8.45 Saluting/Platoon drill, arms drill, ceremonial 9.45 P.T. & B.F. 10.45 Specialists Coy Drill to 12.45 attack & raid practice	As for Monday	8.45 Specialists & Coy Training 10.45 P.T. & B.F. 11.30 C.O. Ceremonial Parade	Stock exercise & shooting	Range -	Dog
D	8.45 Specialists Coy Training attack & raid practice 10.45 P.T. & B.F. 11.45 Saluting, Platoon Drill Arms Drill Ceremonial	As for Monday	8.45 Specialists & Coy Training 10.45 P.T. & B.F. 11.30 C.O. Ceremonial Parade		8.45 Specialist & Coy Training attack & raid practice 10.45 P.T. & B.F. 11.45 Close order Drill & Musketry	Range

Snipers & Signallers under instruction Officers daily
C.O. Conference of Coy Commanders 6 p.m. daily

[signed] A.W. du Rocker
Chief

Training Programme Week ending 3/1/17.   October Appendix III

Coy	Monday	Tuesday	Wed	Thursday	Fri	Sat
A	8.45. P.T. & B.F. 9.45. Coy + Coy Drill Ceremonial 10.45 Specialist & Coy training 12. attack & raid practice.	8.45. P.T. & B.F. 9.45 Specialist & Coy training 11.45 attack & raid practice 13.00 C.O. Ceremonial parade	Pedals Ceremonial	8.45. P.T. & B.F. 9.45 Specialist & Coy training 11.45. Coy in attack for inspection by C.O.	—	Range-
B	Range-	8.45. P.T. + B.F. 9.45 Specialist & Coy training 11.45 attack & raid practice. 12.00 C.O. Ceremonial Parade	Pedals Ceremonial	8.45. P.T. + B.F. 9.45 Coy in attack for inspection by C.O. 10.45 Specialist & Coy Training	To attack	as for Coy & Monday
C	8.45. Annual Coy Drill Ceremonial 9.45 P.T. & B.F. 10.45 Specialist & Coy training 12.45 attack & raid practice.	8.45. Specialist & Coy Training 10.45 attack & raid practice. 11.45 P.T. & B.F. 12.00 C.O. Ceremonial Parade	Pedals Ceremonial	8.45. Specialist & Coy training 10.45 Coy in attack for inspection by C.O. 11.45 P.T. & B.F.	To attack	as for Monday
D	8.45 Specialist + Coy training attack & raid practice. 10.45 P.T. + B.F. 11.45 Annual Coy Drill Ceremonial	8.45 P.T. + B.F. 9.45 Coy in attack for inspection by C.O. 10.45 Specialist + Coy Training 12.00 C.O. Ceremonial Parade	Pedals Ceremonial	Range-	To attack	as for Monday

2–3 Daily. Officer classes in Lewis Gun, Bombs, Rifle Bombs,
Snipers & Signallers under instructing officers
6 p.m. Daily Company Commanders Conference

Cmdg Lt Col Ch Borden

Confidential 87/29

War Diary

of

2nd Battn South Wales Borderers.

Six Appendices —

From 1st/11/17.   To 30"/11/17.
Folio 30.

WAR DIARY
or
INTELLIGENCE SUMMARY.

Army Form C. 2118.

November 1917.

Place	Date	Hour	Summary of Events and Information	Remarks and references to Appendices
BELLACOURT	1st		2/Lieuts F.T.R. ROWLANDS and S.E. LLoyd joined the Battalion with a draft of 3 O.R.	
	2nd		Brigade Ceremonial parade. Decoration presented by G.O.C. Division. Coy Commanders attended demonstration of Tanks and Infantry	
	4th			
	5th		2nd Lieuts H.J. EDWARDS, G. ESMOND, E.F. MALINS arrived from England	
	7th		2nd Lieuts H. EDWARDS, R.S.M. BRUNTNELL and 7 O.R. arrived from England	
	6th		D. Coy. sent on detachment to H.Q. 20th Division, SOREL to prevent area	
	5th to 10th		Training. Lectures by Divisional Commander on the 5th. Semi-open warfare, attack of infantry with Tanks, Pickets, musketry etc. Trained during the week in advanced guard and outpost work. Exercises many areas had found.	
			Selected teams to the Lewis Gun, Lewis Gun, Bayonet & K [illegible] Weather throughout the week variable with heavy showers.	

Army Form C. 2118.

WAR DIARY
or
INTELLIGENCE SUMMARY. November 1917.

(Erase heading not required.)

Instructions regarding War Diaries and Intelligence Summaries are contained in F. S. Regs., Part II. and the Staff Manual respectively. Title pages will be prepared in manuscript.

Place	Date	Hour	Summary of Events and Information	Remarks and references to Appendices
BELLACOURT	12th		Brigade Tactical exercise. Advance and attack of villages in open warfare.	
	13th		Draft of 3 O.R. arrived from England. Lt. Col. G.T. Raikes D.S.O. returned from leave. Major H.G. Garrett proceeded on leave to U.K.	
	14th		Chaplain Rev A.K. Swallow proceeded U.K. on termination of attachment. Capt F.W. PAGE proceeded on leave to U.K. Draft of 107 O.R. joined Battn., 6 being casuals, the remainder new men. Administration instructions received for move to forward area.	
	15th		Divisional Tactical exercise. Attack in open warfare, whole day. Scheme finished.	
	17th		Marched to BOISLEUX and entrained there at 8 p.m. Capt E.N. Le ROY & 2 Lieut H.K. NETHERCLEFT and 61 O.R. remained behind to proceed to Corps Reinforcement Camp as 10% reinforcements. All men sent on leave up to 24th Nov sent with this party. Returned rafts proceeded to Division. 16 An.	
	18th		Detrained at PERONNE about 2.30 am & marched to a camp (huts) about 4 miles from PERONNE on road to HAUT ALLAINES.	

Army Form C. 2118.

WAR DIARY
or
INTELLIGENCE SUMMARY. November 1917 (3)
(Erase heading not required.)

Instructions regarding War Diaries and Intelligence Summaries are contained in F. S. Regs., Part II. and the Staff Manual respectively. Title pages will be prepared in manuscript.

Place	Date	Hour	Summary of Events and Information	Remarks and references to Appendices
HAUT ALLAINES	18th	20:00	Marched to FINS arriving 12 midnight (Huts & shelters)	
FINS	19th		Issued battle stores etc + 2 days rations to men. 3pm – 11.0 pm men slept.	
		11:30pm	Men started blankets + great coats. Issued hot tea. 10% remaining in camp	
FINS	20th	1:10am	Marched off via GOUZEACOURT to assembly area.	Appendix I
			Strength of Battn as follows:—	Map showing Boundaries & Objectives.
				Appendix I a
				Officers	Other Ranks	
			2/10% Staff at Corps Reinforcements	3	65	
			5/10% " at Transport lines	3	147	87:3rd Oven to attack & B.H.Q. instructions issued to Coys.
			Attached 88th Field Ambulance	—	25	
			Attached 4/5 W.Riding Field Coy	1	25	
			Attached 87 BGe HQ wounded Sigrs		6	Includes B.H.Q. Shelter Reserve etc.
			With 1st 1/3rd in attack	19*	596	
				*Does not include Medical Officer.	
			For accounts of Operations on 20th see Appendix. II	Appendix II Account of operations 24/11/17
			1/Royal Inniskilling Fusiliers advanced through 1/4 B Corps evening the Ridge head attack	

WAR DIARY or INTELLIGENCE SUMMARY

Army Form C. 2118.

Place	Date	Hour	Summary of Events and Information	Remarks and references to Appendices
MARCOING	20th Nov 1917	14.00	about 2.0 p.m. They went with considerable opposition from the Ammunition Pits on the S side & were held up short of the final objective. C Coy advanced toward with to 1/R.T.F. taking several Ammunition Pits & machine guns. On the right the Newfoundland Regt held the Western edge of MASNIERES. The village itself was still occupied by German Snipers but further to the right still to 4 Wooden pills - position across square 927.a	Appendix III. Map of position night of 20/21st.
		23.00	The Bn received orders which it is requested to readjust & reinforce the attack at dawn on the RUMILLY Trenches & village. During the night the hour of attack was postponed till 11.0 a.m. It was also stated that 9 tanks would assist the attack.	
	21st	6.0 am	No further information having been received about the tanks, an attempt was made to get in touch with them. No information could be obtained in Marcoing but 7 tanks were found belonging to A.Bn. who were willing to assist though they had been fighting all the day before. The Tank officers came forward to arrange details of the advance & at 12 noon the advance started. (See account of operation Appendix IV)	
			At the time of the attack Masnieres was still not occupied by our troops.	Appendix IV account of Operation 21/11/17.

Army Form C. 2118.

WAR DIARY
or
INTELLIGENCE SUMMARY.
(Erase heading not required.)

November 1917 (5)

Place	Date	Hour	Summary of Events and Information	Remarks and references to Appendices
MARCOING	21st	1400	After the attack started 2.0 pm the B⁺ occupied the line G.20.a-b.0 —	
			G.20.a.3.7. C Coy on the left & the remaining Companies who were much	
			mixed up holding the rest of the line to the Cambrai Rd – B⁺ HQ at abt 200ˣ	
			back in an old Ammunition pit. After the attack had pushed onto were	
			received from the Brigade to return to our original position but this was cancelled	
			when it was proven what line the B⁺ had taken up. The out honour g Masnieres	
			had not been entered & after dark a special party was sent to clear them out.	
			It returned & established a post there. They also done 1 German & 3 civilians	
			were found there & sent back. The B⁺ was left in trench with any troops on	
			our right.	
MASNIERES	22nd		At dawn after Stand to B⁺ HQ moved back to a house at G.20.c.2.7.	
			2ⁿᵈ Lieut Hearden (Signalling Offr) took over command of A & D Coys.	
			2 Lieut Winter " " " C Coy	
			2 Lieut Edwards H.J. " " " B Coy.	
			These were all the officers left except Cmdg Officer & Adjutant.	
			At dusk Companies were reorganised as follows. D Coy on right, A Coy, B Coy & C Coy on left.	

WAR DIARY
or
INTELLIGENCE SUMMARY.
(Erase heading not required.)

Army Form C. 2118.

November 1917

Place	Date	Hour	Summary of Events and Information	Remarks and references to Appendices
MASNIERES	22ⁿᵈ		Capt Esthank 1/Border Regt was attached from Bⁿ Staff to assist, & took charge of the Front line. Continued digging in during the night - little hostile activity.	
	23ʳᵈ		Good progress was made with the digging during the night. During the day movement was difficult owing to Enemy Snipers in the houses on Cambrai Rd. There was obtained with 1/Essex Regt on the right flank.	
	23ʳᵈ		Good progress was made with the digging during the night. Hostile shelling heavy. 2/Lieut Jordan & 26 men 10% from Transport Lines arrived 5·0 am. During the night orders were received to find out patrols & if was thought Enemy were retiring. 2 Patrols went out at about 1·30 am and found Enemy still holding their position. Lance's two took over from 1/Essex Regt on our right at the Somme River taking over our Snipers position in the Cambrai Rd. Relieved by 1/KOSB 7·0 pm & moved over to the Marcoing Bridgehead Defences (See sketch of disposition. Appendix V). Coypus with hot food met the Bⁿ on Canal Approaches V. Mot. Party Tank by Bren Bⁿ H.Q. Coys wanted there for hot meal & then guides to their new defensive position. Brigade Defence line B Coy on right - C Coy on left. A & D Coys in rear in reserve. C Coy had to dig in before dawn.	

Army Form C. 2118.

WAR DIARY
or
INTELLIGENCE SUMMARY.
(Erase heading not required.)

November 1917

Place	Date	Hour	Summary of Events and Information	Remarks and references to Appendices
MARCOING Bridgehead defences	24th		A & C Coys in trenches only. B & D Coys in deep dug-outs. Day quiet except for hostile shelling of Marcoing Ry Station by A Coys left flank. A Coy had a few casualties. At dusk B & C Coys worked on Bridge head defences. Line with R.E. — B & D Coys commenced communication trench from front line back from Bridge head line 200 x dug. Two craters were placed in a shed on canal bank near Bn HQ.	
"	25th		Still quiet on this sector. Heavy shelling to the North. Enemy night A Coy was moved over to its right to keep clear of Marcoing Station which Enemy shell continuously. At dusk Coys worked as 24th. Another 200 x of C.T. dug. Latrines dug —	
"	26th		5·0 p.m. relieved by 4th Worcesters & moved into billets in MARCOING. — B Coy detailed to defence of Ry bridge in care of Alarm & C Coy for Marcoing main bridge. — A B & D Coys in billets at S end Marcoing with only occupied cellars. C Coy in Main St in cellars. A little shelling during the night with occasional 9" Their Manifests about 10·0 p.m. B Coy to cellars close to Ry bridge — C Coy	
MARCOING	27		to cellars near Bridge over river in Main St (there was a available Coy should have gone to	

Army Form C. 2118.

WAR DIARY
or
INTELLIGENCE SUMMARY.
(Erase heading not required.)   November 1917

Instructions regarding War Diaries and Intelligence Summaries are contained in F. S. Regs., Part II. and the Staff Manual respectively. Title pages will be prepared in manuscript.

Place	Date	Hour	Summary of Events and Information	Remarks and references to Appendices
MARCOING	27th		1/(a) Cellars opposite main bridge over Canal. A.D Coy & H.Q. moved to N.W. edge of Marcoing where there were better cellars & a more fireproof sleeping fort just outside the village. Got into new billets at 2 p.m.	
"	28th		Spent the day getting rifles & stores from the cleared up & completing equipment - men still very tired -	
		1630	Again moved up into Bridgehead Defence line relieving 4th Worcesters. Coy B & H.Q. moved into I/Essex H.Q. about 50X from deep dug outs used last time. Immediately after relief Coys worked as follows:- B & C Coys wiring front line from Cavalry Rd. westwards. 340 yds trestles & trakers wire coils put up. A & D Coys worked on C.T. from front line	
Bridge Head Defences	29th		Day fairly quiet. At dusk Coys worked as follows: A & D Coys on Bridge head Defences B Coy on support trench to Boston Regt. C Coy on C.T. to front line. Orders received to relieve I/Boston Regt in front line left sector on night 30/1st	
"	30.		At dawn there was a certain amount of hostile shelling including gas & coy in Bridge head Defences were ordered to "Stand to". At about 10.0 a.m. the Enemy who had broken through the line on the right appeared in large numbers behind	

Army Form C. 2118.

WAR DIARY
or
INTELLIGENCE SUMMARY.

(Erase heading not required.) November 1917.

Place	Date	Hour	Summary of Events and Information	Remarks and references to Appendices
Bridgehead Defences	30.		(Relieved) B. H.Q. + South of the Canal. Received Operation 30: Nov - 3" Secret instructions attached to War Diary for Dec. Little was Known of the situation in rear of the Hindenburg Line but late information was received that the enemy had broken through apparent BANTEUX + had captured La Vacquerie + Gonnelieu - and went up into Welsh Ridge. Counter attack by 88 B⁰ 1/Nos B3 + Greasury Militia drove them back from the Rees Vertes + South of Marcoing & Mar coming Copse. Advanced Bde H.Q. 29" Div at Gouzeaucourt were captured by the Enemy. Enemy to any counter attack by guards Division retook Gouzeaucourt & late La Vacquerie	
		1400	C Coy & B Coy moved to S sector of Canal & support position 230 a facing Les Rees Vertes. B Coy to support 26 B⁰ in Masnieres. Later A Coy also moved over & B3. took over front line from Les Rees Vertes past Encrefuer K.23.c.8.5. Ration arrived at our H.Q. & were got up to Companies. D Coy still remained garrisoning the Bridgehead Defences West of the Canal. Disposition on night of 30" Nov are attached Appendix VI. Capt E.M. Gilton. Capt Tragett and 64 OR from Corps Reinforcements came up each evening	Appendix VI Map of Disposition night 30/1

Army Form C. 2118.

WAR DIARY
or
INTELLIGENCE SUMMARY.
(Erase heading not required.)

November 1917

Instructions regarding War Diaries and Intelligence Summaries are contained in F. S. Regs., Part II. and the Staff Manual respectively. Title pages will be prepared in manuscript.

Place	Date	Hour	Summary of Events and Information	Remarks and references to Appendices
MARCOING COPSE. U.24.b.9.1.	30th		(contd.) carrying 250 rounds S.A.A. in addition to attack order. Capt. Gebbie took over C. Coy & Capt. Traquit B Coy. The men being sent to their companies. D Coy added to B Coy. 31 men 10% relief 1/Royal Inniskilling Fus with two Officers / 1 Batta Regt also arrived, & were kept in reserve.	

Casualties from 20th Nov – 29th Nov were as follows:—

	Killed		Wounded		Missing		Total	
	Officers	Other Ranks	Officers	Other Ranks	Officers	Other Ranks	Officers	Other Ranks
20th Nov.	–	7	1* #9th	47	–	15	1 – 76	69
21st Nov.	–	12	#3 5th	64	3	75	6 – 151	
22nd – 29th Nov.	–	2	–	1	–	–	–	3
Total	–	21	10	112	3	90	13 – 223	

\# Two later died of wounds.

Officer Casualties
20th Wounded. Capt C. MUMFORD – Lieut G.T. BAGGALLY – Lieut H.H. EVANS – 2/Lt C.L. WOOLVERIDGE
\# 2nd Lieut H.T. EDWARDS. Died of wounds Lieut W.H.M. WEEKS – 2/Lt J.C.B. JAMES.
Wounded 22/11/17.
21st Wounded. Capt. F.J.L. MAYGER – 2nd Lt E.W.S. COOKE – 2/Lt J.E. LLOYD
Missing : Capt V.H.M. PIERSON – Lieut A.V.N. COOPER – 2/Lt F.T.R. ROWLANDS

G.J. Parkes Lt. Colonel
Comdg. 9/Royal Welsh Fusiliers

Nov 17
Appendix II

Account of Operations on 20th Nov 1917.

The Barrage opened on the German trenches at about 6.45 a.m.

Ten minutes after Zero the B[attalio]n moved forward in column of fours (companies at 400 yds distance) B Coy finding small advance guard. There was practically no shelling until the B[attalio]n reached VILLERS-PLOUICH where the German counter barrage commenced. The shelling became worse as the B[attalio]n got about 400ⁿ from our old front line. There were about 13 casualties including 1 Officer & 2 O. Sons. The B[attalio]n reached its allotted Position in the old front trench at about 7.15 a.m.

Hostile shelling died down by 7.45 a.m. The B[attalio]n moved forward at 10.15 a.m. in Artillery formation covered by sect[ion]s. The direction was well kept but the formation proved difficult owing to the belts of barbed wire & the broken & deep trenches

Additional account of operations on 20th
Nov. 1917 after correcting fuller information

From further evidence it appears that
the enemy's trenches were shellocked only
with dugouts at intervals. The enemy
machine Guns were in these dugouts
& also in the open behind. As Tanks
came up the M Gunners retired down
the dugouts coming up again as soon
as the Tank passed, so that the machine
Gun fire was continuous & heavy.
The left only reached the enemy's wire
& in the centre & right scattered groups
only got over the German front line.
On the left of the 13th Bn. of KOSB did
not get forward at all nor did any
troops advance on the right. The German
counter attacked at once & drove the left
back, the centre withdrew to a small
cable trench & on the right also the
Germans counter attacked & surrounded
Capt Pearson & about 15 men who it

is believed were captured. The centre therefore was left unsupported on either flank & with no officers. C.Q.M.S. Ruffle who had led these men forward when all officers had become casualties ordered the men to withdraw & himself faced the advancing Germans. He was last seen advancing with fixed bayonet against a party of advancing Germans.

26/11/17

Maurice M'Dowel
Comdg 2/1st W.Bord.

Account of operations on 21st Nov 1917

During the night 20/21st, the Bn received orders to attack the enemy trenches from G.14.C.L.9 to G.20.b.6.9 at 11.0 am 21st Nov. 9 Tanks to cooperate, the 1st KOSB advancing simultaneously on our right.

Before 11.0 am 9 Tanks were obtained 3 of which advanced with 1/KOSB and 4 with SWB.

The Bn was in position with 3 Coys about 250 yds over the canal + 1 Coy well in advance.

Orders for the advance were as follows. The 3 Coys in rear to advance 200x behind the tanks passing through the leading Coy which was to come on as support Coy, that is to say 3 Coys in the front line + 1 in support. The advance had to be made along the spur running up towards Rumilly. + there was about 1100 yds to cover before reaching our front line

Nov '17 Appendix IV

One tank went ahead to deal with a machine gun known to be in a house on Cambrai Rd. just North of Marcieres & which swept the ground to advance over, the other 3 tanks followed about 600ʸ behind it. The advance started about 12 noon & before the leading line had advanced 200ʸ machine gun fire opened both from the Enemy trench and from the houses on the Cambrai Rd. This quickly became very heavy & swept the slope from the right front & left front. A certain amount of cover was obtained by advancing from one ammunition pit to another, there being 8 or 10 rows of these, but after passing these there was no cover at all. The men advanced + with the aid of tanks took the houses on the Cambrai road & got into the german front line where it crosses the road. On the left the leading line reached the German wire, this was not cut as the tanks went through on the flank only then mowing down the trench. The machine gun fire continued very heavy throughout. When the tanks came back after passing along the Enemy trench all the men on the left & centre also came back on the right the men who had reached the German trench I believe held on but there were only a few of them. I received two messages back from the right to say that we were at the houses on the Road & in the trench where it crosses the road. Two wounded officers were brought back from the German trench by a tank, at the time they were picked up the Germans were quite close & advancing on them. As soon as the men came back they were reformed & moved forward to cover Masnières in case the Enemy ~~was appearing on the road~~

advanced & to get in touch with the parties in the Enemy's trench on the right. Whilst taking up this line the Enemy were seen advancing over the crest & past the houses on the Central road. Fire was opened on them & after a certain amount of firing, seeing that the Enemy brought up a machine gun they retired & the line was formed up to the mill house of Namainier. Only two officers of those who advanced were the Company officers W. Birrell & V-ey for N.C.Os. At dusk the men dug themselves in where they were.

24/11/17

Parker W Read
Comdg 2/Strath-Brown

On approaching the Hindenburg
Support, a few bullets came across
the crest of the hill from the right front.
This was from an enemy strong point
which was still holding out in the
Hindenburg support. This did not
interfere with the advance, but the
Newfoundland Regt on our right was
checked until a tank went across.
There was no opposition except from
one or two snipers a gun position pulled ? &a driver
Mouroncopse. There were a few
germans in the copse & on starting to
move forward to the town a machine
gun & rifle fire was opened from the
houses by the brook. the river was crossed
easily but as soon as men started
to get to the tramway bridge over the
canal they were caught by M.G.
fire from a house facing right down
the canal. There was a good deal
of delay here & the right support

company came up in addition to the two leading Companies. A Tank also came up & under cover of its fire the three Companies got across. The Newfoundland Regt also got across by the lock.
These three Coys took up positions about 250ˣ across the canal, the R.I.F. following close behind them.
The KOSB had got across by the Marcoing bridge about ½ hour earlier.
The three companies were across the canal by 1.30 p.m., & the Reserve Coy in position on the Northern edge of MARCOING Copse. We were in touch with the KOSB on the left across the canal & NFLD on the right.
One Coy pushed forward & got into German ammunition pits at about G.19.b.6.6.
Reserve Coy & B⁺ HQ crossed the canal at about 3.0 p.m. at which

C Coy pushed forward when R.I.F. started to advance & pushed farther to far side of the ammunition pits.

hours the situation was as follows:
C Coy forward at G.19.b.6.6.
A, B, + D. Coys covering the bridgehead & lock. D Coy on right. A Coy in centre B Coy on left.
Bn H.Q. at L23.d.6.3. Companies dug in before dark.
On our right we were only in touch with a few men of Newfoundland Regt & nothing was known as to whether MASNIERES had been captured by us or not. A post was therefore pushed out & the houses at about G.19.D.0.5 occupied. It was afterwards discovered that the Newfoundland Regt H.Q. were established near the lock.
During the advance a few small parties of Germans were captured at intervals also 2 Field guns at about L28.b.6.1. No record of prisoners was kept but about 60 were sent

back including a few officers

$\frac{24}{11}{17}$ G T Parker McConnel
         Courtney of Sheals Bowmen

MESSAGE FORM.

To   No.

1. I am at.............................. { Note:—Either give Map Reference or mark your position by a 'X' on the Map on back.

2. My Line runs...

3. My Platoon / Company is at..and is consolidating.

4. My Platoon / Company is at..and has consolidated.

5. Am held up by (a) M.G. / (b) Wire at.....................(Place where you are).

6. Enemy holding strong point.................................

7. I am in touch with...on Right / Left at.............

8. I am not in touch with..on Right. / Left.

9. Am shelled from.................................

10. Am in need of :—

11. Counter Attack forming at...................................

12. Hostile (a) Battery / (b) Machine Gun / (c) Trench Mortar active at.......................................

13. Reinforcements wanted at...

14. I estimate my present strength at.................rifles

15. Have captured........................

16. Prisoners belong to..

17. Add any other useful information here :—

Name....................................

Platoon................................

Time.........................m.   Company.............................

Date......................1917.   Battalion............................

(A). Carry no maps or papers which may be of value to the Enemy.

(B). Give no information if captured, except the following, which you are bound to give :—

    Name and Rank.

(C). Collect all captured maps and papers and send them in at once.

Confidential

War Diary

of

2nd Battalion South Wales Borderers

From 1st December 1917   To 31st December 1917

Folio 29.

WAR DIARY
or
INTELLIGENCE SUMMARY.
(Erase heading not required.)

December 1917

Army Form C. 2118.

Place	Date	Hour	Summary of Events and Information	Remarks and references to Appendices
MARCOING COPSE L.29.6.9.0	1st		Fairly quiet at dawn – at about 9.30 am a very heavy hostile bombardment started on LES RUES VERTES. See account of operations 30' Nov – 3rd Dec attached	Appendix I
			About midday orders were received. Send D Coy which was still operating to account of operations Nov–3rd Dec.	
			Appendix I. North of the Canal to the 86' B⁰ in MASNIERES the Coy moved over about	
			2.0 pm just before the second hostile attack on Les Rues Vertes commenced. The Enemy was in Les Rues Vertes at about 4.0 pm – 86' B⁰ agreed to oversee	
			MASNIERES commencing 11.0 pm. 2/Lt Fortescue (plus 1 Coy HQrs) sent up to reinforce) to form rear front line facing Les Rues Vertes. 3 parties of disposition attached Appendix II. After dark the 76' B⁰ were also attacked & lines on the	Appendix II sketch of disposition taken at night 14/12
			left flank by the Canal. Two patrols of a platoon each were sent out after dusk one from C Coy & one from A Coy to ascertain the situation in Les Rues Vertes. A Coys patrol got in touch with 86' B⁰ at about 9.26 a 3.6. C Coys patrol under	
	2/12		2/Lt Windsor met a Sgt 86' B⁰ on Encicits – Les Rues Vertes Rd who said he could lead them straight into an Enemy party at about G.26.c.6.4 & 2 Lt Windsor too believed them have been captured as remainder of the patrol got back.	

WAR DIARY or INTELLIGENCE SUMMARY

Army Form C. 2118.

December 1917

Place	Date	Hour	Summary of Events and Information	Remarks and references to Appendices
MARCOING COPSE L.29.c.9.0	2ⁿᵈ		Day fairly quiet except for hostile Trench Mortars on front line particularly on "C" Coy. Major H.G. Garnett arrived during night 1st/2nd. The two Coopers Still North of canal were taken back during the night and at B⁹ Stores & blankets from + Lewis Guns. The Trench Mortar was H.Q. towards the canal was continued of Langford also a trench was dug immediately above B⁹ H.Q. parallel with the Rd., both of these proved invaluable on 3ʳᵈ. MARCOING. At dusk "A" Coy post on the canal bridge was increased to 16 men	
	3ʳᵈ		Start of operations in Afterwoon. 1. 1/Border Regt & 1/R.Inniskilling were relieved North of the Canal by 16ᵗʰ B⁹⁵ 6ᵗʰ Div. These regiments were driven in during the day & by dusk we had only a few scattered detachments N. of the Canal. About 7.0 p.m. the 72ⁿᵈ was relieved by 2 Coys Hants Regt & moved back to Reserve trenches L.23d.8.8. near 88ᵗʰ B⁹ H.Q. After recovering her about 1 hour The B⁹ moved back to RIBECOURT & was billeted in the entrenchments. Capt Blake M.C. R.A.M.C. the 73ʳᵈ Medical officer & 48 men went back to the Aid Post at L.29.c.3.2 & carried out 7 of our stretcher cases taking them the whole way back to Ribecourt, Field Ambulance arrangements having	

Army Form C. 2118.

WAR DIARY
or
INTELLIGENCE SUMMARY.
(Erase heading not required.)

December 1917 (3)

Place	Date	Hour	Summary of Events and Information	Remarks and references to Appendices
RIBECOURT	3rd		(heavy) fifteen down. On arrival at Ribecourt men had hot tea & got their blankets.	
	4th	4.00	Received Orders to march at once to SOREL. Men were still asleep having only gotten in the early morning. Dinner was got up at once & everything packed up. Marched 17 2.0 pm. Men marched well arrived SOREL about 5.30 pm, delayed 2 hours trusting billets. Received Orders to be ready to move early following morning. Capt W.F. PAGE rejoined the Battn at Ribecourt. Total Casualties between 30th Nov & 3rd Dec as follows:—	
			Killed — one officer and 12 O.R. Wounded — 3 — — 71 — Missing — 4 — — 100 — Total 8 Officers and 191 O Ranks	
			Officers Killed Major H.C. GARNETT Wounded Capt F.M. GIBBON M.C. 2Lt H.C. CAIN (A.S.C att) 2Lt H.H.K. NETHERCLEFT — missing Capt J.B. TRAGETT (believed killed) 2Lt D.R. WINSOR (believed prisoner) 2Lt T.C. JORDAN 2Lt H.T. EDWARDS — 29th Bn Special Orders to Day. 7. Dec. 1917	Appendix VII

Army Form C. 2118.

WAR DIARY
or
INTELLIGENCE SUMMARY.
(Erase heading not required.)

Instructions regarding War Diaries and Intelligence Summaries are contained in F. S. Regs., Part II, and the Staff Manual respectively. Title pages will be prepared in manuscript.

December 1917

(4)

Place	Date	Hour	Summary of Events and Information	Remarks and references to Appendices
SOREL	5th	02.30	Orders received for transport to move off by road at 6.30am. Battalion to entrain at E.TRICOURT at 11am. Whole Brigade moving in return. Detained at MONDICOURT depot 7.30pm. Tea issued. Moved off about 8.30pm and marched to billets in HENCOURT arriving about midnight.	
HENCOURT	6th to 16th		Billeted in fact billets, they were most of them with windows - Straw issued to everyone, in large pieces & palliasses & small amount of new cloth was taken in, + a complete change of underclothing. Whole carried out was mainly steady drill, organisation of companies & platoons - Programme of work daily. (Appendix 14)	Appendix 14 Programme of work
	10th		Guard inspection by G.O.C. 87 Brigade.	
	11th	8pm	Draft of 8 officers and 73 O.R. joined from England, the majority being men returning with a few new entries. Officers joining were 2 Lieut P.H. FRANKS, H.E. ARNOLD, G.P. DAVIES, J.E.A. GIBBS, W.S. PARRY, W.H. MORRIS, A. REES, E.J. RUSSEL.	
	13th		2nd Lieut I.F. SEAGER joined Battalion.	
	14th		Warned to be ready to proceed on 17th inst to BOUBERS area.	

Army Form C. 2118.

WAR DIARY
or
INTELLIGENCE SUMMARY.
(Erase heading not required.)

December 1917

Place	Date	Hour	Summary of Events and Information	Remarks and references to Appendices
LIENCOURT	16th	12 n	Orders received to move at 7am next to the FRÊVES area, the Division being transferred from IV Corps to X Corps (Second Army)	
CONCHY	17th		Left LIENCOURT at 10.15 a.m. marching by road to FRÊVES area. 13 mile march to CONCHY where we billetted for the night. Good hard road, men marched well (1 in the coy of Transport). 5" snow fell during night fairly, but did not interfere with marching.	
GRIGNY	18th		Five mile march to 9 p.m. CONCHY, roads stuffy going not very good, a lot had flat. Level road.	
EMBRY	19th	8 p.m.	Left GRIGNY at 10 a.m., arriving EMBRY about 8 p.m. Very hilly on to EMBRY. Thin Deep snow drifts on the roads on top of ground. Made hard marching & men tired. Halted 1 hour at Lunch's hut, on hill side. Arrived 10 p.m. Much transport and 4 Brigade following line of march stranded on roadside. All our transport arrived with 4 Bn A & B H.Q. billetted in EMBRY. C & D in RIMBOVAL 1½ miles distant.	
EMBRY	20th 24th		Village very scattered. Billets fairly good no todays rest. Some illness during this period. Programme of work attached. Battn inspection called specially mentioned by Brig Gen M Kerrar. Demonstrations held of the Inspection of Arms [?] by A Coy. Rest well done. (good work did he.) [illegible]	Appendix V
	23rd	10 a.m.	Four and small interfering with Training	

WAR DIARY or INTELLIGENCE SUMMARY

Army Form C. 2118.

Place	Date	Hour	Summary of Events and Information	Remarks and references to Appendices
EMBRY RIMBOVAL	25		Xmas day. Divine Service at RIMBOVAL 10 a.m. General to deliver lecture. Went. Visited the Batt. at 1 p.m. for five minutes. Saw H. by of dinners and addressed them. We were given a good reception by B. By. c. H.A. Men had very good Xmas dinner. Weather continuing fine and nothing of importance to be reported, and little of interest to be seen.	
	26		Nothing to report. Aeroplanes attacked.	
	27		Batt. engaged in cleaning same M.T. and BOUBERS, EMBRY, MANINGHEM. Warning received to march on 30th inst. to XIX Corps area by road.	
	28		Inspection of boys on Lunch-L-Lunch. Attack by commanding officer.	
	29/30		Calm to meet path and 24 hrs. Owing to bad condition of roads.	
AVROULT	31.		Batt. marched off at 8.15 a.m., arriving AVROULT about 3.15 p.m. 15 mile march. Roads wretch and sloppy, rations fed in transit at very convenient café. Following officers arrived with draft from base:— 2/Lt. T.H. PRATT. 2/Lt G.F. SMITH. Draft 133 O.R., including 20 casuals, mostly A+ from furloughed Batt.	

Signed
for Lt. Col. Comdg 8th W.G. Borderers

Dec 17. Appendix I

Account of operations 30th Nov - 3rd Dec.

On 30th Nov the Batt. was holding the bridgehead defences. From dawn on that day increased hostile shelling but not sufficient to indicate an [hostile attack?].

At about 10 am it was reported that the enemy had broken through on the right & [were?] advancing across the sea on to S[?]. [troops?] almost immediately afterwards rifle & M.G. fire was heard from the rear on the B.H. All men available at H.Q. were "turned out" & began holding the [?] on W side of Canal. Several hits of enemy were seen advancing [?] & began to move to [front?] side of [Masar?] bypass & fire opened on [?] on them. The enemy at this [?] [?] but they were still [?] & steady fire was kept up on them at [?] time a Party was detached to the [East?] bank of Canal covering

(Coverley) to look at L24c and the open ground between Marcoing copse and spur in Q25b. One Company (C Coy) was sent up to reinforce the bridgehead garrison line on the right flank.

Shortly afterwards at the request of Capt Innes 20th Bn Staff, 35 men & two Lewis Guns were sent off to assist 20 Bn in Marcoing. These were posted near the Lock / L24c, facing South.

At about 11.0 am our counter attack from Marcoing was seen advancing & between Masnieres & the enemy forces & the enemy began retiring back; few troops were seen to advance as far as the road from Marcoing to Masnieres in L30c & also over the spur L29c.

At about 12 noon a message was received from the Brigade to send 2 Coys across the Canal to Masnieres (vicinity) of Mastoring Copses (orig. place) to report personally to Bde H.Q. Verbal orders were given at Bde H.Q. to dig in live (?) trenches in support from Coys facing Les Rues Vertes. Their Coys did not get across the canal till 2:30 p.m. (these Coys were C Coy & B Coy, less 2 Lewis Guns & 35 men with 86th Bde). On arrival B Coy was sent to the lower spur G.25.b & C Coy dug in close to & parallel with the lock road G.30.a facing East. During the afternoon further orders were received for the Bn to take over the front line from near the Crucifix G.25.d.00/2 to the corner of Les Rues Vertes, getting in touch with 86 Bde at the latter point. The 1/KOSB to take over the line on our right. At that time our front line was 300x short of the Crucifix at about G.25.d.2.5 where it bent N along the spur where ½ B Coy were already

(already) digging in. The 1/KOSB did not come across & consequently the O: had to take over from the ditch (KSLI) to les Rues Vertes. The following arrangements were made. A Coy to come across the canal & to form a line from an advanced post Hants Regt on Linsafer Rd about G 25 6 4 4 past the crossroads to connect with 86th Bde whose situation was not known at the time. C Coy to move from back road & take over from ditch (230 c) up to A Coy. The La B Coy on spur in G 25 6 to swing round & dig in as support to A & C facing South. These dispositions were taken up by about 9 a.m. & coys started to dig in. D Coy still remained on N side of canal. B: HQ moved to dug out at L 29 6 9 0.
The night 30/1st was quiet & coys got dug in. B: HQ was dug & through

(trench) at L29 b 9.1 facing East.
1/12/43: At dawn the situation was quiet, but during the morning the enemy started a heavy bombardment of Les Rues Vertes & Masnières. This bombardment also opened on A Coy by the Canal Junction. The enemy attacked but this could not be seen from our position. A Coy were in touch with the Guernsey Militia in front of Les Rues Vertes. They were still in position when bombardment stopped. At about 2.30 pm the enemy there started very heavy bombardment of Les Rues Vertes followed by an attack. Towards dusk enemy Very lights were seen sent up apparently in Les Rues Vertes, & the detachment of Guernsey Militia on our left flank reported that the enemy were round their flank & & had been in the village. About 4.30 pm orders were received to withdraw our left flank & establish a line about the centre in L30 a

(4.30a) This was carried out almost immediately, & at 10th hour there was informed that the 26th Bde had attempted to see Bois Vitre by a counter attack. At afternoon found was that La Reine Vitre had only been recaptured up to the main Cameron Rd.
During the evening further orders were received that mesures & La Reine Vectie were to be evacuated commencing at 11.0 pm & that the Bn line would be withdrawn as soon as all detachments of 26th Bde had retired. This was successfully carried out & one Coy Hants Regt was sent up to assist in Withytcline. The following dispositions were taken up:
C Coy on the right front along Quarry on Cameron Rd.
½ B Coy in centre about 925 d 2.7
1 Coy Hants with details 26th Bde attached on left G.25.6.2.3 with post of liaison
A Coy in Reserve near Bn Hq North

(North) on the Masnières – Les Rues Vertes
Road & 30 men R.P.F. 10% details
attached south of above road but
the latter facing east. A log formed
detachments at river and lock
bridges. 3 Vickers Guns in the
front line, 2 Vickers Guns in Support
near Bn HQ. 2 others about
Lyc.

D Coy which were N of the Canal had
been sent to reinforce 9/L'Bn
during the day. There were therefore
only 2½ Coys of the Bn present.
During may 1st/2nd the Bn cookers
which were N of the canal were taken
back to Transport Lines, also all
Bn Stores from Marcoing.

2/12/17 Little occurred during the day except
that the Bn front line was trench
mortared intermittently.

3/12/17 During the night the enemy brought
up a machine gun to cover a spot
our post on canal was strong (though) and

(and) no water [not established] between Hawk Coy left flank & Canal as there was a big gap here, it being impossible for day trenches owing to water. Both flanks of the front line were, therefore, unsupported as the Newfoundland line on our right was back at right angles facing South.

At 4.30 a.m. the enemy started a heavy bombardment of our front line, also Canal & Beaucourt copse, this however steadily becoming intense about 11 a.m. It was difficult to make out what was happening owing to smoke, but at 11.15 a.m. it was seen that the enemy in large numbers were over our front line, + a few stragglers of N'F'L'D, Hawks & B Coy'y fell back to our support trench. About this time the enemy having got himself to our support trench + B: H.Q. a steady fire was kept up on the enemy which prevented him advancing

(advancing) beyond our front line which was at that time in our possession. The barrage lifted again to about L29b33. but the Enemy had established a Machine Gun on the N.F.L.D. front & managed to get out part of their sorry front at about L30c05. On the N side of the canal the Enemy was seen in large numbers in L24cc about the bank & he opened fire with M.G. from this side out own position. The trestle bombardment was brought back out our Reserve position & Bn H.Q. & the position swept by hostile M.G. fire. Heavy casualties were caused & all Vickers guns except one put out of action. All survivors of B: H.Q. took up their position in the shell & there was no reserve of our we left. Hostile fire died down gradually towards dusk. After dark the B.

(B=) separated by Heath R.R. Only
75 yrs ahead but with the Banks

7/12/17   by Barker & Cruel
          Cuts a front take
          Browns

December 1917 Appendix II
Disposition taken up by 2/Hoods Bn: in
the 96th R° between from Masnières night 1st/2nd

MESSAGE FORM.

To   No.

1. I am at........................ { Note:—Either give Map Reference or mark your position by a 'X' on the Map on back.

2. My Line runs..

3. My Platoon / Company is at..and is consolidating.

4. My Platoon / Company is at..and has consolidated.

5. Am held up by (a) M.G. (b) Wire at....................(Place where you are).

6. Enemy holding strong point...

7. I am in touch with..........................on Right / Left at..............

8. I am not in touch with........................on Right / Left.

9. Am shelled from...

10. Am in need of :—

11. Counter Attack forming at................................

12. Hostile (a) Battery
           (b) Machine Gun   active at................................
           (c) Trench Mortar

13. Reinforcements wanted at.................................

14. I estimate my present strength at................rifles

15. Have captured........................

16. Prisoners belong to................................

17. Add any other useful information here :—

Name.................................
Platoon..............................
Time...................m.   Company...........................
Date....................1917.   Battalion..........................

(A). Carry no maps or papers which may be of value to the Enemy.

(B). Give no information if captured, except the following, which you are bound to give :—
     Name and Rank.

(C). Collect all captured maps and papers and send them in at once.

SPECIAL ORDER OF THE DAY
by
Major General Sir Beauvoir de Lisle, K.C.B., D.S.O.
Commanding 29th Division.

I wish to convey to the Troops of my Division my high appreciation of their gallant conduct and resolute determination during the operations from November 20th 1917 to the 4th December 1917, and to convey to all ranks the following messages which have been received by me:-

From Sir W.P. PULTENEY, K.C.B., K.C.M.G., D.S.O., Commanding III Corps.

"The Corps Commander would like to place on record his deep appreciation of the fighting spirit of the 29th Division.
The magnificient defence of the MASNIERES-MARCOING line at a most critical juncture, and the subsequent orderly withdrawal reflects the highest credit on all concerned.
In the 15 days in which your Division has been in action on this front, all ranks have displayed an endurance which is beyond praise.
He would be glad if this could be conveyed to your troops."

From General Sir Julian BYNG, K.C.B., K.C.M.G., M.V.O. Commanding Third Army.

"I would like you to express to all ranks my sincere appreciation of the services which have been rendered to the Third Army by the 29th Division.
Both in the attack on the 20th November 1917 and in their defence of their sector on the 30th November 1917 and subsequent days, the Division has more than maintained its splendid reputation.
I ask you to accept my warmest congratulations."

From Field Marshal Sir Douglas HAIG, K.T., G.C.B., G.C.V.O., K.C.I.E. Commander-in-Chief British Armies in France.

"Please convey to General de Lisle and men of the 29th Division my warm congratulations on the splendid fight successfully maintained by them against repeated attacks by numerically superior forces. Their gallant defence of MASNIERES throughout two days of almost continuous fighting has had most important results upon the course of the Battle and is worthy of the best traditions of the British Army."

Beauvoir de Lisle

7th December 1917

Major General,
Commanding 29th Division.

2nd BATTALION, SOUTH WALES BORDERERS.

Appendix IV
December

Programme of Work week ending 15th Decr.

Date	9.30am - 10.0am	10.0 - 11.30am	11.45am - 12.30pm	2.0 - 3.30pm
Monday 10th	Inspection of Batt⁰ by G.O.			Specialists Instruction
Tuesday 11th	Bat⁰ Con. & Squad Drill	R.S.M. Parade Saluting & marching for all men not posted by Coy Comdr.	Coy Lectures & Inspections. Specialists Instruction.	
Wednesday 12th	- Do -	- Do -	- Do -	- Do -
Thursday 13th	- Do -	Adjutant's Parade	Markets under Specialists training O.C. Coys	
Friday 14th	C.O.'s Parade 9.30 - 10.30 am	11.0 - 12.30 Specialist training & Lectures to NCO's	Tactical Exercise for officers.	
Saturday 15th	Coy Drill	Inspection of Coys in Drill order by C.O. Inspection of Transport	- Do -	

Daily conference of Coy Officers &c to Brigade Command
5.0 - 5.30 pm.

M Paulli
Commanding 2nd South Wales Borderers

In the Field
Decr. 9th 1914

APPENDIX III

Dotted Blue line shows approx British front line / Night Nov 20/21st

Disposition of Coys 2/W.R. Battalion shown in Blue.

1. I am at........................ { Note :—Either give Map Reference or mark your position by a 'X' on the Map on back.

2. My Line runs...

3. My Platoon is at..and is consolidating.
   Company

4. My Platoon is at..and has consolidated.
   Company

5. Am held up by (a) M.G. at...................(Place where you are).
               (b) Wire

6. Enemy holding strong point..

7. I am in touch with..........................on Right at...........
                                              Left

8. I am not in touch with..........................on Right.
                                                   Left.

9. Am shelled from..

10. Am in need of :—

11. Counter Attack forming at..

12. Hostile (a) Battery
           (b) Machine Gun } active at...............................
           (c) Trench Mortar

13. Reinforcements wanted at..

14. I estimate my present strength at................rifles

15. Have captured........................

16. Prisoners belong to..

17. Add any other useful information here :—

Time........................m.   Name..............................
                                      Platoon...........................
                                      Company..........................
Date....................1917.   Battalion.........................

(A). Carry no maps or papers which may be of value to the Enemy.
(B). Give no information if captured, except the following, which you are bound to give :—
     Name and Rank.
(C). Collect all captured maps and papers and send them in at once.

2nd BATTALION SOUTH WALES BORDERERS.

Programme of Work.

Date	9 am – 9.30 am	10.0 am – 12.30 pm	2 – 3 pm	5.30 – 6.15 pm
Friday 21st	Bombing and arms Drill	Trench to Trench attack (Platoon)	Specialist training (Coy inspection etc)	Musketry. Lewis Gun – Off's etc. Regtl Musketry "A" & "B" Coys Sergt Sparks "C" & "D".
Saturday 22nd	Bombing and arms Drill	Trench to Trench attack	Specialist training Officers v Lewis Gun class.	Appendix IV Quarter
Monday 23rd	9.0 – 10.30 am Musketry	11.0 – 12.30 Extended order and fire movements		

Date 5-12-17
20-12-17

W. T. Page.
Capt. M. & Adjt.
2nd Batt. S. Wales Borderers.

Appendix V
December

Appendix V

Disposition of Bridgeheads between 4 Front line 23rd Nov 17.

To

1. I am at.................................. { Note:—Either give Map Reference or mark your position by a 'X' on the Map on back.

2. My Line runs..

3. My Platoon / Company is at..............................and is consolidating.

4. My Platoon / Company is at..............................and has consolidated.

5. Am held up by (a) M.G. / (b) Wire at..................(Place where you are).

6. Enemy holding strong point.................................

7. I am in touch with........................on Right / Left at............

8. I am not in touch with........................on Right. / Left.

9. Am shelled from..

10. Am in need of :—

11. Counter Attack forming at...

12. Hostile (a) Battery
        (b) Machine Gun   active at................................
        (c) Trench Mortar

13. Reinforcements wanted at...

14. I estimate my present strength at................rifles

15. Have captured............................

16. Prisoners belong to...

17. Add any other useful information here :—

Name..................................
Platoon..............................
Time......................m.   Company............................
Date....................1917.   Battalion...........................

───────────

(A). Carry no maps or papers which may be of value to the Enemy.

(B). Give no information if captured, except the following, which you are bound to give :—
    Name and Rank.

(C). Collect all captured maps and papers and send them in at once.

Training Programme.   O.C. 1 — 29th/?

Monday. 9-30 - 10-30 am. R.S.M. parade EMBRY – LEBREY R^D
24th. 11-0 - 1-0 pm. Musketry, and Fire and
             Movement.
       2-0 P.M. Lecture to Officers and N.C.O's
           by Divisional Gas Officer.

Wednesday. 9-0 - 9-30 am. Drill parades under O.C. Coys.
26th. 10-0 - 11-30 " Coys attack under Barrage.
       12-0 - 1-0 pm. Specialists and Scouts training.
       2-0 - 3-0 " Bayonet Fighting and Musketry.

Thursday. Inspection of Coys in Trench to Trench
27th. attack.
       "A" Coy   9-0 A.M.
       "B" -"- 10-0 -"-
       "C" -"- 11-0 -"-
       "D" -"- 12-0 NOON.

While other Coys are being inspected Coys
will carry out fire and movement and
extended order practise.
       2-0 - 3-0 pm. Specialist Training.

Friday. 9-30 am Battalion Ceremonial Parade.
28th. 11-30 - 1-0 pm. Musketry and fire and movement.
       2-0 - 3-0 -"- Specialist Training.

Saturday. 9-0 - 9-30 am. Drill parade under O.C. Coy.
29th. 10-0 - 12-30 pm. Open warfare attack under
           O.C. Coys.

Lectures to Officers and Companies will be
arranged in evenings, also Conference of
Company Commanders.

Appendix VI
December.

War Diary

of

2nd Battn South Wales Borderers

From 1st   to 31st

Folio 42.

Army Form C. 2118.

WAR DIARY
or
INTELLIGENCE SUMMARY.
(Erase heading not required.)

Instructions regarding War Diaries and Intelligence Summaries are contained in F. S. Regs., Part II. and the Staff Manual respectively. Title pages will be prepared in manuscript.

Place	Date	Hour	Summary of Events and Information	Remarks and references to Appendices
RENESCURE	1918 1st	7pm 8pm	March continued. Started 10.15 a.m. arriving RENESCURES about 4 p.m. 12 miles march. Lads still chilly and not too happy.	
ROOSENDAEL	2		March cont. 8.30 a.m. arriving ROOSENDAEL at 3 p.m. 13 mile march. Billets very scattered & farmers not very keen. Road conditions rotten for marching and Lorries fast.	
PORTSMOUTH CAMP (PROVEN P.O.H.)	3		Reached PROVEN area about 3 p.m. after 4 days march during which only one man fell out.	
	4		Day devoted to Administration and Reorganization.	
	5		Batt. moved to Forward area Camp at BOESINGHE	
BOESINGHE	6-17th		Batt. engaged on works under the R.E. and 256 N.C.O's and men of the ARMY LINE, work on the STEENBEEK. 10 men and mostly making matting jumpers for trenches. Attached to the 1st Australian Army late during this period. 5 Offrs & 1 O.R. gone to change of climate during this period. Casualties:— On 12th 1 man killed, 3 wounded near FOURCHE Fm all of "D" Coy. On 13th 1 man killed, 3 wounded near BRANDHOEK area on 18th inst.	
	14		Orders received to move to BRANDHOEK area on 18th inst. 10 Officers & 25 O.R. visited 1st Batt. on "intent." Programme included Cinema Show, Divisional Band and concert party, dinner, and D coy concert which father of above 3 so. 15th inst. party returning late in the day.	

Army Form C. 2118.

WAR DIARY
or
INTELLIGENCE SUMMARY.
(Erase heading not required.)

Instructions regarding War Diaries and Intelligence Summaries are contained in F. S. Regs., Part II. and the Staff Manual respectively. Title pages will be prepared in manuscript.

Place	Date	Hour	Summary of Events and Information	Remarks and references to Appendices
BRAKE CAMP BRANDHOEK	18th		Moved to BRAKE CAMP BRANDHOEK over 7 klm march.	
			Camp found to be in a very dirty + desolate condition.	
			Special General Orders of the day by Brig. General issued re relinquishing command of the Brigade.	Appendix I
	19th-24th		Period spent in "smartening up" and cleaning. (R.S.M's parade) and Specialist Train-	
			-ing (Lewis Gunners + Rifle grenade pits.)	
			Parade Divine Service.	
	24th		Practice Brigade Ceremonial parade. Bn Parade found cleaner + walked by Battn.	
	25th		Brigade paraded for inspection of models (miniature of models (miniature aircraft) by Commanding officer.	
			R.E. completed O.Ps Lewis gun posts and also drill March past etc	
			1 O.R carry party food stuff of the period.	
	26th		Move to forward area at ST JEAN, by rail. 3 Coy 3rd HQ in Nunnenhuts ad	
JUNCTION CAMP ST JEAN	26th	1st	JUNCTION CAMP. A Coy in Dug-Out shelters at ENGLISH F.m Divisional Lines – ABRAHAM HEIGHTS – WORST F.m	
			Battn employed on work on Divisional Lines – ABRAHAM HEIGHTS – WORST F.m	
			drawing features. 2 two weeks, 300 men a night 26th–29th; 400 from 30th–1st 2nd	

G.T.Raikes Lt.Colonel
Comdg 2/3rd South Wales Regt.

Army Form C. 2118.

WAR DIARY
or
INTELLIGENCE SUMMARY.
(Erase heading not required.)

Instructions regarding War Diaries and Intelligence Summaries are contained in F. S. Regs., Part II. and the Staff Manual respectively. Title pages will be prepared in manuscript.

Place	Date	Hour	Summary of Events and Information	Remarks and references to Appendices
			The following Honours & Awards were published during this period:—	
			Half-Yearly Brevet Major. Capt (A/Lt-Colonel) G.T. RAIKES D.S.O.	
			The Military Cross. Lieut & Qr. Mr. E.K. LAMAN.	
			The Distinguished Conduct Medal. No 10627 C.S.M. F. HILLIER.	
			Mentioned in Commander-in-Chiefs despatch of 7th Nov. '17. Lt. Colonel G.T. RAIKES. D.S.O. Lieut T.R. WILLIAMS. No 9261 Sgt. BLAIR.T. 13567 DURKIN.A.	
			Immediate awards for Operations at CAMBRAI Bar to D.S.O. Lieut Colonel G.T. RAIKES. D.S.O.	

Confidential

Vol 24

War Diary

of

2nd Battn. South Wales Borderers

From 1/2/18   To 28/2/18

Army Form C. 2118.

WAR DIARY
or
INTELLIGENCE SUMMARY. February '18.
(Erase heading not required.)

Place	Date	Hour	Summary of Events and Information	Remarks and references to Appendices
JUNCTION CAMP ST JEAN	1		Last day of work on GRAVENSTAFEL line.	
	2-3		Tarrib [?] to treatment at the Baths. In every way of Latten.	
			Strong draft of Officers & other ranks arrived from England:—	
			B/Major Lieut G.N. HOLYOAKE. 2/Lt D.R. JONES.	
	2		(Other Ranks. 52. (60% A IV, and 40% returned (B.E.F) from Eng'd.)	
			Lieut Hilyarde took over command of "D" Coy	
	3		2/Lt. J.H. PRATT	actd. to Hospital.	
			W.P. WILLIAMS. }	

WAR DIARY or INTELLIGENCE SUMMARY

Army Form C. 2118.

(Erase heading not required.)

Instructions regarding War Diaries and Intelligence Summaries are contained in F. S. Regs., Part II. and the Staff Manual respectively. Title pages will be prepared in manuscript.

Place	Date	Hour	Summary of Events and Information	Remarks and references to Appendices
JUNCTION CAMP SUFFERN	3	4.0 pm	March forward to take up support at BELLEVUE. B & C companies at Bellevue in Pill boxes & shelters. A Coy in support - D Coy in Reserve in CALIFORNIA CAMP. B & C Coys were shelled on main Road at prefabricated on the way in /15 casualties/ in addition just after arrival at Bellevue two officers were hit by a shell. Killed 2 Lieut W.H. MORRIS. Wounded 2 Lieut W. PARRY.	
BELLEVUE	4th to 5th		Defence of the BELLEVUE Pill Box Companies at Bellevue (B & C Coys) in communication with the Bellevue Defences. A series of half day stronghouses about 300x in front. In event of great very serious enemy penetrate to counter attack. B & C Coys occupied pill-boxes until 10 the clear of 4 out, the Pill boxes shell prof. A Coy in quite good trenches, but no drains. Night 4/5 to looked at Bellevue defences. digging drains & digging 2 trenches, also carrying up sandbag material. Bn HQ shelled with gas shell for short period	

Army Form C. 2118.

WAR DIARY
or
INTELLIGENCE SUMMARY.

(Erase heading not required.)

February 1918

Instructions regarding War Diaries and Intelligence Summaries are contained in F. S. Regs., Part II. and the Staff Manual respectively. Title pages will be prepared in manuscript.

Place	Date	Hour	Summary of Events and Information	Remarks and references to Appendices
BELLEVUE	5th	6.0 p.m.	Moved up to front line right subsector. Relieving 1st Border Regt: A.C. & D. Coys in front line in series of small posts & short lengths of trench – B Coy in Reserve in Gourberg Defence line. VEGETABLE Fm – MEEHELE. Relief Complete 11.0 p.m. B Coy was used for carrying rations & rations etc to all Coys. Only two of Mk Officers had previous experience in the line into the Battn and nearly 400 out of the 500 men with Companies were never under [fire?] work to the 1st night & forming of posts.	
	6th		A certain amount of hostile M.G. fire sweeping the ridge, shelling negligible. The ground generally was a quagmire, shell holes full of water, actually in front the line however it was a little dryer. A Coy's line was more or less connected & Coy consisted of 9 posts of which 2 were joined up, the [?] very excellent fairly deep & tenable. D Coy consisting of 13 posts, the 5 on the right life [?] of which were supporting posts were joined up by a narrow trench, the remaining posts on the right & very small & very scattered covering about 350 x of ground all about 5.3.5 am. N 0.5 posts. D Company were bombed by the enemy under cover of M.G. & Howitzer fire during the night & inflicted	
	7th			

Army Form C. 2118.

WAR DIARY
or
INTELLIGENCE SUMMARY.
(Erase heading not required.)

FEBRUARY 1918

Place	Date	Hour	Summary of Events and Information	Remarks and references to Appendices
Front Line	7th		Shelling. Work on firing up of the trenches progressed well.	
	8th		During the day there was slight intermittent shelling from both sides. Shortly before dawn an enemy raiding party raided Post No 13 on C Coy front. The post were apparently completely surprised. Capt Knight 1/c post + 3 men were captured by the enemy. One of them Pte Bouillon escaped whilst being taken across no mans land and returned to our lines, Lewis gun + rifle post was cleared from the posts on either flank + 304 enemy were reported killed. No 13 post was held by Capt Knight + 5 men. During the periods in the front line, the weather was exceptionally dank, cloudy sky & no water, it rained throughout. By day communication from front to front was impossible + it was very difficult to find the way at night. Relief has to be carried out from Bellevue a distance of about 1700° to the front line. Tour was traveled were much brokn by shellfire + very difficult to track.	
		6.0 pm	Relieve as follows:— B.C. + D Coys by 1/Lancs Fus. A Coy by 1/Border Regt. On relief Coys moved as follows A + B Coys to support positions in shelling	

Army Form C. 2118.

WAR DIARY
or
INTELLIGENCE SUMMARY.   FEBUARY 1917
(Erase heading not required.)

Instructions regarding War Diaries and Intelligence Summaries are contained in F. S. Regs., Part II. and the Staff Manual respectively. Title pages will be prepared in manuscript.

Place	Date	Hour	Summary of Events and Information	Remarks and references to Appendices
Front Line	9th		+ jill trees at INCH HOUSES, - WALLE MOLEN - + KRON PRINZ	
			C + D Coys + Junction Camp. ST JEAN. B"+ Hq. to ST JEAN.	
JUNCTION CAMP	10th		A + B Coys worked on Die Reeier duin.	
			C + D Coys rested. A + B Coys relieved at 6.0 p.m. entrained at WIELTJE	
			A + B Coys to WATOU Area.	
	11th	5.30 am	C + D Coys moved up + worked on Die Reeier duin.	
		12 mid nyte	B"Hq. C + D Coys entrained at WIELTJE. Train did not start till 3.0 a.m. arrived ABEELE about 6.0 a.m. + marched to Bikelo	
			in WATOU area.	
			Casualties while in line: — Offrs. O.R.	
			Killed. 1 2	
			Wounded. 1 27	
			Missing — 5. (3 captured No 13 Pest. I man did not return	
			after having gone out in patrol + 1 man afterwards	
			not known whether C + DH.Q. (probably hit)	
	11th		Capt. P. H. FRANKS admitted to hospital	
			2/Lt. J. B. STEERNDALE-BENNETT took over command of C Coy.	

Army Form C. 2118.

WAR DIARY
or
INTELLIGENCE SUMMARY. February 1918
(Erase heading not required.)

Instructions regarding War Diaries and Intelligence Summaries are contained in F. S. Regs., Part II. and the Staff Manual respectively. Title pages will be prepared in manuscript.

Place	Date	Hour	Summary of Events and Information	Remarks and references to Appendices
HILL CAMP NATOU	12th		Billets very scattered — B Coy H.Q. being 20 min walk from B.H.Q. Billets were three houses and barns, most of which were in good condition and comfortable. Billets with 2 huts at B.H.Q. Following drafts of officers and men, which reported at Bn were H.Q. on 8 Feb. 11th met infantry while Bn was in the line, joined on arrival at NATOU. 5.8. C Coys Ranks from England. A & D men from Graduated Cadre. Officers 2/Lt L. ROGERS-JONES. 2/Lt H. JONES from 13th South Wales — A.W. HARDWICK — W.H. MORGAN. Borderers. (2 only) on Bn. join'd later up. Other Ranks 100. Inspection of ad hoc Lewis Guns by Commanding Officer.	
	12th–20th		Time employed in cleaning & smartening up. Saluting & arms drill under R.S.M., platoon drill, musketry & bayonet training. Each coy carried out 2 practice trench-attacks under a barrage. Rifle range (25) and trenching passed at disposal of Coys daily.	
	16th		2/Lt N. PARRY rejoined from Hospital. (awarded 3/2/18)	
	-		2/Lt C.J. HARDY joined Bn on first appointment.	

(A-283) W+ W609/M1872 350,000 4/17 Forms/C/2118/14

Army Form C. 2118.

WAR DIARY
or
INTELLIGENCE SUMMARY.
(Erase heading not required.)

Instructions regarding War Diaries and Intelligence Summaries are contained in F. S. Regs., Part II. and the Staff Manual respectively. Title pages will be prepared in manuscript.

Place	Date	Hour	Summary of Events and Information	Remarks and references to Appendices
HILL CAMP NATOD	16th		A draft of 3 Officers — 2/Lts Lieutenant, Carruthers, Penny & F.S. Williams and 40 other ranks obtained for training.	
	20th		Practice attack by Bn. scheme for 23rd inst.	
	21st		Divisional conference with G.H.Q. Reshirt.	
	22nd		Bn. Commanders present presentation of medals by G.O.C. 5th Corps Lieut. Gen. Sir. S. ? Bunchtnel (+ Alay + 1 Bay) preach and complimenting Bn. on smart appearance & smartness drill.	
	23rd		Bn. Field Scheme. Attack carried out by 1st K.O.S.B. (+½ Bay) & 1st Borderht. (+Alay + ½ Bay)	
	25th		Bn. training.	
			During this period, every man had a bath & complete change of underclothes.	
	26th		Marched to POPERINGHE, to work on Army Lines.	
			Billeted in Rue des FOURNES; each Coy being together in one billet.	
	27th-28th		400 men per day employed on work on Army Lines, at PLUM, UHLAN & JASPER KEEPS.	
			On the event of enemy attack, Bn. responsible for manning PLUM (A + D Coys) & UHLAN + JASPER (C (A)), GREY (½ B Coy) and RUPPRECHT (½ B Coy) Keeps.	
	28th		Strength draft joined Bn. — B3 O.R. (15 A II, remainder A E.E.).	

Army Form C. 2118.

WAR DIARY
or
INTELLIGENCE SUMMARY.
(Erase heading not required.)

Instructions regarding War Diaries and Intelligence Summaries are contained in F. S. Regs., Part II. and the Staff Manual respectively. Title pages will be prepared in manuscript.

Place	Date	Hour	Summary of Events and Information	Remarks and references to Appendices
			Strength of Bn. (present) 22-2-18.	
			Officers 30 Other Ranks 836	
			Company Commanders	
			A Coy Capt. A.E. CROWDER.	
			B Coy Lieut. J.E. SEAGER.	
			C Coy Lieut. J.B. STERDALE-BENNETT	
			D Coy Capt. W. DAVIES.	
		8/3/18	G. Parkes W. Ward
Comdg 2nd Bn South Wales Borderers	

Confidential

Vol 25

War Diary

of

2nd Battn. South Wales Borderers

From 1/3/18   To 31/3/18

Folios 44

WAR DIARY
INTELLIGENCE SUMMARY
(Erase heading not required.)

Army Form C. 2118.

March 1918.

Place	Date	Hour	Summary of Events and Information	Remarks and references to Appendices
POPERINGHE	1-4th		Bat. continued on Army Line.	
	5th		March 5. Bn. moved by Route to HASLER CAMP, arrived pm.	
	6th		D Coy moved up to WALLEMOLEN & INCH HOUSES, relieved D Coy & HQ BEDFORDS – WALLEMOLEN line.	
			B " " " " KRONPRINZ – relief held up owing to enemy put down barrage.	
			C " " " relief in order of [illegible] Bn. (1st R.N.F.) Machine Guns.	
			A Coy in ENGLISH CAMP as Batt. Res. South.	
ENGLISH CAMP	6-9.		The two companies at English Camp worked each day on KRONPRINZ – WATERLOO LINE (in Divisional Reserve Line). Morning 9th A & C Coys & HQ went through breakfast & breakfast.	
	9.	6.0pm	Moved up here in right subsector. Left Bryant.	
			B Front V.29.a.5.0.50 – V.30.a.5.0.40	
			Frontline B Coy on left, C Coy on right, Batt.ing HQ at VIRILE FARM.	
			Supports GOUDBERG SPUR, D Coy on left, A Coy on right.	
			Bn HQ & RAP at BELLEVUE.	
			Frontline nearly continuous but posts very scattered, the usual listening posts & pickets were sent out, A Coy employed in carrying timber for GOUDBERG Dug-Out & also	

Army Form C. 2118.

WAR DIARY
or
INTELLIGENCE SUMMARY. MARCH 1918.
(Erase heading not required.)

Place	Date	Hour	Summary of Events and Information	Remarks and references to Appendices
FRONT LINE			Digging a Communication trench (none at present in existence) D Coy employed carrying Rations when not on fatal-igs. Rations have to be carried by hand 3000 +	
"	10th		Fairly quiet during night. Trenches dry + fairly good. Wire very indifferent. All improved by day in front of Bn H.Q. in view of Enemy. Bellevue + Gook 6 also Goudberg shelled occasionally. A few casualties in D Coy	
"	11th		Night fairly quiet.	APP. I
		6.30am	Enemy put down sudden barrage on front, support, Gravels + Bn H.Q. SOS signal seen almost immediately. Enemy attacked but was met by heavy rifle + Lewis Gun fire from B + C Coys. Heavy casualties were inflicted + the enemy driven back to their trenches. The behaviour of the men during the enemy attack was excellent. They displayed a fine fighting spirit + to greater possible use was made of rifle + L gun fire. Cap't Seager was wounded during the attack. There were 17 casualties in the Bn. The remainder of the day was very quiet.	Account of Enemy Attack
"	12th		No unusual occurrence. The Bn was relieved by 1/KOSB's + moved back to ENGLISH CAMP. Relief complete by 11.30 p.m. Just on arriving back the SOS was sent up in front line. There were hostile shelling in the back areas. Orders were received	

WAR DIARY or INTELLIGENCE SUMMARY

Army Form C. 2118.

MARCH 1918

Place	Date	Hour	Summary of Events and Information	Remarks and references to Appendices
ENGLISH CAMP	12th		Men ready to move at once, but everything quietened down by about 2.30 a.m. Throughout the last few days Hostile Artillery has been more active & minor attacks have taken place both North & South as well as on our front.	
			Inter Staff till 18 noon, remainder of day cleaning up & inspection of posts.	
	14th		There are a rather large proportion of men sick. 2/Lt E.A. LLOYD left on Command (3 Oy.) with Batta. entrained (light line) 9.20 a.m. up to ASSOUAN thence normally train to KRONPRINZ line where they worked on to Sir Reserve line, returning by S. John train for HELWAN.	
	15th		All Coys went through trench tape treatment. Raiding party (Raid having been indefinitely postponed) rejoined their Coys. moved up with front line in left sector 6.0 p.m. in relief of 1/Border Regt. Bn front Y.28.a.65.15 — Y.29.a.60.30 Front line D Coy on right, A Coy on left. C Coy in Support at WALLE MOLEN & INCH HOUSES. B Coy in Reserve at KRONPRINZ. Relief very quick. D Coy line continuous. A Coy rather scattered posts & proved very boggy. C Coy employed carrying Rations etc. B Coy working under Brigade on Kronprinz line	

Army Form C. 2118.

WAR DIARY
or
INTELLIGENCE SUMMARY.
(Erase heading not required.)

MARCH 1918

Place	Date	Hour	Summary of Events and Information	Remarks and references to Appendices
FRONT LINE /16*			Quiet night. Usual listening posts & patrols sent out. Hostile M.Gs. fired a few short bursts during the night. At dawn a party of the enemy were seen leaving their trenches in full marching order, friends seems hit. There do not seem to be many enemy opposite our left where ground is very swampy. Disposition not altered Appendix II	APP II Map of disposition
	17*		Night again quiet. Some successful wiring was done round Post 12 & trench across bare of salient dug through. Patrol went out to reported M.G. (hostile) on our front but found nothing. It is not proposed to push our line forward at this point to reduce the salient on the left. Heavy aerial fighting between our formations during the morning. Enemy shelled H.Q. with two concentrated shoots at 10.45 pm & 11.15 pm	
	18*		Wiring continued during night. Two patrols went out on left Coy front & submitted reports on enemy positions, wire & state of ground. At 4.0 am heavy enemy shelling started on the left about 200 x away S.O.S. sent up at the same time. Enemy shelled our lines. 4 casualties were caused in D Company. All quiet by 5.0 a.m.	

Army Form C. 2118.

WAR DIARY
or
INTELLIGENCE SUMMARY.
(Erase heading not required.)

MARCH 1918.

Instructions regarding War Diaries and Intelligence Summaries are contained in F. S. Regs., Part II. and the Staff Manual respectively. Title pages will be prepared in manuscript.

Place	Date	Hour	Summary of Events and Information	Remarks and references to Appendices
FRONT LINE V.28.a.65.15 to V.29.a.60.50	18th		Throughout the day continuous enemy movement was observed on Hill 50. Artillery were informed. About 7.0 pm Enemy shelled back between B^n & B^{n}H.Q. heavily with H.E. & gas. 7 men were gassed.	
	19th		Night quiet. At 3.0 am a wiring fatigue from Post 12 was approaching our wire when about 6 enemy were observed immediately outside our wire, simultaneously other parties were seen opposite 12 & 13 posts. The enemy threw bombs when discovered, wounding the two men on wire fatigue, heavy Lewis gun & rifle fire was opened & enemy ran away. Very lights put up by No 19 post on extreme left showed a further party of enemy hurrying back. Lewis gun fire was also opened on these. One German was killed just outside the wire. Rgt 38th Division. Enemy shelled B^n H.Q. at about 11.0 am & 41.0pm. The fine weather broke this morning, rain commencing about 9.0 am, rained all day. B+C Coys relieved D+A Coys respectively in front line. Trenches very wet & for most part 6" water at bottom.	
	20th		Hostile Artillery very active during Tuesday. Krupping & Christie Trench shelled	

WAR DIARY or INTELLIGENCE SUMMARY

Army Form C. 2118.

MARCH 1918.

Place	Date	Hour	Summary of Events and Information	Remarks and references to Appendices
FRONT LINE	21st		Particularly in the evening. Back areas were shelled during tonight & very heavy gas shelling from 6.0am - 9.0am. Ottrien to front line was quick during the night. Trenches here cleaned of water & are again habitable. A little gas at Bn.H.Q. Two Canadian officers attached spent the day in front line. Day quieter.	
"	22nd		Night quiet. Work done wiring & making fire position in trenches. Front trenches are now nearly all duck boarded & are in good order throughout. A certain amount of movement in Enemy front line. Observed in 21st trench 9" several strafes. Foggy morning. Bn.H.Q. shelled 3.15 – 3.30 pm.	
	22/23		B.C. relieved by 1Coy 2nd Monts and 3 coys 4th Worcesters and moved back — by bus from SPREE FM to RED ROSE CAMP BRANDHOEK. Relief complete by 12.30 a.m. The following were the casualties during tour 9th–12th and 15th – 22nd :—	

1st tour
Killed   Wounded
Officers   —   1
Other ranks 7   18

2nd tour
Officers   —   —
Other ranks 5   12 (since died of wounds)

Total
Officers   1 — 1
Other ranks 4 — 29 OR
            9 — 26

WAR DIARY or INTELLIGENCE SUMMARY

Army Form C. 2118.

MARCH 1918

Place	Date	Hour	Summary of Events and Information	Remarks and references to Appendices
RED ROSE CAMP	23rd		Men slept till 12 noon; the afternoon being devoted to cleaning up.	
	24th		Day devoted to inspection, checking of stores and cleaning up. Accommodation - mostly huts - found to be rather crowded, but more tents were obtained.	
	25th		A & B Coys engaged on work on Army line, on BOSSAERT Keep.	
	26th		C & D Coys worked on Divisional Reserve line; D by day, C by night.	
	27th/28th		While B'n rested and delivered. Blankets and greatcoats also delivered.	
	28th		C & D Coys working on BOSSAERT Keep; A & B on Br'gd Res. line.	
	29th		All four coys working on B'd'l line.	
	30th		B'n moved up by train to ST JEAN, as reserve B'n of the Brigade. Three Coys H.Q. at JUNCTION CAMP; D Coy at CALIFORNIA CAMP. D Coy worked on Bged Reserve line at night.	
JUNCTION CAMP	31st		Easter Sunday. Divine Service in Recreation Hut. The following draft joined B'n on 25th :- 33 O.R. from Base (including 1 C.S.M, 5 Sgts + 1 Cpl) in exchange (temporary) for men (or transfer to other Battalions). C/f. 38 O.R. 10.2.7 Strength of Battalion:-	

Arty .... In Major
Comdg 18th W. Yorks Reg't

March 1918 Appendix I

Report on Enemy attack on 11th March.

At 6.5 am the enemy opened up a barrage on front line - Circle Farm - Track 6 - Gwalzany Line. Almost immediately the attack started, enemy advancing in two waves against the whole Battn. front, except for the extreme left posts. The advance was checked by rifle and Lewis Gun fire, though enemy made 2 subsequent attempts to advance.

About ½ hour after start of attack a number of the enemy were seen advancing over the sky-line presumably reinforcements, some of these came over the enemy parapet but did not advance far before turning and running back.

When fire was opened on the advancing waves the enemy bunched particularly the 2nd line, and the thickest part of the attack were V.2.9.660.70 and V 30.a.05.80; at the latter point enemy got a certain amount of cover from the mounds of VOX Farm which is just inside our wire and in front of our trench, these men were however caught under Lewis Gun fire from Nos 9 & 10 posts (on the right)

My Observation post at GOODBERG reports that after the attack there were still a large number of men manning the enemy's front line.

Ammunition which was nearly all used up was replenished immediately after the attack and a further supply sent up at night.

It is estimated that at least 400 groaned to the attack on the Battn. front and that there were quite 50 parties of 2 men each working under the Red Cross afterwards;

These parties carried in and come out again for others, that is to say well over 100 men were carried in. These stretcher parties carried in to all parts of the line but particularly to following points V29a 80-85 and V.7.3.d. 70.10.

A good many of the stretcher parties came back along the road at this latter point. In addition bandaged men were seen going back from these points.

Enemy casualties on this Battn. front must have been 150 or more. Our total casualties were about 17.

3

Enemy barrage was mostly over our trench, only the back part of it hitting the trench itself.

In addition to Rifle and Lewis Gun Fire, Rifle grenades were used against the enemy after he was checked.

Our wire was considerably thinned by rifle fire and Lewis Gun fire.

(Sd) G. I. Raikes Lt. Colonel
Commdg. 1/North W. Borderers

2/3/18

(Weather notes on attack)
Enemy attacked on the front of this Bttn from V 29 c 10.90 - beyond the Battn right boundary V 30.a 5.5, that is about a frontage of 400 x on this Battn front.

I do not know how far the attack extended on the flanks front. Estimated strength 400. this does not include those enemy who came over the crest at about Zero + 15 minutes

The enemy started the advance in two lines but bunched when fire was opened on them.

About ½ hour after the barrage dropped another lot of men appeared coming over the crest of the hill from direction of YPID Farm, these were in small groups estimated total strength 60.

Also at this time my observation post at YALOOR farm reports that the enemy front trench was crowded.

The hostile barrage was indifferent and was for the most part behind the front line.

On the West flank of the attack the enemy had two machine guns at YAT Cottages these opened when the barrage dropped and traversed our

taispel on the left of the line
is just outside the flank of
the attack.

(SD) G.T. Rakes Lt Colonel
Commdg. 1/South W. Borderers

87th Brigade.
29th Division.

2nd BATTALION

SOUTH WALES BORDERERS

APRIL 1918.

Confidential

War Diary

of

2nd Battn South Wales Borderers

From 1/9/18 to 30/9/18

Army Form C. 2118.

WAR DIARY
or
INTELLIGENCE SUMMARY.
(Erase heading not required.)

April 1918.

Instructions regarding War Diaries and Intelligence Summaries are contained in F. S. Regs., Part II. and the Staff Manual respectively. Title pages will be prepared in manuscript.

Place	Date	Hour	Summary of Events and Information	Remarks and references to Appendices
S. JEAN.	1/4/18		In Camp at JUNCTION CAMP. - Battn in Reserve - Strength 9 Bn. are 29 Offs & 897 OR.	
	2/3"		Battn moved into the line and took over right section of the Brigade front from 1/KOSB.	
PASCHENDAELE.	3rd	3.30 a.m.	In front of PASCHENDAELE village itself - Relief Complete 3.30 a.m. - Distribution of the Bn:-	
			A Coy Right front line posts 165 inclusive from D6a 8.3. 85.6 to the line was as follows -	
			A Coy Right front line posts 165 inclusive from D6a 8.3. 85.6	
			D6f 88.18 - B Coy Left front line posts 96.14 inclusive from J6a 85.35 to E1a 05.60 -	
			D Coy in Reserve line at MOSSELMARKT. - 2 Platoons of C Coy in the Intermediate line at	
BELLVUE			BELLVUE, S.E. of BELLVUE - MOSSELMARKT Rd. - 2 Platoons in Divisional Reserve	
			line WATER 60 - Bn HQ. at BELLVUE dugout - Strength 9Bn in line 20 Offs 663 OR.	
PASCHENDAELE.			Line - The line consisted of a series of posts. The largest post (No.2) accommodated a Platoon	
			and the others held a section or less. Forms No. 4 to 14 posts were a continuous C.T.	
			but it was practically impossible owing to the shallowness & lack of drainage	
			and the soil falling in. The ground on the right in front of No 1 to posts was	
			very marshy and much cut about by shell fire. All posts except No 8 were	
			too shallow to stand up in (by day); most of garrison were distributed -	
			N.W. - The main line front 6.20 very bad - 2 or 3 stands on a knee and long	
			Sketch (when known) with the review at all	

Army Form C. 2118.

WAR DIARY
or
INTELLIGENCE SUMMARY.

(Erase heading not required.) April 1918

Instructions regarding War Diaries and Intelligence Summaries are contained in F. S. Regs., Part II. and the Staff Manual respectively. Title pages will be prepared in manuscript.

Place	Date	Hour	Summary of Events and Information	Remarks and references to Appendices
PASCHENDAELE			The Support Platoon were in the Commemorative Trench running from No 8 Post through PASCHEN DAELE. She rest had two posts and supported but not forward slope it was very bad, full of water and not used at all. The Reserve Line posts held a platoon each - not front posts, these being very little shelter from the weather. The Intermediate Line was found with plenty of shelter.	
	3/4/18	10 PM	Quiet day in the whole line - very little shelling from either side.	
	3/4	12 MN	Fighting patrol of 1/NCO and from No 8 Post to a point	
		2 AM	on road 100" in front of EXERT F"m. This was patrolled every two hours from	
		4 AM	10 PM to 4 AM. No enemy has been nor anything heard of them.	
	4.		Quiet day - Observation poor.	
	4/5.	10 PM	An officers patrol of 1 Off and 2 men went out at 10 PM. to reconnoitre Homewood	
		6-4 AM	in front of the Bn section. The ground on the right was very swampy. He began of	
			Enemy patrols or working parties were seen. Where the patrol returned the Standing Patrol patrol went out again to the same place - nothing was seen or heard of the enemy. During the night each platoon	

Army Form C. 2118.

WAR DIARY
or
INTELLIGENCE SUMMARY.
(Erase heading not required.)

April 1918

Instructions regarding War Diaries and Intelligence Summaries are contained in F. S. Regs., Part II. and the Staff Manual respectively. Title pages will be prepared in manuscript.

Place	Date	Hour	Summary of Events and Information	Remarks and references to Appendices
	5th		Examined ground in front of it's own posts - it was found that an advanced wire during the night the Rifle Coy. attempted to improve to C.T. running through PISCHER DREIE. The post which had fallen in were re-dug but the next day they fell in again - Enemy M.G. reported firing from the GASOMETERS at night. It was very misty during the day enabling to be works round the posts during daylight in the morning - a new route to M.G. post was made from the Rifle Coy. H.Q. by way of the main road rather than 97th Church - heavy enemy shelling of BELLVUE line took place about 6 P.M. Two casualties from the 13 Bn. 2 killed, 1 Died of wounds, 5 wounded - Total 8 O.R.	
	5/6		Inter Coy relief - Completed by 2.30 A.M. - Tract. 5 was shelled at various places at intervals during the night - Otherwise the night was quiet.	
	6th		Was a quiet day.	
	6/7	10 P.M.	Very wet and dark night - No patrols was done - 2/Lt PARRY & 5 O.R. went out on patrol in front of own right Coy to reconnoitre EXERT F.M., they found the very muddy & it was impossible to make progress.	
	7th		Very close day for observation	

WAR DIARY
or
INTELLIGENCE SUMMARY.
(Erase heading not required.)

Army Form C. 2118.

April 1918.

Place	Date	Hour	Summary of Events and Information	Remarks and references to Appendices
PASCHENDAELE	2/8		Very fine night - Info from TETE COT and GASOMETERS from action - The enemy about whom our front was stretched a good deal -	
	8/4.		Quiet day - misty -	
	8/9.	1.40 a.m.	Battn relieved by 10th Queens 41st Div. Relief Complete by 1.40 a.m.	
POPERINGHE	9th		Bns: proceeded by light railway to POPERINGHE and thence by march	
ST JANTER		6.30 a.m.	route to ST JANTER BIEZEN arriving there at 6.30 a.m. - Bn:	
BIEZEN			was accommodated in huts -	
	9/4/18.		Following officers joined 1C Battn -	Appendix I.
			Capt. J.R. MORGAN.	
			Capt. R. DENDY.	
			2/Lt. E.J. THOMAS. 2/Lt. J.S. LEWIS.	
			2/Lt. F.H. BEES. 2/Lt. G. GARNER.	
			2/Lt. C.R. THOMAS. 2/Lt. L.G.B. BLACKWELL.	
			2/Lt. L.F. DIXON	
	9/4/18		Capt. J.A. MORGAN took over the command of B. Coy from 2/Lt (T/Capt) E.A. LLOYD on 9/4/18.	

Army Form C. 2118.

WAR DIARY
or
INTELLIGENCE SUMMARY.
(Erase heading not required.)

April 1918.

Place	Date	Hour	Summary of Events and Information	Remarks and references to Appendices
WATOU	10th	2.0am	Battn. (less 16 Officers & 170 O.R. 10%) entrained & moved to OUSTERSTEENE thence to NEUF BERQUIN – Situation as follows :- Enemy in possession of crossings over R. LYS ESTAIRE and STEENWERCKE. Our front line held very strongly by 40th & 50th Divisions who were very exhausted – Orders for 29" Division were to come up close behind the front line & if possible retake ESTAIRE. During evening 87" 18th moved up via DOULIEU to a position from S.W. Bastions on the left 1000X on the right & Bosta Bgd. echeloned on the right flank. 86" Bn. in Rear. The 40th & 50th Divs held a line some 200X in front & beyond our left flank the line bearing due North. Battn. dug in on a long front in a series of holes. B.D.C. Coys in the Front line on right centre & left respectively. A Coy in support close to Battn. H.Q. Battn. strength in the line 20 Officers & 704 O.R. With Major S.H.S. Sommerville.	
LES HAIES BASSES	11th		At dawn the enemy attacked the 40th & 50th Divs after a great mortar barrage. These troops retired at once through the Battn. Some were collected by Major Sommerville & put in a support position on the left flank between where there were no troops behind the front line, therewise fell back about 800X - 900X thus leaving	

Army Form C. 2118.

WAR DIARY
or
INTELLIGENCE SUMMARY.
(Erase heading not required.)

April 1918.

Place	Date	Hour	Summary of Events and Information	Remarks and references to Appendices
JESSAIE'S BASSES.	11th		The left flank of the Bat'n in the air. Some of these troops (40 'odd') were formed up by Major Somerville just in front of Bat'n H.Q. & an N.C.O. was sent down to the left to find out if there was any line of defence on the left. A line was found being formed by Staff Captain 119th Bde. East that line did not rest. ± Captain Stondale Bennett comm'g 'C' Coy to left of front line formed a defensive flank but the distance was too great & the country enclosed. About 1 hour or 1½ hours later the enemy again attacked & worked through the exposed flank. Bat'n H.Q. was taken in flank & rear. Major Somerville was last seen with 1 platoon of A Coy defending a small pulverised trench but the enemy were close & round the flanks. The left flank of the front line under Capt Bennett held on till the enemy was in the trench from behind after this the remainder of the front line fell back constantly very heavy & men became disorganised. Small parties fighting with different units during the remainder of the day. At dusk the various parties of the Bat'n were collected at Bde. H.Q. & reformed under Capt W. Davies, the Bat'n numbers were only 140 & 3 officers. Serving through'ly Capt Davies quickly formed & took up a good position about	

Army Form C. 2118.

WAR DIARY
or
INTELLIGENCE SUMMARY.
(Erase heading not required.)

April 1918.

Instructions regarding War Diaries and Intelligence Summaries are contained in F. S. Regs., Part II. and the Staff Manual respectively. Title pages will be prepared in manuscript.

Place	Date	Hour	Summary of Events and Information	Remarks and references to Appendices
DOULIEU	12.		men in FERME PRINCE. During the morning there was a little advance on the left & the position at la ferme Prince was outflanked. At this time the whole line has become very much mixed up & there was little control. The fighting was continuous during April 10th day & by 4.0 p.m. the line has been forced back to the vicinity of BLEU. About this time the left again went back & the line was forced till the slope North of MERRIS was reached. The Bester Reg.t & details 2/9 Div. however held on to BLEU till about 5.0 p.m. when the line withdrew about 700 x & formed a line along a sunken cutting from VIEUX BERQUIN – LABIS FARM, with the left thrown back. The 31st Div. on the left then connected with the left flank but their line fell back at right angles to our Ldly 2/9 Div. During the evening the enemy attempted an advance against this line but was checked.	
FERME LABIS	18th		Night was quiet. Patrols were sent out & four occasional fire kept up in enemy positions. Our artillery shelled the line BLEU – CORONNE just before dawn, one of the parties was set on fire & a number of enemy were seen infront of it. Fire was opened on these. About 9.0 a.m.? rifle cover of machine gun fire and trench mortars the enemy attempted to	

A6913. Wt. W14422/M1160 350000. 12/16 D. D. & L. Forms/C./2118/14.

Army Form C. 2118.

WAR DIARY
or
INTELLIGENCE SUMMARY.
(Erase heading not required.)

April 1918

Place	Date	Hour	Summary of Events and Information	Remarks and references to Appendices
Zn LABIS.	13"		advance he was checked in front but continued trickling past the left flank inside cover of horses hedges &c. Our Guns at our request fired on this flank & heavy severe Gun fire was opened on the enemy. Enemy casualties were inflicted & enemy checked. About this time Ammunition began to tire & enemy advance explored & continued for about 2 hours, the enemy retired & many were hit as they ran back. Enemy left a fairly continuous barrage of trench mortars on our positions	
		15·00	About 3·0 pm the troops on our right were seen retiring rapidly & the enemy following up. Two parties on the enemy but it was impossible to stop him getting into VIEUX BERQUIN in small numbers. Our left flank was thus turned, at the same time the enemy attempted to advance again on the left but were checked. The position remained thus till dusk. The 31st Div on the left gradually made orders after dark to withdraw. Troops were therefore warned to be ready & covered by Lewis gun fire to this bn filed out (Map Loreng K 290). There was no interference by the enemy & no troops of any sort were met for about 1500x.	
		21·45.	were sent up but did not arrive. The withdrawal commenced at 10·45 pm.	

Army Form C. 2118.

WAR DIARY
or
INTELLIGENCE SUMMARY.
(Erase heading not required.)

April 1918.

Place	Date	Hour	Summary of Events and Information	Remarks and references to Appendices
LABIS.	13		The troops held in the line during the day consisted of about 300 1/Border Regt + a mixed W.G. + S.W.B. R.S.B. 50" Bde details + 40 "Bn Wilts.	
		2400	Received O⁰ H⁰ + units report under their own Officers to a camp near BORRE. None of the Officers who went in with the Batn. got back except 3 who were wounded early at the wire of Batn. Hd. Qrs. were either killed ~ captured on the 11".	
Casualties 11" + 12"			Officers	
			Missing	Major L.H.S. SOMERVILLE M.C.
				Capt J.B. STERNDALE BENNETT M.C.
				2Lieut S.F.S. HEARDER.
				" H.G. ARNOLD.
				" G.F. SMITH.
				" J. PEMBERTON
				" J.S. LEWIS.
				" T. ROBERTS.
				" F.M. BEESE
				Capt W. DAVIES.
				Capt F.J. NATTRASS (RAMC)
				Capt 2Lieut E. LLOYD
				2Lieut E.D. THOMAS
				" L.G.B. BLACKWELL
				" W.H. MORGAN
				" F.T. WILLIAMS.
				" W. PARRY
				P.T.O.

WAR DIARY
or
INTELLIGENCE SUMMARY.
(Erase heading not required.)

Army Form C. 2118.

April 1917

Place	Date	Hour	Summary of Events and Information	Remarks and references to Appendices
Casualties Cont'd			Officers Wounded & Missing Capt W.F. PAGE.	
			2nd Lieut E.F. MALINS.	
			Wounded H JONES.	
			" W.S. PARRY.	
			Officers Wounded, Wounded & Missing Missing	T. Rnks
			Officers 3 1 17	21
			Other Ranks 146 12 335	3 - 11
			Killed	
			Officers --	
			Other Ranks 18	
ST SYLVESTER CAPPEL	14th	2.0pm	The Battn. marched to Camp, 10% from POPERINGHE rejoined + 17 officers (viz:) sections + attended Battn. Ration strength 413	
	15th		Checked equipment etc. Cleaned up.	
			The following Officers rejoined with the 10%	
			Capt. P.A. MORGAN. — Capt E.E.A. WHITWORTH — Capt R. DENDY — o/Capt A.E. CROWDER.	
			Lieut P.H. FRANKS — Lieut J.H. EVANS — 2/Lt D.C.S. DICKINSON — 2/Lt S.W. ANGELL	
			— 2/Lt G.T. DAVIES — 2/Lt E.J. RUSSELL — 2/Lt J.J. PRATT — 2/Lt A.R.C. HALL — 2/Lt C.J. HARDY.	
			2/Lt G. GARNER — 2/Lt C.R. THOMAS — 2/Lt T.J. WILLIAMS.	PTO.

Army Form C. 2118.

WAR DIARY
or
INTELLIGENCE SUMMARY.
(Erase heading not required.)

April 1918.

Instructions regarding War Diaries and Intelligence Summaries are contained in F.S. Regs., Part II. and the Staff Manual respectively. Title pages will be prepared in manuscript.

Place	Date	Hour	Summary of Events and Information	Remarks and references to Appendices
	April 14/6		Also. 2W REES from leave & Lieut. T.C. NEWSON American Army Lieuts.	
			Officers now commands of Companies as follows:-	
			A Coy. Lieut. P.N. FRANKS.	
			B Coy. Capt. T.A. MORGAN.	
			C Coy. Capt. E.E.A. WHITWORTH.	
			D Coy. Capt. R. DENDY.	
				(191 men)
St SYLVESTER	16"		87th Bn. joined into our Composite Batt: S.W. Bertens formed 2 Coys & into Capt. Morgan & Capt. Dendy, these Coys came under orders of 1st April Murray 1/KSLB	
"	17"	9:0 am	Detail. Transport & Bn: H.Q. marched to CAMPAGNE (about 12 miles).	
			Draft of 83 men from 51st Grad Bn. joined Composite Bn: to their Bn.	
CAMPAGNE	18"	10:0 am	Bn. HQ & Details returned by bus to former camp at St SYLVESTER. Transport by road	
			Draft of 114 men from 51st Grad Bn: joined very different Kind billets to Kn.swages finally with the aid of Sanit: from Field Ambulance.	
			Both drafts consist of 18th year troops with about 6 months training No NCO's came with them. Composite Bn: returned after being in support during operation on 17th.	
St SYLVESTER			The two Companies of the Bn: had 18 casualties in charge the following	

WAR DIARY or INTELLIGENCE SUMMARY

Army Form C. 2118.

April 1918

Place	Date	Hour	Summary of Events and Information	Remarks and references to Appendices
S.t SYLVESTER	19th		Capt. I.A. MORGAN Killed. 2/Lt GARNER & 2/Lt RUSSELL Wounded.	
			Returned to White Balls including men from Comptrail B" & new drafts into 2 Companies.	
			N.o 1 & N.o 2 Coys. each of 4 Platoons & 4 Lewis Guns; N.o 1 Coy consisting of A & D Coys under Capt Denby & N.o 2 Coy consisting of B & C Coys under Capt Whitworth.	
			There are at present in the B.n: except excluding staff only 2 Sgts & 12 Corpls & very few Lewis Gunners etc. Strength of the B.n new Companies about 230 each.	
		6.0 pm	Moved to billets about 2000x South.	
	20th	5.0 pm	Moved again to new billets on outskirts of HAZEBROUCK at V.20.B & D much.	
			More NCOs & men Comptrails. 29' Stirs & Coys Reserve ready to move at ½ hour notice by day & 1 hour by night.	
LA HELOGE	21st	9.0 am	250 men under Capt Denby marched up to reserve line E of HAZEBROUCK, & were employed digging trenches returned 3.0 pm. Available Officers & NCOs under Capt Corneta during afternoon to tactical training.	
V.20.d.6.5.	22nd	9.0 am	250 men again employed digging 2.nd zone of defence E of HAZEBROUCK. Continuous heavy shelling of HAZEBROUCK.	
			Tactical exercise for available Officers.	HAZEBROUCK
			during night 21/22.nd Burst of day.	

Army Form C. 2118.

WAR DIARY
or
INTELLIGENCE SUMMARY.
(Erase heading not required.)

April 1918.

Place	Date	Hour	Summary of Events and Information	Remarks and references to Appendices
La Haule	22ⁿᵈ		Batt. billeted in farms on outskirts of HAZEBROUCK ready to move at 1 hours	
Loge HAZEBROUCK	26ᵗʰ		notice. Weather fairly fine. Daily work on 2nd Line of Defence lines E. of Hazebrouck	
			as far as possible. Training was carried out & B⁴ refitted. During this period a few	
			shells burst near the billets & troops were ordered three times on night into	
			camouflage —	
			During this period the following drafts arrived. 2 Lieut MORRIS & 211 MAY 00	
			38. O.R. from 57ᵗʰ Graduated B⁴⁴	
			43. O.R. from 9ᵗʰ entrenching B⁴⁴	
Support B⁴⁴	27ᵗʰ	10.30	Batt⁴ moved up to relief of B⁴⁴ in Support in Left Brigade sector & took up the following	
			dispositions. Sheet 36A NE. 4 Platoons in Main Support line F15C & 21b. — H/platoon in	
			Little le G⁴ See BOIS and SWARTEN BROUCK — B⁴⁴ H.Q. D.18 c.7.4	
			The B⁴⁴ was organized in 2 Coys A Coy & D Coy forming N⁰1 Coy under Lt. Franklin B & C Coys	
			forming N⁰2 Coy under Capt. Whitworth. 6 decree given per Coy only could be	
			manned — Greyancies + 10% under Capt. Denby formed Div. Reserve B⁴⁴	
			Quiet going into position. Look ahead by B⁴⁴ H.Q. was shelled for an hour after	
			arrival.	

Army Form C. 2118.

WAR DIARY
or
INTELLIGENCE SUMMARY.
(Erase heading not required.)

April 1918.

Place	Date	Hour	Summary of Events and Information	Remarks and references to Appendices
	24th		Capt A.B. COWBURN joined as 2d in Command from 1/Border Regt	
SUPPORT	28th to 1st		Quiet day Generally quiet. The 4 Platoons in Main Support line were withdrawn by 6°° Sec Bois and SNARTEN BROUCH to Rest & each day were stood up - Coys worked by night on Petit Sec Bois and Main Support line.	
FIRING LINE	2d	7.30 pm	B.s moved up + took over from 2/Devonshire relief complete by 10.0 pm.. No 1 Coy held right with 2 Platoons in Redoubt line & 2 platoons in Main Support line. No 2 Coy similarly on the left.	Appendix II Nominal Roll Officers
			Strength of Bn 30th April 1918. 23 Officers 698 Other Ranks	
			Cow DENDY in command of No 1 Coy.	
			Capt WHITWORTH in command of No 2 Coy.	
			9th May 1918.	
			G.T. Raikes? Colonel	
			Comdg 2/Welsh Brigade	Appendix II Spec. Order 9th Day.

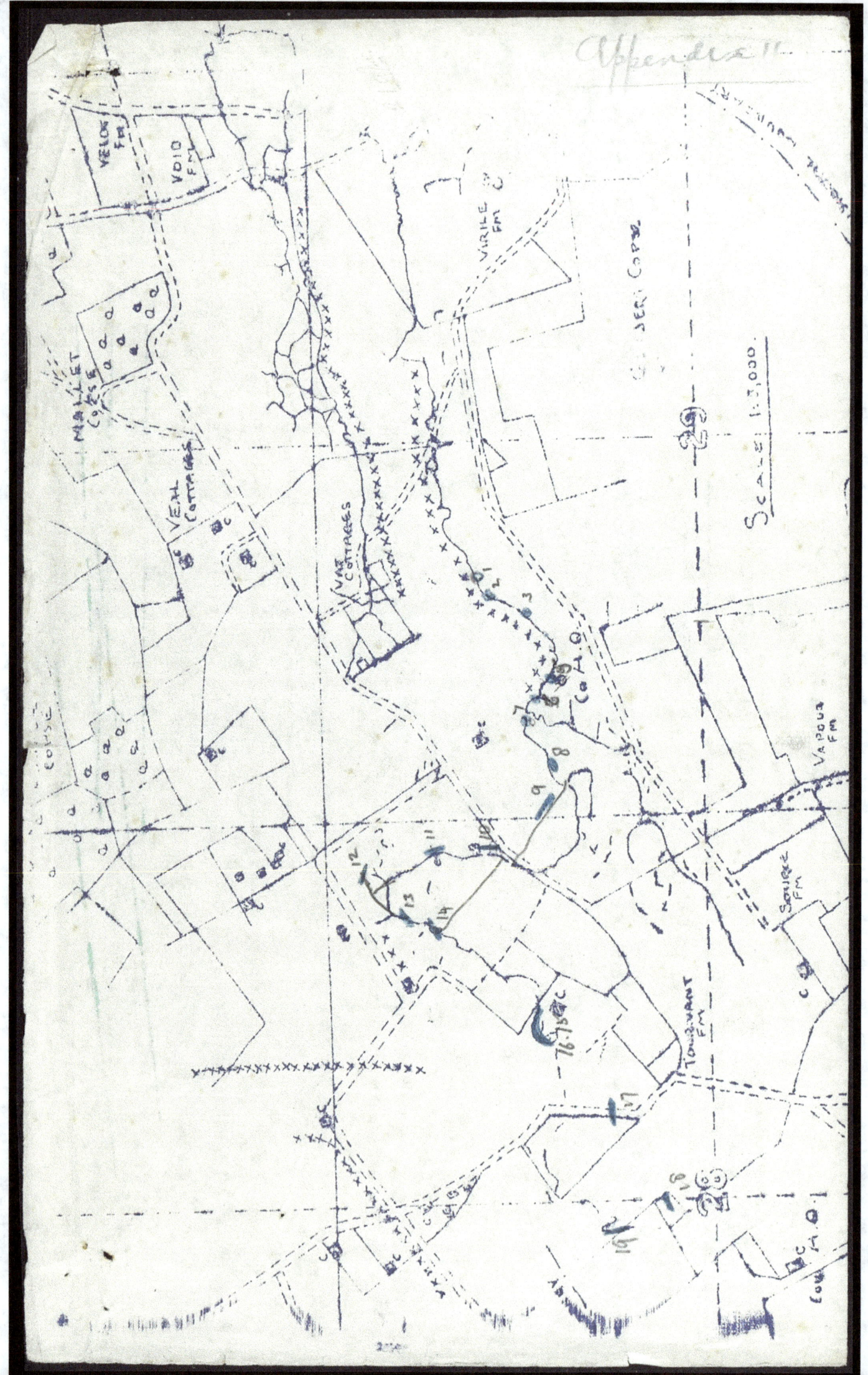

SPECIAL ORDER OF THE DAY
by
MAJOR GENERAL D.E.CAYLEY,C.M.G.,
COMMANDING 29th DIVISION.

In bidding goodbye to the ROYAL GUERNSEY LIGHT INFANTRY on their departure from the 29th Division, I wish to place on ~~regret~~ record my great regret at their withdrawal. During the six months the Regiment has been with the Division, they have constantly displayed high qualities of courage and resolution. Both at CAMBRAI and in the recent fighting about HAZEBROUCK, nothing could have been finer than their conduct. Their record, though short, is one on which they and their fellow Islanders can look back upon with the greatest pride.

I wish Lieut. Colonel DE HAVILAND and all ranks all good fortune in the future.

(sd) D.E.CAYLEY
Major General,
24th April 1918. Commanding 29th Division.

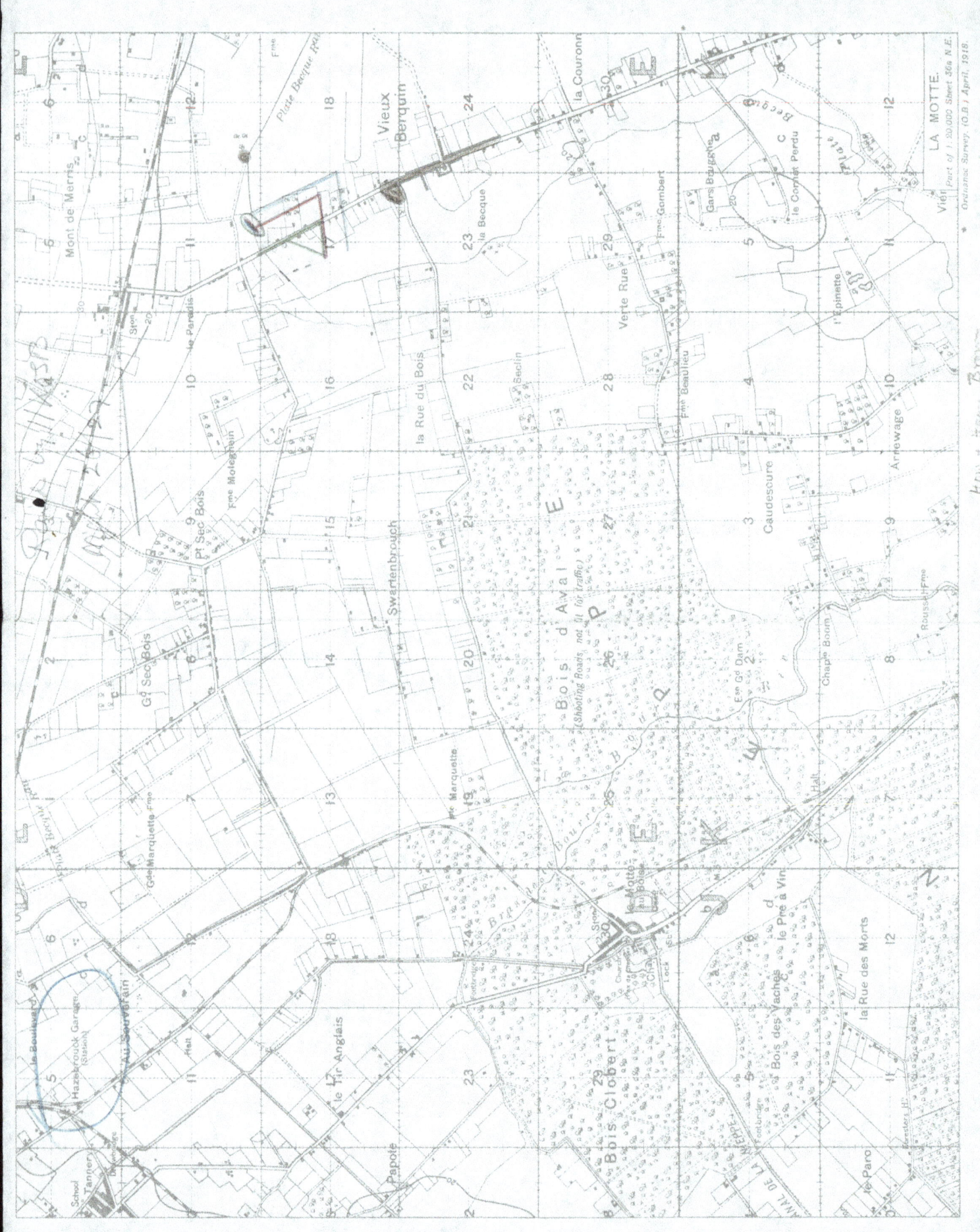

Paid 1/10/18
24/27

2/S.W.B.

Army Form C. 2118.

WAR DIARY
or
INTELLIGENCE SUMMARY.
(Erase heading not required.)

May 1917   Vol 2

Place	Date	Hour	Summary of Events and Information	Remarks and references to Appendices
SUPPORT	1st		Bn in support to 4th Brigade Sect. N°1 Coy SWATTEN BROUCH N°2 Coy C4 Sec B.P.S	
SUPPORT	2nd	7.30pm	Relieved 2/Lincolns in right firing line left B4 sect — Relief completed 10.0 pm.	
			Distribution of Coys.	
			N°1 Coy on right — 2 platoons (outposts) holding outpost line SEELINBURG	
			E.22.C.3.2. 2 Platoons in close support line E.21.C.6 & 8	
			N°2 Coy on left — 2 platoons E.22.C.3.3 — E.16.C.4.9. (Outpost line) 2 platoons	
			in Main Support line E.15.C.6 & 5.	
			B. H.Q. at E.15.C.3.7.	
			Outpost line consists of posts only & probably held merely behind top of	
			a steep crest, invisible & offering the fifteen partially in reserve.	
			Main support line continuous shallow trench with breakworks & well wired	
			for Coy on right to Forest Platoons in Main Support line for defence of	
			line & will act as counter attack.	
FIRING LINE	3rd		Heavy Hostile advanced posts were pushed forward & small concealed patrols	
			made in advance of outpost line. Vanguard Patrol reconnoitred up to E.23 C.1.9	
			but could not penetrate the hedge bordering Parvis Road. On left Platoon established	

WAR DIARY or INTELLIGENCE SUMMARY

Army Form C. 2118.

May 1918.

Place	Date	Hour	Summary of Events and Information	Remarks and references to Appendices
FIRING LINE	3rd		Very fort. Thorny thick hedge in front without aperture a got men in long ditch behind.	
			Coy. extended myself in dinner in Farm - Run by which to B.H.Q. only half of Coy.	
			Quiet - heavy MG fire ordered Capt E.23.0.17 approved no enemy	
			Patrol also reconnoitred hedge E.17.C.21 approved no enemy.	
			Wire was put up in front of SELLIER-built E.22.b & W.E.2.a also a Vickers	
			MG dug pit behind ditch running through E.22.d	
			At midnight enemy dug a M.G. Emery Shell to Rue du Bois Road	
	5th		Rather quiet night patrol again established liaison & found no enemy	
			Wire erected & two strong-points made through the ridge only	
			Enemy approached to the line of The Bocque which is used as his fire line.	
			10th advanced posts put to three hundred yards in advance - very little resemblance seen.	
			10pm Relieved by 1/Hants Regt & returned back & 2" Zone of defence in Vicinity of Gd MARQUETTE Farm. Heavy Rain & trenches & shelters all the time.	

Army Form C. 2118.

WAR DIARY
or
INTELLIGENCE SUMMARY.
(Erase heading not required.)

May 1918.

Instructions regarding War Diaries and Intelligence Summaries are contained in F. S. Regs., Part II. and the Staff Manual respectively. Title pages will be prepared in manuscript.

Place	Date	Hour	Summary of Events and Information	Remarks and references to Appendices
Gd MARQUETTE Farm.	3rd		Draft of 143 other ranks joined from Base (in Reinforcements Camp)	
	6th		On relief Coys were disposed as follows. No 1 Coy Gd MARQUETTE Farm – No 2 Coy in Farm at D.12.a.2.1 – Bn HQ D.12.a.1.8. Men rested & cleaned arms & equipment etc. 2 cases of alarm. Bn wears for this 2nd zone ready to counter attack. Bn was advanced Bn. of Bde in Reserve.	
	7th		Bn HQ caught fire during the night & was burnt down. Officers' mess kit lost but escaped the severe except a few stores. AP & Canteen intake. Bn HQ moved to Gd Marquette farm. Heavy rain during early morning. Coys formed working parties D & him under RE on Reserve line & Petit S&C Bois.	
	8th		Training Cuss & Scouts Section. Reply of working parties to training under selected officers. Staff of 143 mustered above James Coys. Bn Grenade & Lewis Gr m/c 635– Bn HQ again moved to Farm at D.6.d.9.9 Following Officers joined all gazetted 29th Jan 1918	

2/Lt. HAM J. 2/Lt. LLEWELLYN. P.L.
2/Lt. BRADLEY A. 2/Lt. PRITCHARD A.J.
2/Lt. KILBOURN W.E. 2/Lt. DAVIES J.

WAR DIARY
INTELLIGENCE SUMMARY

Army Form C. 2118.

May 1918

Place	Date	Hour	Summary of Events and Information	Remarks and references to Appendices
I 6 d 99	9th		Officers joined (centre) 2/Lt. McPHERSON N.C. 2/Lt. HUGHES M. 2/Lt. SEARLE J.B. 2/Lt. DAVIES R.G. Training of new drafts, scouts & rifle grenadiers - Making of shelters in vicinity of each Coy "Billets" - At night 3 parties of 1 officer + 100 W/Men found for work'g parties R.E. to	
	10th		Fine day - Quiet - Carried on with Specialist Training - working parties of 4 Off + 100 W/Men as for 9th	
	11th		The Bn. was reorganised into 4 Coys again of 3 platoons each with four Lewis Gun teams per Coy. - Coy. Commanders as follows:- A Coy. 2/Lt. HALL A.R.C. B Coy. 2/Lt. PRATT J.H. C Coy. Capt. WHITWORTH E.E.A. M.C. D Coy. Capt. JERRY R. Working parties & training as for 9th & 10th. Reorganisation of Coys & Platoons during the day.	
	12th		Quiet day. Specialist Training. 4 Offs + 100 men to work w/ water R.E. at night.	
	13th		Training of Specialists - Coys employed making preparations to relief.	

Army Form C. 2118.

WAR DIARY
or
INTELLIGENCE SUMMARY.
(Erase heading not required.)

May 1918

Instructions regarding War Diaries and Intelligence Summaries are contained in F. S. Regs., Part II. and the Staff Manual respectively. Title pages will be prepared in manuscript.

Place	Date	Hour	Summary of Events and Information	Remarks and references to Appendices
	13th		B. Coy - Command of B Coy taken over by 2/Lt. G. ESMOND from 2/Lt. J. H. PRATT.	
	13/14	9.15 P.M.	Relieved Battn in 15 line & Spts -	
			B Coy relieves 1 Coy 2/LEINSTERS in SWARTENBROUCH area	
			C Coy " " " " Reserve line at E.13.d	
			A Coy " " 1 - 4/WORCESTERS " Left Support line E.9.a & c	
			D Coy " " 1 Coy " " PETIT SEC BOIS Defences	
		11.50 P.M.	Relief Complete 11.50 P.M. - Bn. H.Q. at E.7.a. 75.75	
	14th		Quiet Day. Dispositions of the Bn. are as follows -	
			A Coy - (134 OR) Left Support line - 3 Platoons to A Support line ab from E.9.b.99.70	
			6 E.9.d.25.60. - Coy HQ. at E.9.a.50.65 in farm with HQrs of D Coy	
			D Coy - (135 OR) PETIT SEC BOIS defences - 2 rifle with LG. in Support line at	
			E.9.a.20.40 - 1 Pn + LG at E.90.95.60 - 1 Pn + 2LG at E.9.a.00.65	
			+2 Sec close support to Rm	
			D Coy are responsible for the defence of defences around PETIT SEC BOIS.	
			B Coy - (4 Off + 146 OR) responsible for defences of SWARTENBROUCH area.	
			1 Pn + L.G. at E.14.n.80.40 - 1 Pn + 2 L.G. at E.20.a.90.60 - 1 Pn in	
			Coy H.Q. at E.14.c.00.80 - (line in billets during day)	
			Reserve at E.14.c.99.20 Coy. H.Q. at E.13.d.	
			C Coy - In Reserve line at E.13.d - Men liven in billets during day	

Army Form C. 2118.

WAR DIARY
or
INTELLIGENCE SUMMARY.
(Erase heading not required.)

May 1918.

Place	Date	Hour	Summary of Events and Information	Remarks and references to Appendices
			The Coy (4 Off & 137 OR) are available for Counter attack under the orders of the G.O.C. Bogaze. — Coy H.Q. at E 14 c 0040	
E 13 d & E 14 C.	14th/15th	10.45 P.M. 4 A.M.	Commencing at 16.45 P.M. the enemy put down a heavy bombardment of Gas Shells in the area of E 13 d & E 14 c which lasted until 1 a.m. & then intermittent Gas shelling from 1 a.m. to 4 a.m. The gas used appeared to be phosgene & mustard oil Gas — Up to 8 A.M. casualties were 10 — Delayed action of Gas but no effect on the men of C Coy — During the day casualties arose	
	15th		to 4 Off. & 90 OR. — Men casualties were 2/Lt J.C.D SEARLE, 2/Lt A. BRADLEY, 2/Lt T R JONES, 2/Lt J.H. PRATT — During the day training as far as possible of 1 survivors & Stores — At night practise night patrols —	
	16th		Quiet Day — Bn in the line handed over by Lt Col G. T. RAIKES D.S.O. to the 2nd in Command, MAJOR A.B. COWBURN M.C. for duty in the line —	
Egypt Suffolks	17th	12 M.N. 6.30 A.M.	Enemy artillery active on left support line from 12 M.N. to 3.30 A.M. French were hit 3 times but only 2 casualties occurred — Remainder of day quiet — Men employed in Specialist training by day & working parties by night.	

Army Form C. 2118.

WAR DIARY
or
INTELLIGENCE SUMMARY.
(Erase heading not required.)

May 1918.

Instructions regarding War Diaries and Intelligence Summaries are contained in F. S. Regs., Part II. and the Staff Manual respectively. Title pages will be prepared in manuscript.

Place	Date	Hour	Summary of Events and Information	Remarks and references to Appendices
	18th		Quiet day - Men employed on R.E. work at night + Lewis Gun training during day.	
PETIT SEC BOIS.	14/19.	10.45 P.M.	4th Tank Bn relieved from the line - 1D Tank Guns of Tank Bn in PETIT SEC BOIS deferen relieved by Six Guns of D Coy S.W.B. approximate position of D Coys Six Guns. E9C 20.15, E9C 05.50, E9C 85.75, E9a 80.45, E3d 25.25 - Relief Complete 10.45 P.M.	
	19th		Working parties under R.E.'s. Days + nights as for other days - Fine day - Two shelters at Bn: H.Q. Completed to-day -	
	20th		Fine day - Working parties for R.E.'s found and work on trenches - Relieved by 2 battns in front line Taking our whole Brigade sector - Relieved 1/Border Regt- in Right Firing Line + Supports with B. + C. Coys respectively and 1/KOSB in Left Firing Line and Support with E + A Coys in Front Line + Support respectively - Relief	
Front Line	20/21st	1.30 A.M.	Complete 1.30 A.M. -	
	21st		The disposition of the Battn in the line are as follows Right Firing Line - B. Coy - 3 platoons - Right platoon from E22 C 85.25 -	

WAR DIARY
or
INTELLIGENCE SUMMARY.
(Erase heading not required.)

Army Form C. 2118.

May 1918

Place	Date	Hour	Summary of Events and Information	Remarks and references to Appendices
			to E.22.b.40.20. with L.guns at E.22.c.40.99 and E.22.b.15.10. - Centre Platoon from E.22.b.40.20 to E.23.a.10.35 with L. gun post at E.22.b.60.30 + E.20.b.90.55 - Left platoon from E.23.a.10.35 to E.16.d.80.Nth L gun posts at E.22.b.90.70 + E.22.b.35.90. - Coy HQ at E.22.b.35.90. Coy HQ E.16.a.30.60. Left Firing Line. - D Coy - 3 Platoons with 6 Lewis guns. Holds left front line from E.16.d.80.20 to road at E.11.c.20.10 inclusive - Lewis gun posts are at E.16.d.80.20, 75.40, 75.90, E.16.b.80.00, 90.40, E.17.a.10.90. The front line is held as a series of posts. - Wire in front is good. Single apron. Two platoons KOSB are in immediate support to left firing line at E.16.a.90.80 + E.10.c.50.60. Right Support line. - C Coy - Consisting of 3 Lewis Guns S.W.B. will 4 guns/Powder Regt. - This line is held with a series of seven Lewis gun posts as follows - 3 S.W.B guns at E.21.d.10.80, E.21.d.20.60, E.21.c.20.40. - 4 Powder guns at E.21.b.10.60, E.15.c.75.25, E.15.c.75.40. E.15.d.30.70. - Coy HQ at E.21.a.65.25. - Wire in front of Support line is good. Single apron in most places.	

WAR DIARY
or
INTELLIGENCE SUMMARY.
(Erase heading not required.)

May 1918.

Army Form C. 2118.

Place	Date	Hour	Summary of Events and Information	Remarks and references to Appendices
			Left Support Line - A Coy -3/Platoons with 4 Lewis Guns - From road at E.15.b.10.90 to E.15.d.00.80 - 6 guns at E.15.b.20.10, E.22.b.60.30, E.20.b.90.55, E.22.b.90.70 B Coy H.Q. at E.22.b.35.90	
SWARTENBROUCH			Bn. H.Q. and Reliefs at E.14.d.60.40	
			Work - Very little work to advise by day - At night work on wire & making parapet of posts bullet proof -	
		11.5 PM	A patrol of 2 officers & 10 O.R. left our lines at 11.5 P.M. at E.16.a.8.9.4 to reconnoitre N.Man's Land previous to the raid - Coloured lights seen in E.17.b were put up for 10 mins - Patrol returned to our lines at 12.30 A.M. owing to slight concentration of gas.	
Enclosure 21/7 at E.23.C.20.90		11.36 P.M.	A successful raid was carried out by 3 Off & 67 O.R. with 3 Lewis guns from E.23.C.20.70 to E.23.C.20.99 - Raid was on the enclosures about E.23.C.20.70 & E.23.C.20.99 - The object of the raid was to obtain prisoners & accurate identification - Full report on raid	Appendices I to VI See App V for App not included
E.23.c.20.99			Carried out under a Barrage - Zero 11.36 P.M. - The object of the raid & it's organisation see Appendices I to IV - OC raid was 2/Lt. G. ESMOND + other officers 2/Lt. L.E. DIXON & 2/Lt. W.H. MORRIS.	

WAR DIARY
or
INTELLIGENCE SUMMARY.

Army Form C. 2118.

May 1918.

Place	Date	Hour	Summary of Events and Information	Remarks and references to Appendices
	22ⁿᵈ	12.5 A.M.	The raid was quite successful + party finally returned to our lines at 12.5 A.M. 2 prisoners (172 + 221 Regt) were obtained + 1 Light M.G. In addition 2 enemy were killed with bayonet + about 20 killed or wounded by L.G. fire. Our casualties were 2/Lt T.E. Dixon killed + 6 O.R. wounded - For information given by prisoners see Appendix VI.	
	22ⁿᵈ	1 A.M.	A Cy. relieved B Cy in the front line after the raid - Relief was quite quiet - Disposition B.A.Cy. exactly same as them taken over from B.Cy.	
		3 A.M.	Relief complete.	
		4 A.M.	Hostile aeroplane flew over our support line + dropped several small bombs - No damage was done + it was driven off by our L.G. + M.G. fire - Quiet day - Weather fine -	
	night 22/23		Quiet night - In front line + supports men engaged on strengthening posts all along line - At dawn hostile planes came over as far as Bn HQ but was driven off by L. gun fire - Enemy artillery was active during day particularly with 4.2 cm shells on	

WAR DIARY
or
INTELLIGENCE SUMMARY. May 1918

Army Form C. 2118.

Place	Date	Hour	Summary of Events and Information	Remarks and references to Appendices
BOIS D'AVAL	23		Eastern edge of BOIS D'AVAL - From 8.50 P.M. to 9.20 P.M. a low flying aeroplane came over our lines & dropped several hand bombs	
		8.50 P.M.	on BOIS D'AVAL - Generally the day was quite quiet. There were actual grenades -	
	23/4	P.M.	Night was employed, men were employed during night shewing trench paths	
Ten BECQUE		10.30	At 10.30 P.M. a patrol of 1/Lt. 9.B.R. went out from our left Coy. to reconnoitre the BECQUE in front of the Bde. sector. hostile was	
			seen of the enemy The patrol returned at 12.30 A.M.	
	24th	1 A.M.	No further patrols were sent out this night as Gas Projectors were due to go off at 2 A.M. on Bde. front. This however was eventually postponed. During the night enemy's M.G.s & T.M.s were more active - Day was well during the early part -	
VIEUX BERQUIN		11.30 A.M.	Observers reported that they heard sound of an enemy tram at 11.30 A.M. coming from the direction of VIEUX BERQUIN.	
	24/25		Left Support Coy. wiring for carrying of R.E. material to front line Coys. During the whole of the night each Platoon in the front line	

Army Form C. 2118.

WAR DIARY
or
INTELLIGENCE SUMMARY.
(Erase heading not required.)

May 1918

Place	Date	Hour	Summary of Events and Information	Remarks and references to Appendices
	20/25		actively patrolled its own front – Wire was found to be intact along whole front.	
	25"	2.50 A.M.	2 enemy patrols left our lines during the night – 1 OTR + 3 OR. left our lines at E 23 a 20.30, crossed our wire + patrolled ground in front of E 23 a 20.30 – No enemy movement was observed – Patrol returned at E 23 a 20.30 at 3.30 A.M. – 1 OTR + 4 OR. went out from E 16 d 84.94 at 2.40 A.M. to reconnoitre homesland from our line to the BECQUE – patrol went N along our wire to 200× then E.S.E. to line of BECQUE then W.S.W. to our line – coming in on front of departure at 3.40 A.M. – Draft of 1 Off + 70 OR. arrived from Reinforcement Camp following officers joined the Battn in the line. Capt Givens 2/Lieut H. JONES (24/5/18) from Hospital to B Coy (took over command) Capt. A.J. GIVONS (25/5/18) from Base. to B Coy. of B Coy.	
		2 A.M.	Gas Projectors were put over at 2 A.M. from two pts. to blink front line – whole of D Coy & left of line were withdrawn to line of front trenches from 1.50 A.M. to 2.35 A.M. as a precautionary measure –	

WAR DIARY or INTELLIGENCE SUMMARY

Army Form C. 2118.

May 1918

Place	Date	Hour	Summary of Events and Information	Remarks and references to Appendices
			When the projectors went over there was no enemy action except the putting up by him of various coloured lights. Fine day. Observation poor.	
	25/6	12 M.N.	Under cover of a patrol of 1/KOSB left platoon 16 left front line Coy. commanded by 2/Lt. C.R. THOMAS silently penetrated into Nomansland and dug in at E.17 a 5.8. The night was light	
E.17 a.5.8.			& the platoon wired & & there to occupy the line as push forward. On their battle at practice B the two front Coys. were out by allow the flank Guns of each Coy. to open from both extremes beyond support Coy. were occupied completing the wires of the support Coys.	
E.15 a.7.4. E.21.6.6.1.			Guns at E.15 a.7.4 & E.21.6.8.1. with assistance of 2 OR's + SOOR Border Reg. 400 yds wire (apron fence) were put up. Others his own beats.	
E.15 cent. 26.		11.00	Enemy Artillery were hostile - suspect him at E.15 central was shells from 11-12 noon causing Cy. H.Q. as far as the E.a.e. cord. Fine Day. Observation poor.	

Army Form C. 2118.

WAR DIARY
or
INTELLIGENCE SUMMARY.
(Erase heading not required.)

May 1918.

Place	Date	Hour	Summary of Events and Information	Remarks and references to Appendices
	26th		Capt E.F.A. WHITWORTH M.C. admitted to Hospital – Command of C Coy (temporarily) taken over by 2/Lt. V.C.C. DICKINSON.	
	26/27	2.15AM	A raid was carried out by 1/KO SLI on enemy posts opposite our Left Coy. front – 3 prisoners + M.G. taken – raiders returned after 20 mins – No damage was done by the enemy barrage to the remainder of the night was quiet – Support Coy's employed on completing two saveno heads of lines to front of Support position –	
	27th		Quiet day – fine – Draft of 3 Offs. + 27 O.R. arrived at the Transport Lines including following Officers, all from Reinforcement Camp. Lieut T.R. WILLIAMS (assumed duties as Transport Officer) 2/Lt. R.G. GLOVER posted to C Coy 2/Lt. B.G. DAVIES do do	
			During day Support Line was shelled intermittently but no damage was	
		9pm.	done – From 9p.m. 6.10 P.M. enemy put over harassing fire around Bn. HQ. but no further shelling followed.	
	27/28		Bn. relieved by 2/K. Fus. – Quiet relief – Relief Complete 12. 45 A.M.	

Army Form C. 2118.

WAR DIARY
or
INTELLIGENCE SUMMARY.
(Erase heading not required.)

May 1918.

Place	Date	Hour	Summary of Events and Information	Remarks and references to Appendices
MORBECQUE D.13.a.4.3.	28th		On relief Bn. moved into Bivouac Camp N. West of MORBECQUE at D.13.a.4.3. – Bn. has part of the Bde. in reserve & liable to turn out at an hours notice to man line of defence "B" & "D" – Draft of 12 O.R. arrives from Reinforcement Camp – Capt. A.J. GIVONS took over the command of "A" Coy from 2/Lt. MRS. HALL. 2/Lt. REES took over temporary Command of "B" Coy.	
	29th		Offrs. men have noted Day spent in cleaning up, inspection of equipments & clothing & checking of Lewis Guns & battle stores. Coys. at disposal of Coy. Commanders – Party of 100 for work under R.E.s found at E.25.c. – 1 Off. & 17 O.R. joins from Reinforcement Camp. 2/Lt. ANGELL S.W. rejoined Bn. from Hospital.	
	30th		2 Off. & 100 O.R. found for work under R.E. as for 29th. Bn. training under O.C. Coys. as per training Programme attached. In the afternoon a Special class of 4 Off. & 1 Pte. N.C.O's were held under an Offr. & N.C.O. for instruction in No. 36 Rifle Grenade. – Draft of 5 O.R. arrives from Reinforcement Camp.	Appendix VIII

Army Form C. 2118.

WAR DIARY
or
INTELLIGENCE SUMMARY.

(Erase heading not required.) May 1918

Place	Date	Hour	Summary of Events and Information	Remarks and references to Appendices
	31st		100 O.R. r 3 N.J. found for work in the R.E's as above — Coys. training in accordance with Training Programme. Strength of Bn: On last day of month 20 Officers & 740 O.R. Nominal Roll of Officers attached	Appendix VIII

C Parker Lt Col.
Commdg. 2/North Wales Borderers

CONFIDENTIAL.

WAR DIARY

OF

2nd. BATTN.   SOUTH WALES BORDERERS

FROM 1-6-18.   TO 30-6-18.

Army Form C. 2118.

WAR DIARY
or
INTELLIGENCE SUMMARY.
(Erase heading not required.)

June 1918.

Place	Date	Hour	Summary of Events and Information	Remarks and references to Appendices
Camp N.W.	1st		Training in accordance with programme - Work party furnished for RE - Grenade instruction under Australian bombing instructor - Draft 6 O.R's arrived - 2/Lieut G. Esmond took over Command of 'B' Coy: from 2/Lieut R. Ross.	
MORBECQUE				
G^{de} MARQUETTE	2nd		Bn. moved into Res: to 86 Bde. re-occupied old around GRANDE MARQUETTE. - Capt Kilmurth rejoined from hospital & took over command of C Coy.	
Div. 6				
LEGRAND	3rd		Less A Coy. Bn. moved back to Bns in Res: of 87 Bde in line. all in 11:30 A.m. 'A' Coy. detached as Support Coy: to left front Bn. in relief of 1 Coy. 4/Manchesters at PETITE MARQUETTE E.19.a	
HAZARD				
"	5th		2/Lieut T.J. Williams rejoined from Hosp: & reported 'A' Coy: - Working parties to A Coy. & 40 B - B, C & D Coys. training	
		11.30pm	Gas shelling - no damage - remainder of night quiet.	
"	6/7/8		Training - RE parties	

Army Form C. 2118.

(2)

WAR DIARY
or
INTELLIGENCE SUMMARY.
(Erase heading not required.)

Instructions regarding War Diaries and Intelligence Summaries are contained in F. S. Regs., Part II. and the Staff Manual respectively. Title pages will be prepared in manuscript.

Place	Date	Hour	Summary of Events and Information	Remarks and references to Appendices
Le Grande Hazard	9th		D Coy. relieved A Coy (latter) remaining in Camp 2.30pm.	
"	10th		Capt M.J. Dickinson joined the Bn. Took over Adjutancy - Capt N Roberts joined & took over Command of "B" Coy. - 2/Lieut R.G. Davies rejoined from hospital & reported to B Coy. - 2/Lieut Thomas rejoined from L.G. course - 2/Lieut N Hughes rejoined from a funeral course - 5 OR's reported to Bn.	
"	11th		D Coy. relieved by 1 Coy of 1/Border Regt. & returned to Camp at 2.30pm.	
"	12th		4. OR's reported to Bn. - 2/Lieut Thomas returned from L.G. course.	
"	13th		2/Lieut Davis returned from TMB course - 1 OR reported - 9a0 shelling 11.30pm - 1.10am no damage	
"	14th	2.0pm	2/Lieut MacPherson rejoined from hospital & reported to B Coy. Bn. received orders to relieve Bn. in left Section, right 87th Inf. Bde. Order No. 112. Operation orders have issued accordingly.	App: A
"	"	"	No. 2 " " on Right of 87th Inf. Bde. No. G.S. 51/15	" B

A6943. Wt. W14422/M1160 350,000 12/16 D.D.&L. Forms/C/2118/14.

Army Form C. 2118.

WAR DIARY
or
INTELLIGENCE SUMMARY.
(Erase heading not required.)

Instructions regarding War Diaries and Intelligence Summaries are contained in F. S. Regs., Part II. and the Staff Manual respectively. Title pages will be prepared in manuscript.

Place	Date	Hour	Summary of Events and Information	Remarks and references to Appendices
E.14.C.7.0.	15th	12.30 A.m.	Relief reported complete to Bde. Hqrs. No. D/4.	
		1.15 "	88th Bde. Carried out a raid against TERN FARM & inclosures in E.17.b Central.	
		3.30 "	Report to Bn. Bde. No. SWTS 03/30	App. C
		9.0 "	" " "	" D
		4.45 p.m.	Reference Bde. Hqrs. order No. 110 (d. 10.6.18) Code word (a) received - forwarded to firing line under No. D/12 (acknowledged 4.30 p.m.)	
		7.2 "	Ref: Bde. Hqrs. Order No. 110. Code word DOG received - forwarded under D/15 to firing line. - Post located 10.40 p.m.	" E
			Further instructions to O.C. C Coy; No. D/19. (vide 87th Bde. Order G.S. 24/7).	
		10.40 "	Ref: Bde. Hqrs. No. 110 Evacuated posts reported to Bde. under No. D/23.	
		11.52 "	" " 110 " "	
16th		3.25 A.m.	" " " " JUSTICE received 3.25 A.m. & forwarded to firing line D/25	
		4.10 A.m.	Report of position of Bn. on our left.	" F
		11.30 "	B.M./2. ten Bde. warning us to provide 100 men from the Bn. to working parties brought under the Staff Capt.	
		4.30 p.m.	Ref: Brigade Order No. 110. BOSTON Received (acknowledged D/31)	

Army Form C. 2118.
(4)

WAR DIARY
or
INTELLIGENCE SUMMARY.
(Erase heading not required.)

Place	Date	Hour	Summary of Events and Information	Remarks and references to Appendices
	16th	8.20pm	Ref. Brigade Order No 110. Code word DOG received (acknowledged D/33) - forwarded to C. Coy. D/34	
	"	"	" Divisional Defence Scheme No 24 " " (" ")	
		10.25"	Ref. " Order No 110 code word DARLING sent to Bde (f D/35)	
	17th	1.40 AM	By Bde No 24/8 received + communicated to OC "C" Coy	
		3 AM	Situation reported normal to Bde. Styles (D/36) with exception of small gas shelling at E.20 Central.	
		5.0 AM	No F1 tied from Bde M/f. green lights from MERE FARM (E16A) Signifying re-occupation of posts in connection with Bde Order No 110 - communicated to OC "C" Coy under D/37	
		8.0 AM	Instructing OC C + D Coys that no patrols were to be sent out on the flanks of the geo owing to it being daylight - If posts were to be re-occupied by day then only small patrols to be sent out - If re-occupied by night then all original garrison to be sent forward.	
		12.15 pm	Ref. Bde No 24/8 code word SALOME with received (acknowledged D/42) - forwarded to OC C Coy under No D/41.	
		1.0 pm	Permission asked from Bde to interchange Coys from front line to Reserve under Rea - Sanctioned G.S/25.8	

Army Form C. 2118.

WAR DIARY
or
INTELLIGENCE SUMMARY.
(Erase heading not required.)

Place	Date	Hour	Summary of Events and Information	Remarks and references to Appendices
	17/5	2.30pm	Operation Order No 3 re digging/jumping off trenches	App. G.
		3.0pm	Ref: No G5/5/18 from Bde informing us Bn moved to relieve tonight (acknowledged D/46)	
		3.45"	Ref: Bde Order No 110 Code word JUSTICE received forwarded to Bde (D/48)	
		5.0"	Bde Order No 113 received ref: being relieved by 2/R Fusiliers acknowledged D/49	
	18/5	2.17 pm	Ref: " " " Code word EMPIRE despatched (D/51)	
		4.30"	Report 15 pushed to aviation effects of gas	App H
		5.0 "	Bn arrived back in Camp at MORBEQUE CHATEAU	
MORBEQUE	19/5	12 noon	Operation Order No 4 issued in conjunction with Bde Order No 114.	" J
"		12.30 pm	BM.39 Received cancelling Bde Order No 114 - acknowledged D/52.	
		12.55".	" HQ " Stating Bn will relieve 2/R Fusiliers in left sector of front line,	
			6.00 Bde Order No 115 confirming this (acknowledged D/53).	
		4.0 pm	Operation Order No 5 issued [Enemy aeroplane brought down S of MORBEQUE at 7.0pm.)	.K
		10 pm	Ref: Bde Order No 115 Code word ENOUGH sent (D/53)	
	20/5	7.30 Am	Report to Bde :- Slight gas shelling during early part of night - one enemy aeroplane over our lines - FANTASY FARM E12b heavily shelled (D.54)	
	"	3.0pm	Report to Bde Situation normal (D/57)	
E14.c.7.0.	21st/5	3.0 Am	Situation normal (D/60) - Rain during night	

Army Form C. 2118.

WAR DIARY
or
INTELLIGENCE SUMMARY.
(Erase heading not required.)

Instructions regarding War Diaries and Intelligence Summaries are contained in F. S. Regs., Part II. and the Staff Manual respectively. Title pages will be prepared in manuscript.

(6)

Place	Date	Hour	Summary of Events and Information	Remarks and references to Appendices
	21st	10.0 a.m.	Operation order No. 6 in connection with Bde. order No. 116 issued (Relief by 92nd Bde.)	App: L
		3.0 p.m.	Situation normal. Reported to Bde. (D/60)	
	22nd	12.30 a.m.	Relief complete. Reported " ("/65)	
			All companies arrived in Camp by 3.0 a.m.	
		2.0 p.m.	Battalion moved off + arrived at Camp near RACQINGHEM by 4.30 p.m. B14 b 55	
RACQINGHEM	23rd		Battalion at rest.	
B14 b 55		11.0 p.m.	Received St/58 from Bde. moving to be ready to move at 1 hour notice, acknowledged by D/68 at 11.30 p.m.	
	24th	6.0 p.m.	All officers attended lecture by Bg. "Bde. Cmdr. — Wet all day	
		10.30"	Received St/62 ref having on 1 hour notice – acknowledged D/69	
			Programme of work for 1st week's training	App: M
	25=27		Training as per programme	
	28	11.0 a.m.	Practice for Bde. Ceremonial Parade. — Lieut Hardy returned from Course.	
	29	11.0 a.m.	Bg. "Bde. inspected by the G.O.C. 89" Div.: — Draft of 19 O.R's arrived + posted to Coys	
		7.0 p.m.	Operation order No. 7 issued	App: N

Army Form C. 2118.

(7)

WAR DIARY
or
INTELLIGENCE SUMMARY.
(Erase heading not required.)

Place	Date	Hour	Summary of Events and Information	Remarks and references to Appendices
ROCQUIGNEM	30th	10 am	Attached is strength of Bn. nominal roll of officers present with the Bn.	
B.14.6.85				

W. Dickinson Capt & adjt.
2/5n Borderers

WAR DIARY   APPENDIX "A"

OPERATION ORDER NO.1 BY,
LT.COLONEL G.T.RAIKES D.S.O.,
COMMANDING 2nd. BATTN.SOUTH WALES BORDERERS.

In the Field.   June 14.18.

1. The Battn. will relieve 1st. Border Regt., in front and support line tonight, and 1st. Lancashire Fusiliers in Reserve position.

2. "C" Coy. will take over the front line) from 1st. Border Regt.
   "D" " "   "   "   "   support line)

   "B" " "   "   "   "   E.20.Central) from 1st. Lancashire
   "A" " "   "   "   "   PETIT MARQUETTE) Fusiliers

   Coys. will move off as follows:-
   "A" Coy. :- 6.0 pm.
   "B" "   :- 6.45 ".
   "D" "   :- 7.30 ".
   "C" "   :- 9.0 ".

   "A" "D" & "B" Coys. to move off in half platoons at 100 yds. distance.
   "C" Coy. to move by platoons at 200 yds. intervals.
        "A" & "B" Coys. will meet guides at the Coy. Hd. Qrs. they are taking over from.
        "D" & "C" Coys. will meet guides at the Saw Mills E.19.d.10.05

3. One limber will accompany each Coy. for Lewis Guns and Ammunition, Water and R Rations.
        One Cooker will accompany "A" Coy.
   Two Cookers will accompany "B" Coy. These Cookers will be at GLYNN Farm and will cook for "B" Coy. at E.20.Central, and also tea etc. for the two forward Coys.
   Coys. will march up via LE TIR ANGLAIS - SPOOK COTTAGE - FETTLE FARM N TRACK X - SAW MILLS.
   Limbers will go via LA MOTTE and thence up yo LA RUE DE BOIS.
   Coys. must send a reliable man with the limbers.

4. All Packs will be dumped by 5.0 pm. at Coy. Hd. Qrs. ready for Transport to take them to Transport Lines.

5. Men will go up in Fighting Order, with all Battle Stores etc. complete, and water bottles filled.

6. All trench stores, maps, defence schemes, etc. will be taken over and receipts given, and copies of receipts sent in to Battn.Hd.Qrs.
        Coys. will also take over the work in progress.

7. Relief complete to be sent in by telephone and runner, the time followed by Coy. Commander's name being the code for telephone message.

8. Battn. Hd. Qrs. will parade at 9.30 pm.

9. Advance Parties as follows:-
        Battn. Hd. Qrs.   2 Signallers and 1 N.C.O. to take over Stores.
        Coys. 1 Officer & 1 NCO. per Coy.
   The front line Coy. Hd.Qrs. are at E.27.b.9.2.
   "   support   "   "   "   "   " " E.29.b.9.3.

10. Regtl Aid Post will be at E.19.b.9.8.

11. 10% will be left behind as follows:-
        6 Lewis Gunners per Coy.
        1 Sgt. 1Cpl., & 1 L/Cpl..
    N.C.O.'s detailed as Battn. Hd. Qr. Instructors will be taken on Battn. Hd. Qr. strength, and will go to Transport Lines. They will be sent to Divl. Reserve Coy. on 15th. inst...
        10% and Sick from Coys. will parade at Battn Hd.Qrs. at 5.30pm.

                                           W.B.Dickinson   CAPTAIN,
                                           ADJUTANT 2nd. SOUTH WALES BORDERERS.

Copies to :- No. 1. O.C. "A" Coy.
"   2.   "   "B" " .
"   3.   "   "C" " .
"   4   "   "D" " .
"   5   "   Signallers.
"   6.   Medical Officer.
"   7.   Quartermaster.
"   8.   Transport Officer.
"   9.   1st. BORDER RGT.
"   10.   File.

WAR DIARY   APPENDIX "B"

OPERATION ORDER NO 2. BY,
LT.COLONEL G.T.RAIKES D.S.O.,
COMMANDING 2nd. BATTN. SOUTH WALES BORDERERS.

In the Field.   June 14 1918.

1. Information has been received that a hostile attack on this Sector is likely at any date, possibly at dawn, on the 16th.

2. The Code word "PERCY" will be sent from these "HQ" if information is received that the attack is imminent.

3. On receipt of this message.:-
   (a). All troops will mann their battle positions.
   (b). The front line will be thinned out, i.e., held chiefly by Lewis Gunners. 4 or 5 men per Lewis Gun Section should be sufficient, and other posts from Riflemen Sections as necessary. All men removed to be put in the main support line.
   (c). The Battn. in Brigade Reserve will mann "B" line in readiness to counter-attack.

4. In the event of fogs or a smoke barrage, an additional S.O.S. Signal will be short blasts (about 10 seconds each blast) on the strombus horn.
   3 Strombus Horns are being sent up to "C" Coy. tonight, 2 will be placed in the front line, and one at Coy. Hd. Qr.
   This signal will only be used, when there is fear that the ordinary SOS. will not be seen. It must be explained to all men that short blasts denote SOS. only.

5. Wireless and Power Buzzer Stations have been notified to Coys.
   The most important are
   Wireless E.22.b.6.8.
   Power Buzzer E.26.b.6.1.
   "   "   E.22.b.6.1.
   These must be known by all Officers.

6. Coys. are warned that in the event of an hostile attack, the enemy will probably drop a heavy barrage on front line, and H.E. and Sneezing Gas on Supports and Reserves. These will lift back by jumps of about 400 yds.. Sneezing Gas has a very irratating effect and effects the eyes, but does not last, and the air is clear a minute or two after the shelling stops.

7. "C" Coy. will have a patrol out 200 yds. in front of the line for an hour before dawn, to give warning of any hostile assembling. they can crawl in under cover of crops when it is light enough to see 300 or 400 yds.. (Reports from these patrols must be taken with a certain amount of reserve).

8. Stand to will be:-   3.15 am to 4.15 am.
                          9.30 pm. "10.30 ".

9. A C K N O W L E D G E.

                                                          WS Dickinson
                                                                 CAPTAIN,
                          ADJUTANT 2nd. SOUTH WALES BORDERERS.

   Copies to :- No.1. O.C. "A" Coy.
                " 2.   "   "B" ".
                " 3.   "   "C" ".
                " 4.   "   "D" ".
                " 5.   Medical Officer.
                " 6.   File.

WAR DIARY   APPENDIX "C".

      To 87th Brigade,
          Headquarters.

     SWB No. 0330,   15/6/18.   AAA.

About 2-30 am. the enemy opened a moderate barrage on what appeared to be our front line and shelling is still continuing (6-25 am.)   Our guns have replied slightly.   Only a few shells have been falling in support and Reserve positions.

My front line Company sent through "Situation Normal" at 3-20 am., on fullerphone but nothing further.

My telephone line to Brigade is cut and also Liason Officer's wire.

                                                               Lt.- Colonel,
                      Commdg. 2nd Battn South Wales Bordrs.

15/6/18.

WAR DIARY.   Appendix "D".

To Headquarters,
    87th Brigade.

        At 2-30 am this morning the enemy put down a barrage
of T.M.'s and 77's, on our front line with heavier shells
on the edge of the wood. This lasted till about 4-10 am. but
was light during the latter part.

        My left Platoon Commander reports that he saw numbers
of the enemy and men extended across our front about 100 yds
from our wire. Lewis Gun and Rifle Fire was opened on these,
and they did not advance. This Officer put up the S.O.S.
Signal but it was apparently not seen as our guns did not open
Some time after the barrage started a German Aeroplane flew
over (while still dark) this aeroplane dropped white lights
which were replied to by the enemy apparently from about
E.22.b.20.40.

        All my posts are intact. Casualties 3 killed and 7
wounded.   I am in touch only on the left with a Lance Corpl.
and 4 men of the Hants Regt.

                                    W.D.Dickinson. Capt.
                                        for Lt. Colonel,
15/6/18.   Commdg. 2/South Wales Borderers.

WAR DIARY   APPENDIX "D".

NOTES ON PARA. 6, OF OPERATION ORDER NO. 7.

Each Company will go into the line or into action with the
following numbers :-
```
        Company HQ.     C.S.M.          1 )
                        Signallers.     4 )
                        St. Bearers.    4 )
                        Gas N.C.O.      1 )            15
                        Runners.        3 )
                        Batmen.         2 )

        Each Platoon (4 Platoons.)            )
          Pl. H.Q. Sgt.         1 )           )
                   Runner       1 ) 3         )
                   Offr's Servt. 1 )          ) = 28   112
                                              )  per
        Lewis Gun Section 1 N.C.O. and 10     ) Pltn.
        2 Riflemen Sectns. ea.1 N.C.O. & 6.   )

                                Total....    127
```

These numbers may be increased to a total of 135, but if Coy.
Cooks are taken up, they will count in the numbers.

The Administrative portion of Companies are as follows:-
```
        C.Q.M.S.        1.                    )
        Storeman        1.                    ) Total 4.
        Sanitary Men    2. (May be taken up.) )
```

Everyone else in the Company will form the 10%.
This 10% should include 1 Sgt., 1 Cpl. 1 L/Cpl., 1 Lewis Gunner
per Gun, 1 Scout and 1 Rifle Bomber, also any Signallers in
excess of four.

These 10% will be told off by Companies now, and a parade state
giving numbers for the line and numbers left out sent in to
Orderly Room.

A Nominal Roll of numbers left out to be entered on the back of
the parade state, shewing what each man is, i.e. L.Gunner,
Scout, etc.

                                        W. D. Dickinson
                                                    Captain,
                            Adjutant, 2nd. Bn. South Wales Borderers.

In the Field,

WAR DIARY.   APPENDIX "E"

O/C.,
  " C " Company.
      Ref. "Dog" tonight.

1.   Please detail an Officer specially to see to this
     Posts 9, 10, and 11, will be evacuated. These may be
     taken back to main support line. The Officer detailed will
     as soon as all these posts are evacuated go straight to your
     Coy. HQ and send through "CORN" on fullerphone.

2.   In the events of the gas not being discharged after
     evacuation you will be prepared to reoccupy these posts
     by counter attack if necessary. In any case a patrol
     will go out in advance to ascertain if they are clear of the
     enemy.

3.   If gas is successfully discharged you may be called upon
     to send out a patrol on flank of gas cloud to discover results
     The safe area will be notified to you.

4.   If "PERCY" is sent up tonight I think you ought to leave
     not more than 8 or 10 in each of your 6 posts, i.e.
     not more than 60 all ranks.

        Your Coy. HQ. will move back to one of the posts
     in main support line not occupied by "D" Comapny.

5.   There is no doubt that Corps Commander expects attack
     by 4 Divisions to take HAZEBROUCH.

                                    W. D. Dickinson Capt.
                                             Lt.-Colonel,
                                    Commanding 2/South Wales Bdrs.

WAR DIARY.   Appendix "F".

To N O F A ,

Am holding FANTASY FARM with 3 platoons line continues along old trench E of wood Coy HQ and support platoon in E 22.b.3.3, posts established in same trench in touch with your left at SECLIN.

My left in touch with Worcesters, exact position not yet ascertained probably on line joining E.16.d.7.1. and E.22.b.8.8.

No report from LUG FARM posts .

Can you give me any information about latter.

(Signed)
A.F.C.V. Prendergast,
Captain,

From H O Z E
4.10 am.

WAR DIARY.   APPENDIX "G"

OPERATION ORDER NO.3 BY
LT.COLONEL G.T.RAIKES D.S.O.
COMMANDING 2nd BATTN. SOUTH WALES BORDERERS.

In the Field.   June 17th/18.

Forming-up Trenches for the attack will be dug along the front edge of the wood and carefully camouflaged, trenches to be short lengths 2' wide and 2'6" deep.   Work to commence tonight. The area will be divided up as follows:-

"C" Coy. from Ditch, N, of No. 6 post for 100 yds South.
"D" Coy. from right of C Coy to where Wood bends back at E 28.c.5.9.
"A" Coy. from E28.c.5.9. to where hedge runs forward at E28.c.55.65.
South of this is allotted to the 1/Border Regt.
"B" Coy. will make three lengths of trenches for their 3 platoons close behind the fronts allotted to C, D & A.   They may make use of No. 5 post.

To-night " B " Coy. will relieve " C "

and "A"   "   "   "   " D "

" C " will leave a party of 35 men to dig their trench.

"A" and "D" will each detail a party of 40 to dig their sections of forming-up trench.

" B " Coy. will find as many men as possible for work on their sections of trench.

All these trenches will be dug in the bushes as close as possible to the forward edge of the wood and must be concealed the bushes will be as little disturbed as possible, and branches placed over the trenches.

" A " Companies will be behind the hedge in front of No. 5 Post.

An officer from A, B, and D, will meet the C.O. at "D" Coy. HQ at 5-30 pm. to reconnoitre these positions.

W.F.Dickinson
Captain,
Adjutant, 2/ South Wales Borderers.

In the Field,   Copy No1. to O/C "A" Coy.
17/6/18.   " 2.   "   " "B"
                          " 3.   "   " "C"
                          " 4.   "   " "D"
                          5.5.   "   " File.

WAR DIARY.   APPENDIX "H".

To Headquarters,

    87th Brigade.

Herwith Patrol Report.

The enemy kept up continuous bursts of M.G. fire from his front line during the night.

The M.G. which opned on the patrol was in advance of his shell hole line.

At about 9-30 pm. whilst posts between LUG FARM and SECLIN were being reoccupied, parties going out were sniped at from LUG FARM amd from about E22.d.75.20.

Enemy also opened fire from BEAULIEU FARM.

                                     W.A.Dickinson Capt

                                            Lt. Colonel,
                                Commdg. 2/South Wales Borderers.

18/6/18.

                      PATROLL REPORT.

Strength   --   2/Lt. Dickinson and 5 men.

Object   --   Reconnaisance to see if gas had caused evacuation of line in E.28.b.

Narrative --   Patrol proceeded up N. side of stream from edge of Wood at No. 6 post. Road. VOLLEY FARM-BEAULIEU FARM was reached and the patrol was fired on by an enemy M.G. on or close behind the road.
The patrol withdrew according to instructions from Company Commander.

Ground   --   A very definite track marks the N. side of the stream.

Time   --   Left No. 6 Post 11-30 pm.
               Returned 12-30 am.

                            (Signed)   D.C.C.Dickinson,
                                                   2/Lt.

WAR DIARY.　　　　　　　　　　　　　　　　　　　　　　　APPENDIX "E".

OPERATION ORDERS NO. 4.

1. The 87th Bde. with 2nd Hants. Regt. on left and 8th Division on right will carry out an attack at a time and date to be notified later.

2. Objectives and Boundaries are shewn on attached map.
   The 2nd SOUTH WALES BORDERERS will attack on the left and the 1st K.O.S.B. on the right.
   Two Companies, one Border Regt. will take the enclosed area on either side of the Road including Beaulieu Farm & enclosures E 29.c.1.5.

3. The Battalion will attack with three Companies in the front line and one Coy. in reserve as follows:-
   "C" Coy. on left, 2 Platoons 1st wave, 1 Platoon 2nd wave,
   "D" Coy. in centre, 2 Platoons 1st wave, 1 Platoon 2nd wave.
   The above Coys. go right through to the final objective.
   The support platoon in each case mopping up shell hole positions in front line E.28.d.75/90, - E.29.a.30/00.
   "A" Coy. in reserve till Border Coy. reach objectives, when "A" Coy. will pass to the north of the enclosure E.29.c.15/50. and capturing VERTE RUE and enclosures East (vide Objectives Map) -
   "B" Coy. will be in reserve and will follow with one platoon behind each of D and C, to mop up first objective, and hold it.
   One platoon to follow on after "A" Coy. and mop up VERTE RUE.

4. Forming up will be as shown on Objectives Map.

5. **Method of Advance.**
   General direction of advance is 94 deg. Magnetic.
   Frontage per Coy. :- 170 yards at start and 270 yds on the sub objective.
   Distance of final objectives from our front line:-
   "A" Coy.　　　1500 yards
   "D" "　　　　1400 "
   "C" "　　　　1300 "
   The leading line of the 1st wave will be extended.
   In all other lines and waves, sections will advance in file.

6. Dress:- Fighting Order.
   170 Rds. S.A.A. per man.
   1 Aeroplane Flare per Man.
   1 Bomb per Man.
   3 men per Riflemen Section to carry 4 No.36 Grenades.
   24 Magazines per Lewis Gun. (These men carry 120 rounds S.A.A. only)
   3 S.O.S. per Coy.
   25 Shovels per Coy.
   As many men as possible to have Wire-Cutters, large,
   Billhooks:- 1 per section.
   Each Company will carry 4 light Bridges for crossing ditches.

7. A dump for S.A.A., Bombs, Wire Pickets, etc. is being formed at E.28.a.4.1.　　On completion of the advance "B" Company will be prepared to send one platoon back to the Dump to carry S.A.AM, to the Front line Coys.
   After the attack, and at dusk, a party of the Divisional Pioneers, will put up 300 yards of wire, astride the Road about E.29.b.9.1. This wire will be carried up by a party of the 1st Border Regt. An Officer will be detailed to have a tape laid from the dump to N. edge of VERTE RUE enclosure as guide for carrying parties.

8. **Communication.** Each Coy. will carry 1 Lucas Lamp, and flags, also two pigeons.
   As soon after the advance as possible a forward Signalling Stn. will be established at about E.29.a.20.05 and a telephone line laid out to it from Battn. Hd. Qrs.
   Flares carried by the men will lit in groups of 3, each flare 2 yards apart when called for by contact aeroplane, by Klaxon horn or by firing a Very's Light.

9. **Headquarters.** Battn. Hd. Qrs. will be at E.29.c.1.8.
Coy. Hd. Qrs will be established at about the following points.
"A" Coy.   E.29.d.20.95.
"D" "   E.29.a.95.15.
"C" "   E.29.a.80.65.
"B" "   E.28.b.40.95.

10. **Medical Arrangements.** Regtl. Aid Post will be established at about No. 5 Post E.28.c.50.70.
Advance Dressing Stations will be at E.20.a.9.1.

11. As soon as objectives are gained, Coys will send information to Battn. Hd. Qrs. by runner and by lamp, and as soon as possible a rough detail of dispositions, casualties and position of Coy Hd. Qrs., also stating whether they are in touch on the flanks.

12. The Barrage will fall and move as on Barrage Map attached. The rate of advance will be 100 yards in 4 Minutes. On C & D Coys front the barrage advance is somewhat slower in order to get a straight barrage line as early as possible. There will be a 10 minute halt after passing first objectives, as shewn on the map attached.

13. 2 Vickers Guns will accompany the Battn., and on the objectives being taken they will take up positions at about E.29.b.3.4. firing in the direction of E.30 Central.
A Stokes Gun will advance with the rear platoon of "A" Coy. This gun will be available to fire on VERTE RUE if required and after the capture of the objective will take up a position from which it can cover the bridge at E.20.a.4.4.

14. **Prisoners.** No man is allowed to escort prisoners to the rear unless detailed by an Officer. When an Officer sends prisoners back he will if possible give the escort a slip of paper with the man's name and the number of prisoners. The escort will take prisoners to the dump E.28.a.4. where they will be handed over to the Regtl. Police who will give a receipt, and the escort will return to the Coy.
Under no circumstances, are men other than stretcher Bearers permitted to take wounded to the rear. After the objectives have been taken an Officer may detail extra men to carry the wounded, but he must give the men a note, giving their names and sign it. Battle police will be established, and the names of all men, (other than runners with messages) going back from the front line will be taken.

W.V.D.Dickinson
Captain,
Adjutant 2nd. South Wales Borderers.

Copy. No.1.   O.C.   "A" Coy.
 "   " 2   "   "B" "
 "   " 3   "   "C" "
 "   " 4   "   "D" "
 "   " 5   Quartermaster.
 "   " 6   Transport Officer.
 "   " 7   Medical Officer.
 "   " 8   Signalling Officer.
 "   " 9   Assistant Adjutant.
 "   "10   File.

WAR DIARY   APPENDIX "K"
                        OPERATION ORDER NO5, BY
                    Lt.-COLONEL G.T.RAIKES D.S.O.
                 Commanding 2nd BATTN. SOUTH WALES BORDERERS.
    In the Field.   June 19th/18.

1. All previous orders with regard to operations to-day are cancelled.

2. The 2nd Battn South Wales Borderers will relieve the 2nd Battn.
   Royal Fusiliers tonight in left sector.

3. Coys. will be in position as follows:-
       "B"   Coy.   Front Line ..... March off 7-45 pm.
       "A"   "   Support Line....   "   " 6- 0 pm.
       "D"   "   E.20 Central....   "   " 6-45 pm.
       "C"   "   P.Marquette .... Parade at 7-15 pm.
       "HQ"   "   As before. .....   "   " 8-15 pm.

4. "A", "D" and "C" Coys to move in half platoons at 100 yards distance
   "B" Coy. to move by platoons at 100 yards distance.

5. One Limber will accompany each Coy. for Lewis Guns, Ammunition,
   water and rations. One Cooker will accompany with "C" Coy.,
   2 Cookers will accompany "D" Company. These latter 2 Cookers will
   be at GLYN FARM, and will cook for "D" Company, and also tea, etc.,
   for the two forward Comapnies.

6. Companies will march up via LE TIR ANGLAIS- SPOOK COTTAGE- FETTLE
   FARM- TRACK X- SAWMILLS. Limbers will go via LA MOTTE and thence
   up to LA RUE DE BOIS. Companies must send a reliable man with
   the limbers.

7. All packs will be dumped by 4-30 pm. at Coy. HQ ready for Transport
   to take them to Transport Lines.

8. Men will go up in fighting order with all Battle Stores etc., complete
   Water Bottles filled.

9. All trench Stores, Maps etc., Defence Schemes will be taken over
   and receipts given. Copies of receipts to be sent to BattnHQ.
   by not later than 8 am. 20th inst.

10. Working progress will be taken over by the Coy. and continued
    tonight. Relief complete to be sent in by Telegraph and runner
    by the word "BRECON" followed by the time, and Coy. Commdr's name.

11. Advance parties will proceed ahead, and will consist of One Officer
    1 N.C.O. and 2 Signallers per Company.

12. Regimental Aid post is at E.29 Central.

13. Coys. will leave behind in addition to their sick, 3 Lewis Gunners
    and 2 N.C.O.s if possible a Sergeant and Corporal.

14. Officers' surplus kit will be placed on G.S.Waggon outside the
    Orderly Room at 5-30 pm. Those men being left behind by Compys
    will parade with these waggons and march back to Transport Lines.

15. Coy. Commanders will see that their Coy. Lines are left in a clean
    state, particular attention to be paid to this. A report will be
    rendered to Orderly Room to this effect, previous to the Coys.
    marching off.

16. Medical Officer's stores and Kit, will be placed on "D" Coy's limber
    and dropped at Regimental Aid Post.

17. One day's rations per Coy. will be carried on Coy. Limbers and one
    on the man.

                              (1.)

18. Coys. will return NOW to Orderly Room the special S.O.S. Lights issued to them today.

W. Dickinson

Captain,
Adjutant 2nd. South Wales Borderers.

```
Copy No.  1   "A" Company.
          2   "B"    "
          3   "C"    "
          4   "D"    "
          5   Quartermaster.
          6   Transport Officer.
          7   Signalling Officer.
          8   Medical Officer.
          9   File.
```

WAR DIARY.   APPENDIX L.

OPERATION ORDERS No. 8. by
Lt. Colonel G.T. Raikes D.S.O.
COMMANDING 2nd. BATTN. SOUTH WALES BORDERERS.

In the Field.   21st June 1918.

1. Battalion will be relived tonight by the 11th Bn. East Lancs. Regt., and will proceed by march route to LE ROMARIN (C. 17.d.2.8.)

2. Company's will be relieved as follows:-
   "A" Company 2nd. South W.B. Relived by "Y" Coy. 11th E. Lancs.
   "B"   "   "   "   "   "   " "Z" "   "   "   "
   "C"   "   "   "   "   "   " "X" "   "   "   "
   "D"   "   "   "   "   "   " "W" "   "   "   "
   Coys will send 4 Guides per Coy to report at Bn. H.Q. at 2-30 pm. These will be taken by Capt. Crowder M.C. to FETTLE FARM whence Coys of the 11th East Lancs. will march off at the following times (approx.)
   "Y" Coy.   6.20 pm.
   "W" "   6-45 PM.
   "X" "   7-30 "
   "Z" "   9-15 "
   H.Q. "   9-15 "

3.

3. One limber per company will as near Coy H.Q. as possible at the following times. These limbers will be loaded with Lewis Guns Ammunition etc. and will proceed to Camp where they will be unloaded AT ONCE, accompanied by No. 1 of each Lewis Gun under and N.C.O.
   "A" Coy.   7 - 0 pm.
   "B" "   6 -15 "
   "C" "   8 - 0 "
   "D" "   7 -45 "
   H.Q. "   9 -30 "

4. Guides will be waiting for Coys at 9-0pm. (onwards) at the Anti-Aircraft Station in LE GRAND HASARD.
   Coys will march by Plattoons at the usual interval distances, to LE ROMARIN.

5. Water Tins and all Pack Containers will be sent to the Coy Cookers NOW.

6. Coys. will hand over to relieving Units as Trench Stores the following Stores which were brought into the Line by the Battalion. Bangalore Torpedoes - No. 36 R.G. Bombs. 1 Bomb and Aeroplane Flare per man - Surplus S.A.A.

7. Breakfast for A.C. & D Coys will be at 9-0am tomorrow - B Coy 10 am. Dinners for all provided the Battn does not move off before 2 pm. will be at 12-30 pm.

8. All receipts for Trench Stores etc should be sent in as soon as possible.

9. Relieve Complete will be reported to B.H.Q. by wire and Runneer by The Code word "HURRAH" followed by time and Coy Commdr's Name.

10. Coy Commdr will forward to Battn. H.Q. NOW all orders, Documents, Maps etc. issued in connection with the recently cancelled attack.

11. 1 Map. Sheet No. 36 A 1/20,000 attached.

12. Medical Officer will pack his Stores etc. on "D" Coys Limber. O.C. "D" Coy will inform the M.O. as to his whereabouts.

                                                          W.S. Dickinson
                                                              Captain,
                                        Adjutant 2nd. South Wales Borderers.

WAR DIARY.   APPENDIX M.

2nd. BATTN. SOUTH WALES BORDERERS.

TRAINING PROGRAMME.

COMMENCING TUESDAY 26th JUNE 1918.

Tuesday, 25th.   8-30 am. to 9-15 am. Drill Parade under R.S.M.
                 9-30 " to 1- 0 pm. Platoon and Company Marching
                                       and arms Drill - Extended Order - Fire and
                                       Movement - Musketry.
                                       Ranges alloted to A. B. and C. Coys.

Wednesday 26th   8-30 am. to 9-15 am. Drill Parade, O.C. Coys.
                 9-30 " to 1- 0 pm. Extended Order - Fire and
                                       Movement - Musketry and Specialist Training.
                                       Ranges allotted to B.C. and D Coys.

Thursday, 27th. 9-0 am. to 10-0 am. Bn. Ceremonial Parade.
                 11-0 " to 1-0 pm.   Demonstration of Platoon attack
                                       on Strong Point.

Friday   28th.   Probably Brigade Ceremonial Parade.

Saturday 29th.   Ceremonial Parade for presentation of Ribands
                                       by G.O.C. Division.

ALLOTMENT OF RANGES.

The following are 30 Yards Ranges :-

  "A" Range.   B.3.a.8.0.
  "B"   "   B.3.d.9.6.
  "C"   "   B.4.a.1.8.

These are allotted as follows :-

  "A" Range. "C" Coy. 25th, 26th and 27th.
              ("B" "   25th and 26th.
  "B" Range. (
              ("D" "   27th.

  "C" Range. ("A" "   25th and 27th.
             ("D" "   26th.

                                                              P.M.
Companies may use the Ranges any time of the day before 5-0 O'Clock.

Every man to fire One Grouping Practice.

Other firing to consist of Section competitions, or competitions
between Rifle Sections and LewisGun etc.

                                            W. A. Dickinson
                                                    Captain,
                            Adjutant 2nd. South Wales Borderers...

In the Field.
  24/6/18.

WAR DIARY.   APPENDIX "N"

OPERATION ORDER NO.7, BY
LT. COLONEL G.T. RAIKES D.S.O.
COMMANDING 2nd. SOUTH WALES BORDERERS.

Map. Sheet 36a.

1. **Move.** On receipt of orders to move Brigade will assemble at U.17.d.

2. **ROUTE.** The 2nd SOUTH WALES BORDERERS will march to U.17.d. independly via PONT ASQUIN, LYNDE.- WALLON CAPPEL.

3. **ORDER OF MARCH.** "A" Company will form the advance guard, "B" "C" "D" "HQ" and Transport with 100 yards interval between Coys and HQ and 25 yards between Columns of 6 vehicles.

4. **DRESS.** Battle Order, with extra Bandolier per man,

5. **TRANSPORT.** On limber for Lewis Guns per Coy. This will follow immediately in rear of Companies.
One limber for tools and Signalling stores, and a Maltese Cart will follow immediately in rear of HQ. Three limbers for SAA One Limber for Grenades, four Cookers, two Field filled water carts, carrying empty petrol tins and Mess Cart will accompany the Battalion.

6. **STRENGTH.** HQ and Conapnies will march out at Strengths as laid down under new organisation. The remainder will form 10%.

7. **TEN PER CENTERS.** The Ten per Centers including the Battalion instructors under Captain Givons will, on departure of Battalion march to U.18.c.8.9. by PONT ASQUIN- EBBLINGHEM. They will be accompanied by one limber.

8. **PACKS, OFFICER'S KITS ETC.** These will be stacked in Q.M. Stores immediately on orders to move being received.

9. **QUARTERMASTER'S STORES.** Q.M.'s Stores and remainder of Transport will remain in present location until receipt of further orders.

W.T.D. Dickinson
Captain,
Adjutant. 2;South Wales Borderers.

```
Copies to    No. 1.    Commanding Officer.
                 2.    2nd in Command.
                 3.    O/C., "A" Coy.
                 4.    O/C   "B"  "
                 5.    O/C   "C"  "
                 6.    O/C   "D"  "
                 7.    O/C   "HQ" "
                 8.    Quartermaster
                 9.    Transport Officer.
                10.    File.
```

NOMINAL ROLL OF OFFICERS
JUNE 30th. 1918.

APPENDIX O.

Lt. Colonel	G.T. Raikes D.S.O.		Commanding.
Major.	A.B. Cowburn M.C.		2nd in Command.
Captain.	E.K. Laman M.C.		Quartermaster.
"	W.V.D. Dickinson M.C.		Adjutant.
"	A.D. Givons.		Commdg. "A" Coy.
"	N. Roberts.		" "B" "
"	E.E.A. Whitworth M.C.		" "C" "
"	R. Dendy		" "D" "
"	A.E. Crowder M.C.		
"	G. Esmond M.C.		
Lieut.	T.R. Williams.		Transport Officer.
"	C.F. Dutton. M.C.		Scout Officer.
"	H.H. Evans.		
"	S.A. Fearby.		
2/Lt.	A.W. Hardwick.		Assistant Adjutant.
"	T.J. Williams.		
"	M. Hughes.		
"	J. Ham.		
"	J.W. Mayou.		
"	R.R. Rees.		
"	R.G. Davies.		
"	A.C. McPherson.		
"	G.P. Davies.		
"	D.C.C. Dickinson.		
"	E.O. Nicholas.		
"	A.N. Glover.		
"	A.J. Pritchard.		
"	C.J. Hardy.		
"	W.E. Kilbourn.		
Captain.	E.V. Morrow.	M.O.R.C.	Medical Officer.

STRENGTH OF BATTALION
JUNE 30th./18.

Officers.   Other Ranks.
   30   835.

Army Form C. 2118.

WAR DIARY
or
INTELLIGENCE SUMMARY.
(Erase heading not required.)

July 1918

Place	Date	Hour	Summary of Events and Information	Remarks and references to Appendices
RAQUINGHEM	12th-13th		Company Training, including extended order work - artillery formation and fire orders and discipline - limited amount of Range work.	
B14 & 88			2nd Brigade Staff Ride - 3rd 10 ORs arrived from Base	
			8th 87th L.I. Bde Ceremonial Parade for G.O.C 4th Army. 2/Lieut Rawlins joined Bn. on 1st appointment. 2/Lieut. Thomas returned from hospital - 11th 2/Lieut H. Jones returned from leave to U.K. - 13th 2 ORs joined from Base. - 10th A/Capt. Carden took over B Coy from A/Capt. Roberts	
	14th	13th	Bn. ordered to move under 87 Inf. Bde Order N°. 117.	
		10:20am	Bn moved on pre Operation Order N°. 9 (Appx A) - arrived camp 3:30 p.m.	Appx A
F3 C 1 &	15th	6:0pm	Bn moved into support re Operation Order N°. 10.	Appx B
		8:55=	Relief reported complete to 87 Bde. by wire D/4.	
		9:0	D/5 issued to Coys, regarding "Stand to" etc	Appx C
			Standing Orders re H.Q. reviewed	Appx D
	16th	3:0 am	Situation reported Normal to 87 Bde. (D/10)	
			4 ORs Casualties last night (wounded D Coy:) - Coys detailed working parties under R.E. Supervision	
	17th	3:0 pm	Situation reported Normal to 87 Bde (D/15).	
		3:0 Am	" " " " " (D/20)	

Army Form C. 2118.

(2)

WAR DIARY
or
INTELLIGENCE SUMMARY.
(Erase heading not required.)

Place	Date	Hour	Summary of Events and Information	Remarks and references to Appendices
ESCLIN	17	3.0 am	Hrs occupied MOEGHEIN FARM with 1 Platoon from Right Reserve line.	
"	17	3.0 pm	Situation reported Normal to Bde (D/25)	
"	18	3.0 am	" " " " (D/32)	
"		7.30 pm	Bn. Relieved by 18th Bn. F. Lancs - relief reported complete to Bde.	AppA
			Map showing Bn. Dispositions whilst in Support	
			Bn. marched back to Billets.	
LINDE	19		Bn. " " into Billets	
HON DEGHEM	23		Bn. moved into Billets in the village + vicinity	
St MARIE CAPPEL	24		Bn. Carried out individual training by Coys, also Bn. field days and Bn.	
	25-30		Exercise to Officers - 150 Officers reconnoitred the Area to which the Bn. would	
	31		have moved in case of attack	

M. Mukken
Gring of Stock Bn St...

2nd. BATTN. SOUTH WALES BORDERERS.

Lt. Colonel	G.T. Raikes	D.S.O.	Commanding.
Major.	A.B. Cowburn	M.C.	2nd in Command.
Captain.	W.V.D. Dickinson	M.C.	Adjutant.
"	E.K. Laman	M.C.	Quartermaster.
"	A.D. Givons		Commdg "A" Coy.
"	G. Esmond	M.C.	" "B" "
"	E.E.A. Whitworth	M.C.	" "C" "
"	R. Dendy		" "D" "
Lieut.	T.R. Williams		Transport Officer.
"	C.F. Dutton	M.C.	Intelligence Officer.
"	R.S.P. Rawlins		
"	H.H. Evans		
"	G.N. Holyoake		Signalling Officer.
"	S.A. Fearby		
2/Lt.	A.W. Hardwick		A/Adjutant.
"	J.W. Mayou		
"	J. Ham		
"	N.C. McPherson		
"	H. Jones		
"	E.O. Nicholas		
"	A.N. Glover		
"	B.G. Davies		
"	S.W. Angell		
"	A.J. Pritchard		
"	C.J. Hardy		
"	I. Griffiths		
Capt.	E.K. Swallow	M.C.	Chaplain.
Capt.	E. Vause	R.A.M.C.	Medical Officer.

STRENGTH OF BATTALION MONTH ENDING JULY 31st/1918.

OFFICERS.	OTHER RANKS.
28	855

CONFIDENTIAL.

WAR DIARY

OF

2nd. BATTALION

SOUTH WALES BORDERERS

FROM. 1.8.18   To. 31.8.18

VOLUME No. 43.

Army Form C. 2118.

WAR DIARY
or
INTELLIGENCE SUMMARY.
(Erase heading not required.)

August 1918

Place	Date	Hour	Summary of Events and Information	Remarks and references to Appendices
STRAZEELE	1st		Bn Training - open warfare - Bn advance on Fm"Huet" - Diamond formation (1.) 2/Lieut. I. Erwin rejoined from Hospital. - (2.) 2/Lieut. A.C. Hare struck off strength of Bn. (B1)	
"	3rd	5.0 pm	Marched to V17 C 9 3 (3 miles) - Bn. accommodated in Bivouacs & Huts - Bn. Hqrs. in Farm - Per. Moore.	
LA KREULE	3.75"		Platoon & Coy Training daily - Coys. worked on the same Scheme throughout, patrolling, raids, working up Enemy detached posts etc. - all Coys tackled.	
V17 C 9 3			(4) 2/Lieut. P.H. Fawkes Struck off strength of Bn. (B1) - (5) 2/Lieut. L.G. Kilbourn admitted to Hospital. (7) 2/Lieut. R. Nicholson struck off strength of Bn. Classified B2 (6) Capt. J.M. E.K. Lamman MC left Bn. for 6 months tour of duty at Home. - (3.) Lieut. & Qm. J.H. Laidler MC joined Bn. from Base. (15.) 2/Lieut. Col. G.T. Raike D.S.O. took on temporary Command of 27 Inf. Bde. Major G.R. Cotton MC took over temp Command of Bn.	
	15th	7.0 pm	Bn. moved up into front line & relief of 7/Hants. Regt. - A+C Coys in front line - D Coy in Support. +B Coy. in Reserve - for disposition see app: I - Front line consists of a series of He too posts about 150 x apart. Relief complete by 11.50 pm. A certain amount of hostile Shelling during Relief. The following officers were in command of Coys :- "A" Capt: R. Gima - "B" Capt. A.F. Crowder - "C" 2/Lieut. W.C. Dickinson - "D" Capt: G. Edmond.	App. I
Front line MERRIS SECTOR	16th		Quiet day a certain amount of daylight scouting was done in front of the posts; and enemy position approximately located - Our own heavy Shelling on	

Army Form C. 2118.

WAR DIARY
or
INTELLIGENCE SUMMARY.
(Erase heading not required.)

Instructions regarding War Diaries and Intelligence Summaries are contained in F.S. Regs., Part II. and the Staff Manual respectively. Title pages will be prepared in manuscript.

Place	Date	Hour	Summary of Events and Information	Remarks and references to Appendices
Front Line	16th		One of "C" Coys posts – 2/Lieut. J. Davis wounded – one O.R. killed & one wounded. Patrols went out during the night from A&C Coys. Enemy located in both instances –	
MERRIS SECTOR 17th			Very little hostile shelling	
	18th		Morning very quiet – at 11.00am 87th Bde attacked in conjunction with 9th Divn: on the left attack was made recently from N to S – Bn: took no part in original attack. After Capture of original objectives patrols were pushed out and two fort: Bn: Coys advanced on own initiative as patrols moved forwards – there was no damage on the Bn: front. Coys moved forward well & pushing forward rapidly smothered successfully tracking objectives. Capturing M.G.s and prisoners. Heavy hostile shelling on OUTTERSTEENE Ridge during afternoon & evening & communication to Coys was very difficult.	App: IV App: V App: III Bn: Order App: IV Objectives Maps App: V Accounts
		11.30pm	In order to attack objective vacant of Battn Sec Appendices 2 Coys 2/Hants Regt: blued on Rly line ALERT CROSSING – Rly BRIDGE on BECQUE (protecting Right Flank) – C Coy: moved into Ravin west F&a Central – 1 Coy: 2/Hants blued A Coy: in original front line – B Coy: moved up into front line taking over from A Coy. Covering Southern portion of OUTTERSTEENE RIDGE.	Officers from

WAR DIARY
or
INTELLIGENCE SUMMARY.
(Erase heading not required.)

Army Form C. 2118.

(3)

Place	Date	Hour	Summary of Events and Information	Remarks and references to Appendices
Trst Line	18th	11:30p	A Coy: Side-Slipped to the left relieving 1 Coy. 1/Border Regt crossing Eastern Side	
YPRES SECTOR			of OUTTERSTEENE. Night was fairly quiet but Enemy Shelled heavily from	
			1am onwards - Rations tanks got up to all Coys.	
			2/Lieuts RCE Dickinson & CR Thomas killed. Capt. N Roberts wounded 9 ORs killed	
			and 11 wounded. 2/Lieut Gibson took over command of C Coy.	
OUTTERSTEENE	19th		Enemy put down heavy barrage at 7:30 A.M. Again at 10:30 A.M. on OUTTERSTEENE Ridge - front	
R. DGE.			and Support line trenches.	
		5:0p	2/Pstn on our right attacked and cleared the ground up to and including the line	
			of the Road from FFC 65:10 to F13a.7.2. South of the Railway	
		10:0p	A Coy: Relieved A Coy in left portion of Bn. front line - latter came back to Support	
			line - Hostile Shelling intermittent throughout night. Capt. Grove provided Stretcher bearer parties	
	"	10:0p	Morning + afternoon fairly quiet. Bn. was relieved by 4/Worcester Regt. - Relief took over	
			complete 10 A.M. 21/8/15 - On Relief Bn. returned to camp at DA KREULE V17C9.3.	
			Total casualties throughout operations 2 Officers killed + 1 wounded. 30 ORs killed, 47	
			wounded + 2 missing believed killed. Following officers joined Bn. from Base Lincoln:	
			At Newman, RG Grave, + 2/Lieuts. JM Handy, GE Smith + JC Bonham. 2/Lieut. JR Jones rejoined	
			from hospital (wounded gas)	

Army Form C. 2118.

WAR DIARY
or
INTELLIGENCE SUMMARY.
(Erase heading not required.)

Place	Date	Hour	Summary of Events and Information	Remarks and references to Appendices
LAROEULE V17c9.3	24.7.72		Bn. in furnaces - 1st/10 Bn. started & relieved.	
	25th		Bn. relieved 1/Bord. Regt. in 2.line. STRAZEELE defences - relief complete 11.15 pm.	
	25/26		Bn. making tactical under RE supervision to town on 2.line. 1 O.R. wounded through rifle being fired. - Drafts of 28 + 52 other ranks joined Bn. from Base - former consisting of returned wounded men also from 6th 10 Bns. - latter all from 51st Grad. Bn. SNTB.	
OUTTERSTEENE Ridge	26th	6.10 pm onwards	Bn. relieved 2/Hants. in front & support line in Northern of OUTTERSTEEN. left Bn. 1/Bord. front.	
	27th	3.0 am	Relief complete. Hvy. enemy hostile shelling during relief. - Distribution C & D Coys in front line, a/two platoons from found by C. Coy. around DERMOT HOUSE - A + B Coys in support line. - Following officers commanded Coys :- A. Coy. 2/Lieut. Meyer - B 2/Lieut Norman & 2/Lieut. Evans & D. Coy. Capt. Edmond - 2/Lieut. J.R. Evans killed - C. Coy. taken over by 2/Lieut P.G. Davies - 2/Lieut J.R. Jones wounded (slight) - Lieut. R.S.P. Rawlins admitted to hospital. 2/Lieut G.M. Angell transferred to M.G. Corps. Enfield School. Slight shelling by day. - 30 R.o A. Coy. killed.	
	27th	10 pm	Redistribution of Bn. :- 2 platoons C. Coy. on outpost around DERMOT HOUSE - Coy Hqrs C. Coy + 2 platoons together with Coy. Hqrs D. Coy + 2 platoons in "J" line (front line) - remaining two platoons D. Coy. in support line - A. Coy. in old front line between GARDE DIEN FARM (F1B) and SCHARP COTTAGE (F 26 J) - B. Coy. in Z line between W 30 a.2.0 and W 30d 1.3.	

WAR DIARY or INTELLIGENCE SUMMARY

Army Form C. 2118.

Place	Date	Hour	Summary of Events and Information	Remarks and references to Appendices
WESTONE RIDGE	29/10		Normally quiet – B Coy in 2" line furnished bombing party of 32 ORs under O.C. Supervision for 4 hour duty for work on the portion of 2" line. – At night "D" Coy furnished bombing party of 30 ORs under O.C. Supervision to work on C.T. between Support & 2" lines. 2/Lieut. R.G. Davies admitted to hospital. – 2/Lieut. J.R. Jones injured. Brighton Hospital – 2/Lieut. G. Garner injured Boris sea wounded.	
	30"	7 pm	In conjunction with 1/Border on the left & 7th Bde on the right one platoon of C Coy & 2 from D Coy pushed out with objective line joining BAILLEUL Rly STATION – CEMETERY (F12) – NOOTE BOOM (F11) – objective line reached at 10.0 p.m. Opposition slight.	
		10.0 pm	A Coy: came up into 2" line & D Coy into Support line.	
		9.0 pm	A & B Coys moved out & relieved 2 platoons on outpost position – B Coy on right in touch with 86th Bde. A Coy on left in touch with 1/K.O.S.B. on line Bailleul-Poperinghe AJ 2.11 – B16 2.9. C Coy: nearer of 2" line and D Coy in Support line. Casualties 2 ORs wounded. 2/Lieut. E.T. Shaw joined Bn. from Base.	
	31"	10 am	Advance continued. Outposts on line Agf 20.28 – A3d 60.05" – Opposition slight.	
		10 pm	Two forward Coys were relieved by 1/Border Regt who took over the whole outpost line. A Coy: came back to Y & Support lines between F3d Central & OUTTERSTEENE,	

Army Form C. 2118.

WAR DIARY
or
INTELLIGENCE SUMMARY.
(Erase heading not required.)

Place	Date	Hour	Summary of Events and Information	Remarks and references to Appendices
	30th		3 Platoons in front line & 1 in Support - 0×D Coys moved off to the Right & occupied the same lines between OUTTERSTEENE and HAUTE MAISON.	
	31st		Strength of Bn: 26 officers and 802 O.Ranks. Nominal roll of officers attached	App: V.

Marker Mhnee
Comg 2° B° Southwark Borderers

SECRET   Appendix 11

87th. Infantry Brigade Order No. 125.

Reference Map
STRAZEELE Sheet
1/20,000 and
 TmSm260, 6/8/18
1/10,000

1.   On 18th. inst at 11.0 a.m. the 87th. INFANTRY BRIGADE
will attack and capture the enemy Front Line System
on approximately an East and West Line between GARBEDOEN
HOUSE and the METEREN BECQUE with the ultimate object of exploit
ing the situation and making good the OUTERSTEENE RIDGE.

          The 9th. Division are attacking on the left.   The
86th. Infantry Brigade on the right will be active with
Trench Mortar, Machine Gun and Rifle Fire during the attack,
and will cooperate in any subsequent exploitation.

          The position of the objective is shewn on attached map
"A" in blue.

2.   DISPOSITIONS.
     1st. KING's OWN SCOTTISH BORDERERS on left.
     2nd. SOUTH WALES BORDERERS on right in present front line.
     1st. BORDER REGT. in Brigade Reserve.
     6th. KING's OWN SCOTTISH BORDERERS (27th. Brigade 9th. Divn)
     are attacking on the immediate left of the 87th. Brigade.

3.   BOUNDARIES   are shewn on attached map.

4.   METHOD OF ATTACK.

     (a).   The attack will commence at Zero hour under a
barrage which commences at ZERO minus 1 minute.   There will
be no preliminary bombardment.

     (b). 1 Company, 1st. KING's OWN SCOTTISH BORDERERS will
advance from present front line (X.26.d.5.8 - X.26.b.9.8 to
the Red Line SCARPE Cottage - METEREN MECQUE, mopping up
the area through which it passes and maintaining close
touch with the 27th. Brigade on left.

     (c). 1 Company, 1st. KING's OWN SCOTTISH BORDERERS plus
half Company Pioneers will advance from AFRICAN TRENCH
following in rear of the right of the 27th. Brigade.

     (d). The barrage will halt in front of the Red line
until ZERO plus 45, when the advance will be renewed to
the Blue Line.

          2 Companies, 1st. KING's OWN SCOTTISH BORDERERS
in present Front Line will take part in this renewed advance
on the right, their objective being the Blue Line from
GARBEDOEN HOUSE to METEREN BECQUE.

     (e)   1 Company 1st. KING's OWN SCOTTISH BORDERERS in
the Red Line immediately West of the METEREN BECQUE will
then cross to the East side of the METEREN BECQUE and take
up a position in reserve South-West of BELLE CROIX FARM.

     (g). As soon as the Blue Line is reached, 1 Company,
1st. KING's OWN SCOTTISH BORDERERS plus half Company
Pioneers from African Trench will take over Blue Line
between METEREN BECQUE and TERRAPIN HOUSE (inclusive)
and hold and consolidate this line.   For this purpose,

(1).

2.

the Company 1st. KING's OWN SCOTTISH BORDERERS will carry 50 coils concertina wire, and the half Company Pioneers 70 coils.

(h). The 2nd. SOUTH WALES BORDERERS will keep touch with the right of 1st. KING's OWN SCOTTISH BORDERERS during the advance.

5. EXPLOITATION.

(a). On the Blue Line being established, patrols will be at once be pushed forward up to the Barrage and onwards as soon as the barrage lifts at Zero plus 90. In the event of these patrols getting into OUTERSTEENE they will be supported and 1st. KING'S OWN SCOTTISH BORDERERS will form a defensive flank from TERRAPIN HOUSE to about F.9.a.6.8. and will arrange to cover the East and South of OUTERSTEENE.

(b). The 2nd. SOUTH WALES BORDERERS will then push forward and occupy the line of the Railway to ALBERT CROSSING. —Fq a 5 5

xxx.

6. MACHINE GUNS.
(a). 4 Vickers Machine Guns of 29th. MACHINE GUN BATTALION will be placed at the disposal of Officer Commanding 1st. KING's OWN SCOTTISH BORDERERS who will be responsible for supply of ammunition to these guns.

(b). A Machine Gun Barrage conforming generally to the Artillery barrage will be put down. In addition 4 Guns will be sited about F.1. central to engage with direct fire targets about OUTERSTEENE.

7. TRENCH MORTARS.

Instructions are being issued later.

8. ROYAL AIR FORCE.
(a). A contact patroll will be over during the whole of the attack.

(b). It will be marked as follows :- Black flap on trailing edge of under plane and coloured streamer on tail.

(c). All troops detailed to go through to the Red Line and also those detailed to go to the Blue Line will be provided with Red Flares and pieces of tin about 8 inches square.

(d). When the contact plane goes over it will call for signals by sounding a Klaxon horn or firing a White Very Light. The Infantry in the Front Line will then light flares in groups of 3 or more or will shine their pieces of tin, or Vigilant periscopes if the sun is shining. This signal is more clearly visible than flares.

(e). A counter-attack patrol will watch the front from Zero hour onward until dusk. A red Very Light dropped from the plane means that HUN Infantry is about to attack.

(f). POPHAM signalling panels will be put out by 87th. Brigade Headquarters, also Battn. Hd. Qrs.

9. SYNCHRONIZATION. Watches will be synchronised by an Officer

3.

from 87th. Brigade Headquarters at Battalion Headquarters of 1st. KING's OWN SCOTTISH BORDERERS and 2nd. SOUTH WALES BORDERERS on "EF" night.   1st. BORDER REGT. will send an Officer to synchronize at 87th. Brigade Headquarters at 9.0 p.m. on "E/F" night.

10. HEADQUARTERS.

87th. Brigade advanced Headquarters will move to IONIC HOUSE (present left Battalion Headquarters) W.18.d.2.9. on "E/F" night.

1st. KING'S OWN SCOTTISH BORDERERS HQ. ⎫
1st. BORDER   REGIMENT   ⎬ Will be issued later
2nd. SOUTH WALES BORDERERS   ⎪
86th. INFANY. BRIGADE H.Q.   ⎭
27th. INFANTRY BRIGADE H.Q. ....X.14.b.8.4.
6th. KING'S OWN SCOTTISH BORDERERS H.Q......X.21.d.4.7.

11. LIGHT SIGNALS   The following Signals will be used :-

Objective gained................Blue Smoke, Rifle Grenade
Lengthen range 100 yds..........White to Green, Rifle Grenade
S.O.S.   by day.................Red Smoke   do.
S.O.S.   by night...............Ordinary S.O.S. Signal.
S.O.S. if in mist...............Short blasts on Strombus Horn
                                 in addition to light signals.

12. COMMUNICATIONS.

1st. KING'S OWN SCOTTISH BORDERERS will establish a lamp signal Station at TERRAPIN HOUSE to communicate with 87th. Brigade Headquarters at IONIC HOUSE.

13. LIASON.

1st. KING'S OWN SCOTTISH BORDERERS will detail a liason party of 1 N.C.O. and 4 men to proceed with right Company 27th. Infantry Brigade.
27th. INFANTRY BRIGADE will similarly send a party to liaise with left Company, 1st. KING's OWN SCOTTISH BORDERERS.
Officer Commanding 1st. BORDER REGIMENT will detail 1 Officer to report Headquarters 27th. Infantry BRIGADE at X.14._.8.4. at 6 a.m. on "F" day, and 2 cycle orderlies.
Artillery liaison will be notified later.

14. DUMPS.   Dumps of R.E. Material, SAA. Grenades and Water have been established at X.26.d.20.65 and F.1.a.7.4.

15. CARRYING PARTIES.

1st. KING'S OWN SCOTTISH BORDERERS will be responsible for carrying to the Blue Line the R.E. Material necessary for the consolidation of this line on their own front.

16. BRIDGES.

R.E. are arranging to throw bridges across the BECQUE. Approximate locations will be issued later.

ACKNOWLEDGE.

(sd).   Rm MARX   Major,
A/ BRIGADE MAJOR 87th. INFTY. BRIGADE.

Issued through
Signals at

Copy No.   Appendix 3

2nd South Wales Borderers
Orders No 14   Aug 14th/1918

Reference Map Strazelle Sheet 1/20,000. TS 260 1/10,000.

Para I   On 18th August at Zero hour the 87th Inf. Bde will attack and capture enemy front line system on approx. an East & West line between GARBEDEON and METEREN BECQUE. With the ultimate object of exploiting the situation and making good the OUTTERSTEENE RIDGE.

    The 9th Div. are attacking on the left. The 86th Bde on the right will occupy LABIS and LYNDE FARMS, also the line of Railway trucks just East of CELERY COPSE. The position of the 1st Objective is shewn in red on the attached map A (already issued) and second objective in blue.

Para II   <u>Dispositions</u> 1st K.O.S.B. on left, 2nd S.W.B. on right in present line. 1st Border Regt in Bde Reserve.

—" — III   <u>Boundaries</u> Shewn on attached map B.

IV   <u>Method of attack</u> The attack will commence at Zero hour under a barrage which commences at Zero minus one minute. There will be no preliminary bombardment. The barrage will fall in front of the red line until Zero plus 45 when the advance will be renewed to the Blue line. Two Companies 1st K.O.S.B in present front line will take part in the renewed advance, their objectives being the blue line from GABBEDOEN HOUSE to METEREN BERQUE. "A" Coy will maintain touch with these two Coys. 1st K O S.B.

V   (i) <u>Exploitation</u> On the blue line being established patrols from 1st K O.S.B. will at once be pushed forward up to the barrage, onwards as soon as the barrage lifts at ZERO plus 90. In the event of these patrols getting in to OUTTERSTEENE they will be supported by 1st KOSB who will form a defensive flank from TERRAPIN HOUSE to about F.9.a.6.8. and will arrange to cover the East and South of OUTTERSTEENE.

   (ii) In the event of 1st K O.S.B. patrols getting in to OUTTERSTEENE the 2nd S.W.B. will then advance and occupy the line ALERT CROSSING along the

(1)

railway F 8 d # 5. 60. and thence to F 9. a 15 00.

Para VI Instructions On arrival 1st KOSB. at Blue line (Zero plus 90)
O.C. A & C Coys will each push forward small patrols
supported by One platoon. to reconoitre the ground between
their present positions and to the METEREN BECQUE
in expectation of receiving orders ~~from Battn HQ~~ to
~~occupy line mentioned in~~ PARA V (2) On receiving
orders from Battn HQ. to advance, AND NOT TILL THEN.
A and C Coys will do so taking up the following positions
A Coy (O.C. A Coy will maintain touch with KOSB on left)
less 1 platoon B.
F 9 a 15 00. - METEREN BECQUE (left Bank)
C Coy Less 1 platoon D. METEREN BECQUE (right bank) O.C. C Coy
ALERT CROSSING and will consolidate on arrival there.
will maintain faison throughout with 86th Bde (2nd R.F.)
D Coy will move forward, pick up No 16 platoon and take up a
defensive position outside the road at F 8 A 95 35 (approx)
They will be in immediate support to A & C Coys. B Coy will
occupy posts vacated by C Coy. No 6 platoon will rejoin
B Coy on its arrival in their new positions.

VII Signalling Officer will be prepared to maintain communication between
B.H.Q and A and C Coys in the event of these Coys advancing
If possible both by visual (Lucas Lamp) and wire

VIII 1st Border Regt will occupy positions vacated by B & D Coys

IX A proportion of smoke shell will be included in the barrage
No artillery fire will be brought North or West of a line
F 4 a 0 0, F 10 a 00 F 9 c 00
In addition to the Artillery barrage there will be a MG
over head barrage

X Aeroplanes A contact patrol will be over all during the whole of the attack
Aeroplanes will be marked as follows. black flap on trailing edge of
under plane and colored streamers on tail.
When the contact plane goes over it will call for signals by
sounding Claxon Horn or firing a white very light.
Infantry in the front line will then light flares (red) in
groups of 3 or more, or will shine their pieces of tin
(already issued to Coys) if the sun is shining
A Red very light dropped from the plane means that
Hun Infantry is about to attack. Signalling Officer
will have POPHAM signalling panel at B.H.Q

XI Light Signals The following signals will be used.
Objective gained - Blue smoke Rifle grenade
Lengthen Range 100 yds - White 2 Green R G
S O S. by day - Red smoke R G
S O S by night - Red - Green - yellow, as usual.

2

XII. A Battn Dump has been formed at BOTHA FARM (W 29 d 1.3) of SAA, Water, Reserve Rations and No 36 R.G. There is also a forward dump at F.1.a.4.4. 170 Rounds S.A.A, 2 R.G. Bombs and one red ground flare will be carried per man.

XIII. Regt'l Aid Post W 29 C.4.4.

XIV. Rations including pot stew and tea will be brought up on night of 18/19 as previously. Details as to carrying parties will be notified later.

XV. Prisoners will be sent under escort to Battn HQ where they will be taken over by Regt'l Police and marched to Bde HQ (IONIC HOUSE) W.18.d.2.2

XVI. O.C. D Coy will detail 2/Lt Griffiths to act as liaison Officer at Hd Qtrs 1st Border Regt. He should get in touch with them as soon as possible.

XVII. The importance of sending back the earliest possible information of progress made must be borne in mind by all ranks.

XVIII. Battn HQ will be at BOTHA FARM W 29 d 1.3 from 9 am on 18th inst.

Issued at 3-0 PM.

Capt. Adjt.
2nd South Wales Borderers.

Copies issued to.
1. A Coy
2. B —
3. C —
4. D —
5. Signalling Officer.
6. Intelligence —
7. M.O.
8. 1st K O S B
9. 2nd R.F.
10. HQ 87th Bde

APPENDIX V

Account of Operation 18th August 1918.

The barrage started at 11 a.m. 9th Divn & 1st KOSB advanced under this barrage to blue line reaching this line at 12.10 p.m. Barrage then moved on to Outtersteene and ridge but no Art. fire was put down on this Bn. front.

As barrage moved on, 1/KOSB pushed forward patrols from blue line south, while 2/ Bdrs pushed out patrols from original line, East; the whole converging on Outtersteene and Outtersteene Ridge.

The following orders were received as regards this exploitation:—

Front line bns to push forward patrols supported by platoons as soon as blue line taken. If these were successful front line bns were to move forward on their own initiative clearing all ground to Outtersteene and N of Rly and holding Outtersteene and Railway on South bank. 86th Bde on right were to push forward S of Rly if possible. In addition a code word was arranged by Brigade on receipt of this word the whole Bn was to move forward to allotted positions for holding the Outtersteene Ridge.

At 12.15 p.m. A & C Coys pushed patrols and platoons forward and followed up almost at once with the remainder of their coys on their own initiative. The advance was excellently carried out with plenty of dash and initiative by individual and junior commanders. Enemy M.Guns were rushed or outflanked & rifle grenades were freely used and found of great value. C Coy who were on the right pushed rapidly down the Rly line & secured the right flank. A Coy who got a little too much over to the right crossed the Becque partly at the Railway Bridge and partly at MERRIS-OUTTERSTEENE Road bridge. "A" Coy got in touch with 1/Border Coy in Outtersteene.

On the right 86th Bde failed to get the line of Rly tracks in F.13 a 6.8. & were driven back to blue fold. The Bn therefore on completion of the attack held the line from A ERT crossing on the right along rly line to Rly bridge on Becque to about F9 a 2.3. A front of about 1800 yds. At 1.32 p.m. the code word from Bde was received and orders at once sent to B & D coys to move. These coys moved forward quickly to following positions:—

APPENDIX I

Spindyn - 18.4.18 contd.

"B" Coy to old German trench just W of Oultersteene & "D" Coy to the old front line between MERRIS & CELERY COPSE Bn. HQ moved to MONT DE MERRIS. Touch on the flanks was obtained in front, support and reserve lines.

The following captures were made by the Battn.
      3 Officers - 132 unwounded other Ranks
      16 M Guns & 3 Trench Mortars.

Minor concentrations of the enemy were reported but no counter attack developed. Oultersteene and forward area were heavily shelled by the enemy during the afternoon and evening. Coys. got quickly dug in.

The success of the exploitation and small casualties were due to the dash and go shown by all ranks. Hostile opposition was invariably dealt with promptly by the man on the spot and mutual assistance by platoons in outflanking enemy machine guns was very well carried out, with the result that enemy resistance was smothered or outflanked before it could inflict heavy casualties.

Coy advances were made with platoons in Diamond formation well opened out.

The value of previous training in these formations was very noticeable.

Total Casualties

Killed   Offrs   O.Ranks.
           2   20
          2/Lt D.C.Dickinson }
          2/Lt C.R.Thomas   }

Wounded   1   37
          Capt N Roberts   }

Missing   2

APPENDIX No. VI.

NOMINAL ROLL OF OFFICERS. - 31.8.18.

Major	A.B.Cowburn	M.C.	Commanding.
Capt.	W.V.D.Dickinson	M.C.	Adjutant.
"	R.Dendy		Commanding "D" Coy.
"	G.Esmond	M.C.	Commanding "B" Coy.
Lieut.	T.R.Williams		Transport Officer.
"	T.H.Waldron	M.C.	Quartermaster.
"	C.F.Dutton	M.C.	Intelligence Officer.
"	H.H.Evans		A/Adjutant.
"	G.N.Holyoake		Signalling Officer.
"	A.L.Newman		
"	S.A.Fearby		
2/Lieut.	J.Ham		Commanding "A" Coy.
"	B.G.Davies		Commanding "C" Coy.
"	J.W.Mayou		
"	M.Hughes		
"	T.J.Williams		
"	N.C.McPherson		
"	J.E.A.Gibbs		
"	G.Garner.		
"	A.N.Glover.		
"	F.W.Hardy		
"	S.F.Shearer		
"	A.J.Pritchard		
"	I.Griffiths		
"	G.E.Smith		
"	T.C.R.Bronham		

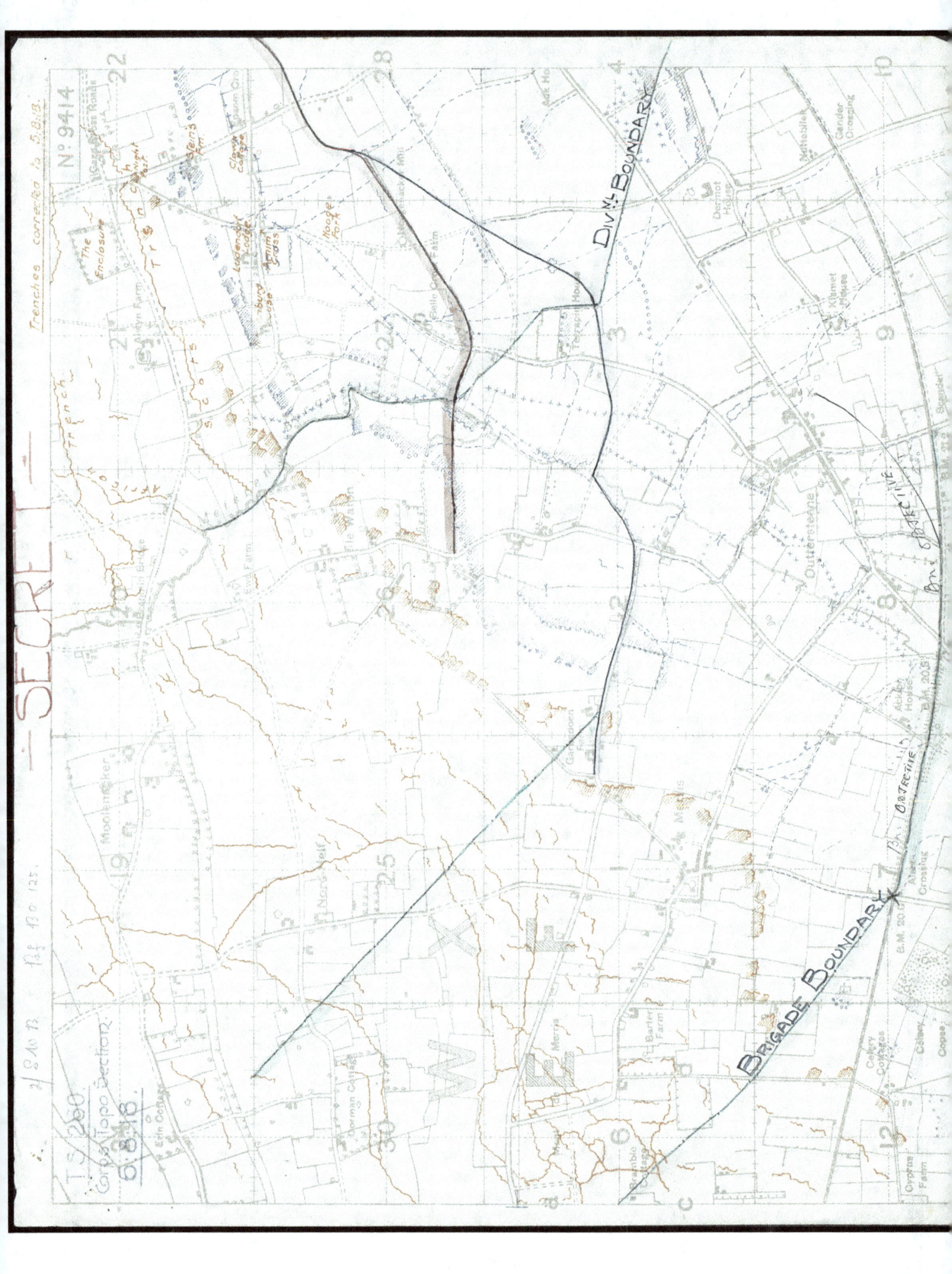

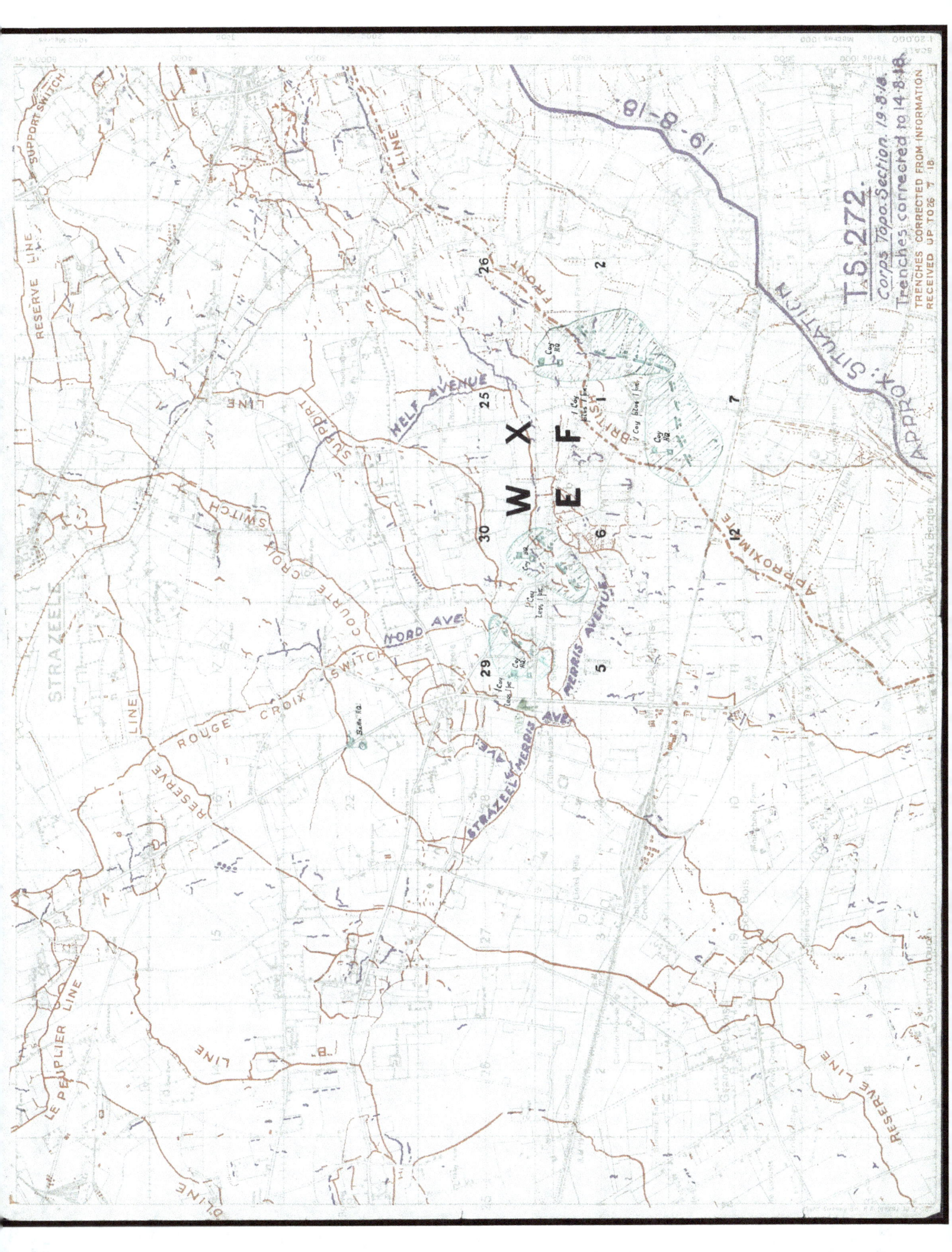

Army Form C. 2118.

2nd M.O.B.
September 1918

WAR DIARY
or
INTELLIGENCE SUMMARY.
(Erase heading not required.)

Instructions regarding War Diaries and Intelligence Summaries are contained in F. S. Regs., Part II. and the Staff Manual respectively. Title pages will be prepared in manuscript.

Place	Date	Hour	Summary of Events and Information	Remarks and references to Appendices
OUTTERSTEEN RIDGE	1st	2.0 pm	Bn. turned off independently by Coys from strength positions of line and took up positions along road from NOOTE BOOM – F.11 f.9.2 – F.5d.50.35 as support to the 1/Border Regt.	
		7.30 pm	Bn. moved forward to relieve 1/Border Regt. dispositions. A Coy (2/Lieut. Ham) Coy HQrs X Roads A.23.a.3.8 – A.23.f.4.7, A.23.a.3.6, VINTAGE FARM A.23.a and A.23.c.3.1	
			B Coy (Lieut. At Newman) in Reserve at Bn. HQrs. – C Coy (2/Lieut. Davis). Coy HQrs WHISKER 12 Pill DGE A.11.c.9.1 Platoon – 1 Platoon A.17.c.75.95 – 1 Platoon just E of NICKY FARM – one platoon with 2 guns A.12.a.40.20 + A.2.a.70.20	
			D Coy (Capt Simond) Coy HQrs at Platoon PITCH BEND A.95.a – 1 Platoon A.12.a.1.7 – 1 Platoon A.6.c Build – 1 Platoon A.6.a.7.7 – Bn. HQrs DOOK FARM A.3.a	
			Relief completed by 12 mn.	
			88th Bde on our left during the night moved on to road running NNE from DE SEULE (B.16 Central)	
			In conjunction with this B Coy moved forward and took up positions as follows :-	
			Coy HQrs + 1 Platoon A.6.c.7.7 – One Platoon A.12.a.9.1 – One at B.1.c.3.0 + 1 at B.1.c.6.5.	
"	2nd	9.15 pm	Bn. ordered to advance – objective NIEPPE (B.16) – TROIS PIPES (B.11) both inclusive. R.L.B. I	
			Owing to strong hostile machine gun fire Companies were unable to advance until dusk when the line MURDER FARM (A.18.D) TROIS ARBRES (B.13.A) – PONT D'ACHELLE (B.84) ?	

A8915 Wt. W11422/M1160 350,000 12/16 D.D. & L. Forms/C./2118/14.

Army Form C. 2118.

WAR DIARY
or
INTELLIGENCE SUMMARY.
(Erase heading not required.)

Instructions regarding War Diaries and Intelligence Summaries are contained in F. S. Regs., Part II. and the Staff Manual respectively. Title pages will be prepared in manuscript.

Place	Date	Hour	Summary of Events and Information	Remarks and references to Appendices
			was tacked – Casualties 4 O.Rs killed 9 O.Rs wounded *[illegible]*	
	2/4	10.0pm	Bn: was relieved by 1/KSLI – Relief complete 1.50 pm (3.9.18) – Bn. relief Bn. returned to DOUX FARM (A3.a) & bivouaced	
DOUX FARM A3.a.	3/4	5.0 pm	Bn: marched to OUTTERSTEENE and bivouaced about F.9.a Central	
	4/4		Coy checked Barr. & New Stores – Whole Bn bathed at 5" – Lieut. Y.R Williams proceeded on 1 month's leave to U.K – Capt A.D Givens rejoined Bn. from leave to U.K – Lieut H.H Evans proceeded	
OUTTERSTEENE	5/4		on 14 days leave to U.K	
	6/4	6 a.m	Bn furnished working party of 300 workers at 2nd BARRIERE CALIER DAYS (X.18.c) and marched to new camp at A.3.d Central on completion of task	
A.3.d Central 7/4		9.15 am	Remainder of Bn: marched to New Camp A.3.d Central. Owing to the heavy rainfall for two days Owing to continual rain, no training was possible. 2/Lieut. W.F Kitchin rejoined Bn from sick leave to U.K	
	8/4	6am 1pm	Bn furnished two working parties of 100 workers each, found of A1.13 Corps at wood junction in X.17.c – on completion of task returned to new camp at ERIN COTTAGES (W.29.d)	
			D.Coy: furnished two working parties of 50 workers each at Bid. 35E (mine crater) & returned to camp at A.3d Central – Remainder of Bn: moved to new camp at ERIN COTTAGES W.29.d (5½ miles)	

WAR DIARY
or
INTELLIGENCE SUMMARY.
(Erase heading not required.)

Army Form C. 2118.

③

Instructions regarding War Diaries and Intelligence Summaries are contained in F. S. Regs., Part II. and the Staff Manual respectively. Title pages will be prepared in manuscript.

Place	Date	Hour	Summary of Events and Information	Remarks and references to Appendices
ERIN OSTREHOVE	10th	10 am	Owing to continual rain no training was possible.	
	12th	9.0 am	Bn. moved by Route march to MAHON CAPPEL Area USd via ROUGE + LANGUE CROIX (11½ miles)	
			A Coy at Hque in Billets, C, B & D Coys in huts & bivouacs	
MAHON CAPPEL	13.5		Bn. halted – owing to continual rain no training was possible	
USd	16th		Bn. moved to S.t TRENTER BRITZEN (Sheet 27)	
			Transport by route march (10 miles) – Bn. marched to HOTT DEG HEM (4½ miles) thence by tram (metre gauge). Whole Bn. in Nissen huts.	
ST TRENTER BRITZEN	17-18		Platoon training with special attention to No 36 & 37 Rifle Grenade Gun 13th C" Coy, here. Gas range (KG) in morning D Coy, in afternoon - All Lewis Guns + rifles inspected by Bde. Armour. Sergt.	
BOMBES PORT	19th	6.45 pm	Bn. moved in full marching Order + proceeded to LANCASTER STATION 27/F19c – thence	
	28.15 + 3.2		by Train (A & D Coys in first train – B, C & HQrs in second train) and took up position. o. a. fcs. attached Graph A, in Support to 1/KOSB – A Coy relieved 1 Coy 33rd London Bn.(?) MOBE All Coys in new positions by 11.15 Pm. Machine trained Road Coys 27/FZs Cavth were OBL Coops – 74 were transport to Lieut. Colonel Rankin Adjutant + Intelligence Officer moved to a forward Bn. Station in the outskirts of YPRES Tue/16 – Rear Bn. Hqrs moved to POPOSTA/ CASTLE HILL	PSF – HZK A 21a 7.4

Army Form C. 2118.

WAR DIARY
or
INTELLIGENCE SUMMARY.
(Erase heading not required.)

Instructions regarding War Diaries and Intelligence Summaries are contained in F. S. Regs., Part II. and the Staff Manual respectively. Title pages will be prepared in manuscript.

Place	Date	Hour	Summary of Events and Information	Remarks and references to Appendices
YPRES	20th		Major Curtis and the Assistant Adjutant came up from Transport Lines and took charge of the Bn: - Situation quiet - Coy: Comdrs A Coy: Capt Quinn - B. Lieut Norman - C. Capt Dutton D. Capt Hardy	
"	21st		Situation Normal - Coy Officers reconnoitred the country forward of YPRES.	
"	22nd		Situation Normal	
"	23rd		Bn: relieved by I/5th Kings Regt - proceeded by train (light Railway) to ROAD CAMP	
			F25C - All Coys in by 2.0 am	
Road Camp	24th		Coys inspected in Battle Dress - 145th Bn. started Horses, but Kitchens proceeded to UK to Report at PRONTHAM to M.G. Corps	
			Lecture on trading situation to all NCO's	
"	26th		Bn moved up into first line Right Sectr of the Divisional front - Coys.	
			disposition as per map A - Relief completed by 12.45 am (27.9.18) - Coy: Map A A Capt Givers - B Lieut Norman - C. Capt Dutton - D. Capt Hardy	
			Nucleus party d up to Bebbelo in POPERINGHE and Transport Lines & Spare Stores to Folly Camp 287 G1.d - Night quiet.	
YPRES	27th	2.0 am	Situation quiet	

Army Form C. 2118.

WAR DIARY
or
INTELLIGENCE SUMMARY.
(Erase heading not required.)

Instructions regarding War Diaries and Intelligence Summaries are contained in F. S. Regs., Part II. and the Staff Manual respectively. Title pages will be prepared in manuscript.

Place	Date	Hour	Summary of Events and Information	Remarks and references to Appendices
YPRES	27th	10.0 pm	Bn moved up into front line trenches and posts, and at 12 am formed up on the tape which	
			had been laid out earlier in the evening.	
	28"		87th Bde. Order to attack	App: 2
	29"		Bn. Order to attack	" 3
	30"		Account of operations	" 4
			Total Casualties throughout the 3 days operations were:-	
			Killed Wounded Missing.	
			Officers 2 6 nil	
			ORs 94 84 2	
			Killed. 2Lieuts. G.P. Davies & R. Skeen.	
			Wounded Capt Greene, 2Lieut A.R. Norman, 2Lieuts. Huntly, Garner, Griffiths	
			Strength of Bn on 30.9.18 Officers 25 (including M.O & Chaplain)	
			ORs 710	
			W.D. Dickson Capt.	
			Adjt. 2/ Staffs Borderers	

SECRET.   Apendix 1

87th INFANTRY BRIGADE ORDER No 134.

Reference Map,
MERRIS No.1/20.000.   Sept. 1st /18.

1. The gneral line at present held by the Brigde is:-
A.29.a.2.4. - A.23.c.7.0. - A.17.d.5.0. - A.15.a.2.5. -
A.12.a.3.8. - A.12.a.5.3. - S.30.d.2.5.

2. To-morrow (Sept. 2nd) the line will be advanced to the gneral line :-
   ORPHANS REST   (B.25.c.7.9.)   - TANDY FARM (B.20.a.3.5.)
   KELOW CROSSING (B.14.c.9.3.)   - PRESETON FARM (B.8.c.4.6.)

3. For this operation Cyclists will move out in front of the outposts and locate the enemy's positions.
When located the Infantry will be communicated with, and the latter will move forward and deal with the situation.
   One Platoon Cyclists will report to Officer Commanding "D" Company, 2nd South Wales Borderers at 8.20 a.m. at their Headquarters at A.5. Central.
   One platoon Cyclists will report to Officer Commanding "B" Coy. 2nd South Wales Borderersat 9-30 a.m.at their Headquarters at A.11.d.2.8.
   One Platoon Cyclists will report to Offcer Commanding "A" Company 2nd South Wales Borderers at 8.30 a.m. at A.22.a.8.0.

4. Movement on the Brigade front will commence about 8-30 am.

5. Acknowledge.

                                    (SIGNED)

                                            P. CUDDYN
                                                    Captain,
                                Brigade Major, 87th INFANTRY BRIGADE.

Issued thro.Signals
at 11-30 p.m.

   Copies to:-   1. G.O.C.
                  2. B.M.
                  3. S.C.
                  4. Signals
                  5. S.W.B.
                  6. K.O.S.B.
                  7. Bordr Regt.
                  8. T.M.B.
                  9. Lt. Col Brine 15th Bde. R.H.A.
                  10. "A" Coy. 25th M.G.Bn.
                  11. O/C., 15th Corps Cyclists
                  12. 25th Div, G.
                  13. 88th Bde.
                  14. 121st Bde.
                  15. War Diary.
                  16. File.

APPENDIX 1

Headquarters,
    2nd. S.W.B.

Orders for the advance today are as follows:-
Brigde objectives are :-

    NIEPPE in square B.16 to TROIS PIPES
       (Square B.4) both inclusive.

On reaching the above, troops will push forward and occupy our old G.H.Q. line running thro. B.16, B11 and B4.
2nd. SOUTH WALES BORDERERS will move thrir right Company in a N.E. direction, heading for NIEPPE and protecting the flank of their centre Company. 121st. Brigade have orders to take over the present front South of the Grid line A.18. central - B.15. central. The 87th. Brigade are responsible for the capture f NIEPPE. 121st. Brigade have ordered the ROYAL IRISH REGIMENT to concentrate now in A.19 and to move forward at once to take over our line from STEENWERCK (inclusive) southwards.
A Brigade Staff Officer will be sent to get in touch with this Regt. and give them the situation. There need be no delay in the change of plan. The S.W.B. will move with their auxilary troops, i.e. the Cyclists etc. at 8.30 a.m. and will head for the objectives given above. Officer Commanding 2nd. S.W.B. if he thinks advisable, will move part of his riht Company echeloned in rear of his right, in order to protect that flank.
Cyclists objectives are allotted as follows:-
Two platoons NIEPPE
one " TROIS PIPES.
This can be amended by Officer Commanding S.W.B. as the situation develops.
88th. Brigade at present hold the line- DE SEULE NEUVE EGLIS RD. & are already moving forward. S.W.B. will keep in touch with the 88th. Brigde right. In case of a gap the 88th. Brigade intend to fill it with Machine Guns.

                                (Sd). A.H. WATOU   CAPTAIN,
                      BRIGADE MAJOR 87th. INFANTRY BRIGADE.

Sept 2/18.

S E C R E T. Appendix No. 2.

87th INFANTRY BRIGADE ORDER NO 147.

Reference Map
Sheet 28 1/40.000.   27th Sept. /18.

NOTE.   These orders are issued in conjunction with Y.B. Circulars
        already issued. If this order differs in any detail
        already mentioned in the Y.B. Circulars, this order will be
        taken as final.

1. OPERATIONS.
   (a). The 29th Division in conjunction with flank Divisions
        will attack the enemy on the 20th inst.   The Division will
        attack on a two Brigade front.
            87th INFANTRY BRIGADE on the right.
            86th INFANTRY BRIGADE on the left.
        The 166th INFANTRY BRIGADE will be on the right of the
        87th INFANTRY BRIGADE.
   (b). The Boundaries and objectives are as shown on Map "A",
        which has been issued to Battalions.
   (c). The extended Boundaries and objectives are shown on Map "B"
        (issued to Battalions only.)

2. OBJECTIVES.
   (a). The high ground CLAPHAM JUNCTION AND STIRLING CASTLE.

   (b). TOWER HAMLETS. and VELDHOEK.
                The direction of the attack will be , until the
        aproximate GREEN LINE is reached, on a compass bearing of
        102 degrees.
                Each Battalion will detail an Officer with a compass
        to be on each flank to prevent loss of direction during
        the different stages of the advance. This Officer will wear
        some distinctive mark.

3. INFANTRY.
   (a). The 2nd SOUTH WALES BORDERERS, will attack and make good
        the JACKDAW SWITCH PLANK ROAD. The Barrag at this point will
        be on te RED LINE on Map "A".
   (b). The 1st BORDER REGIMENT will leapfrog the 2nd SOUTH WALES
        BORDERERS at this point and will attack the high gound, and
        ain the first aproximate objective marked on MAP "A". If the
        resistance is great on the ridge the 1st KING'S OWN SCOTTISH
        BORDERERS WILL probably be used to aid the 1st BORDER REGT.
   (c). If hostile resistance is easily overcome the 1st KINGS
        OWN SCOTTISH BORDERERS WILL BE used to capture TOWER HAMLETS
        - VELDHOEK.
   (d). The 86th INFANTRY BRIGADE will be moved up through the 87th
        INFANTRY BRIGADE to exploit success.

4. ARTILLERY.
   (a). The Field Artillery barrage opens at ZERO minus Five. on
        the North and South line I.22.b.68.90.- I.16d.68.20.
   (b). At Zero the barrag will lift 100 yds. and advance due east
        at the rate of 100 yards every three minutes up to a line
        1.500 yards East of and parallel to the opening line; thence
        it will advance to the final line at the rate of 100 yards every
        five minutes, with the exception of extra pauses marked on
        barrag map as follows:-
                Total pause of six minutes at line -   500 yards.
                   "   "   " six   "   "   " - 1.000 "
                   "   "   " five   "   "   " - 1.500 "
                   "   "   " 15   "   "   " - 2.500 "

(2).

(c). On arrival at the 2,500 yards line, all guns will fire Thermit for two minutes, and thus indicate long pause at which time, the 1st BORDER REGT. will leapfrog 2nd SOUTH WALES BORDRS.
This indicates that the RED Line has been reached.
<u>Thermit will not be fired on the Final Line.</u>

(d). At Zero plus 156 mins. the Field Artillery Barrage will reach the final (BLACK) Line and will remain on that line until Zero plus 178 mins., when it will cease East of this Line.
The advance to the Green line and beyond the GREEN LINE will be supported by Corps Heavy Artillery.

(e) The total pause at the BLACK LINE will be:

    (1.)   20 Minutes for Field Artillery.
    (11.)   12 Minutes for Heavy Artillery 1st Line.
    (111.)   20 Minutes for Heavy Artillery, 2nd Line.

        Total Halt.---- 52 Minutes.

When the Heavy Artillery Barrage moves from the line Zero plus 210, the Infantry will be able to move to its objective.
From Zero plus 234 the barrage will move forward in lifts of 200 yards every 6 Minutes.

(f). Barrage Maps are issued herewith (Battalions only.).

5. <u>MACHINE GUNS.</u>
Machine Guns will be distributed as follows:-

    4 Guns with 2nd SOUTH WALES BORDERERS.
    4 "   " 1st BORDER REGT.
    8 " In Reserve.

From Zero Hour it is left to the discretion of the Battalion Commanders as to the policy i.e., whether the guns are manhandled or go forward on pack.

6. <u>TRENCH MORTARS.</u>
Will work in accordance with instructions already issued.

7. <u>Royal Engineers.</u>
The policy of work for the R.E. during the attack is the repair of roads. These roads have already been enumerated in Y.B. Circular No.5.

8. <u>REPORTS.</u>
Situation and Progress reports will be sent by Battalions at least every hour to Brigade Report Centre. Any special reports will be sent in in addition.
The Brigade Intelligence Offr. with Bde. Observers, will make arrangements for keeping touch with the situation.
Brigade Report Centre will be at I.16.c.2.7.
The Brigade Flag on a stick will at any time denote the position of the Brigadier.

9. <u>AIRCRAFT.</u>   Attention is called to Y.B. Circular Nos. 3 & 4
It is essential that when flares are called for by contact planes, these be shewn.
The following lights will be fired :-

A RED PARACHUTE LIGHT fired from the Aeroplane means that a hostile attack is impending. The direction in which the light is fired, gives the direction from which the attack is expected.

BELGIAN aeroplanes doing contact work with the BELGIAN Division on our left will fly a flag at the extremity of the lower wing.

(3).

10. PRISONERS.

Attention is drawn to Y.B. Circular No. 10.

Battalions will detail reliable men to search Headquarters, Dugouts etc., for documents. These documents will be forwarded to Brigade Headquarters Report Centre. Documents will be only be taken off Officers and N.C.O.s at time of capture. Men detailed for this work will wear a distinguishing mark.

All prisoners will be sent to Brigade Advanced Headquarters where arrangements will be made to take them back to the Divisional P.O.W. Cage.

11. MEDICAL ARRANGEMENTS.

These remain as detailed in Y.B. Circular No. 6

12. POSITION OF HEADQUARTERS.

Advanced Brigade Headquarters will be at Report Centre.

2nd. SOUTH WALES BORDERERS and 1st. BORDER REGT at I.15.c.2.7
1st. K.O. SCOTTISH BORDERERS ARCADIA HOUSE (I.15.b.65.35)

1st. BOUND.   Brigade Hd. Qrs.   -   RIDGE STREET TUNNELS.
2nd. BOUND.   JACKDAW DUG-OUTS.

13. SYNCHRONISATION OF WATCHES.

A Divisional Staff Officer will visit Brigade Hd.Qrs between 6 p.m. & 7 p.m. on the 27th. for the purpose of synchronising watches.

2nd. SOUTH WALES BORDERERS will send an officer at 7 pm. to Brigade Headquarters for the purpose of synchronising watches.

A Staff Officer of the Brigade will visit the 1st. KINGS OWN SCOTTISH BORDERERS and 1st. BORDER REGIMENT for the above purpose.

14. DUMPS.

Dumps are situated as follows :-
(1). SCHOOL DUMP B.9.d.15.65.
(2). SALLY PORT DUMP - AT SALLY PORT, YPRES RAMPARTS.
(3). I.15.d.80.42.
(4). I.9.a.7.0. - 60 Boxes T.M. Smoke Shell.
(5). I.5.c.1.0.   -   Divisional Dump.

15. LIAISON

Battalions will detail one Sergeant and 5 other Rks. to establish liaision at the following points :-

Northern Boundary
2nd. SOUTH WALES BORDERERS with 1st. LANCASHIRE FUSILIERS.
                I.17.c.7.8.
                I.17.d.5.7.
                J.13.c.15.80

1st. BORDER REGT. with 1st. ROYAL DUBLIN FUSILIERS
                J.13. d.55.55. (CLAPHAM JUNCTION)
                J.14.d.9.6.   & N.E. Corner of
                                INVERNESS COPSE)

Southern Boundary.
2nd. SOUTH WALES BORDERERS with 1st INFANTRY BRIGADE.
                I.92.b.8.2.
                I.24.a.2.3.(N.E. Corner of Maple COPSE)
                I.24.b. 3.3.

(4).

1st. BORDER REGIMENT with 100th. Brigade.
J.10.b.15.10 (30).

16.
SIGNALS.   The Signal denoting that the STIRLING CASTLE - CLAPHAM
JUNCTION Ridge has been captured will be a rocket which on bursting
releases a large flag attached to a parachute.
The 1st. BORDER REGIMENT will be provided with two of these
Rockets as soon as they are received from Division.

ACKNOWLEDGE.

(Sd).   A.H. WATOU   CAPTAIN,
BRIGADE MAJOR 87th. INFANTRY BRIGADE.

Issued through
Signals at.......

To all recipients of
Y.B. Circulars
Nos. 1 - 10.

SECRET.   2nd. SOUTH WALES BORDERERS   Appendix. 3
                            ORDER No. 25.

Ref. Map.
YPRES   1/10.000
GHELUVELT
----

1. In conjunction with other troops, the 87th. Brigade will carry
    out an attack on a date and hour to be notified later.

2. Boundaries and Objectives are shewn on the attached map. The
    2nd. SOUTH WALES BORDERERS will attack up to the Road T.13.c.
    2c.52. - I.24.D.74.24.
    At this point the 1st. BORDER REGT. will pass through and take
    up the final objective — attack up to the final objective
    2/K.O.S.B.'s will be in Reserve.

3. Formation of advance is attached.
    "B" & "D" Coys will attack on the right and left respectively up
    to the Blue Line - "A" & "C" Coys. will then pass through and
    take up to the Road mentioned in Para 2. (Barrage Line shewn in
    Red).
            Bn. Frontage   750 yards
            Coy.   "   375
            Direction of advance 102 deg. magetic.
            Assembly position to Objective   2400 yds.

4. FLANKS.   A left flank detachment will be formed by C Coy.
    and right flank detachment by A Coy.   These detachments will
    consist of one platoon and two Vickers guns each.   They will
    advance along the N.& S. Bn. Boundaries respectively.   They are
    detailed for the protection of flanks both during the advance
    and on reaching the objective.   They are not to be used for any
    other purposes.   They will keep 80 - 100 yds. behind the leading
    troops.   Should troops on the flanks be held up, these detachments
    will take up suitable positions to cover the flanks of advancing
    troops.

5. LIASON. Each Coy. will detail a small party of 1 N.C.O. and 3 men.
    These parties will advance with the flank of the troops of
    Brigades on either flank.   They will report
    progress of neighbouring units to their Coy. Guides at certain
    fixed points to be detailed by Coy. Comdrs.

6. RATIONS. for Y and Z days will be brought upon X/Y night. On Y/Z
    night hot food only will be brought up and will be issued
    to the men at 10.0 p.m.   Hot food containers will be brought
    up by a party from 10 % and will afterwards be dumped at Coy.
    Hd. Qrs.

7. ASSEMBLY.   The Battn. will assemble on Y/Z night in the old
    trenches, in line with the present forward posts from I.16.d.2.3
    to I.22.a.9.3.   A white tape will be laid out by the Battn.
    Intelligence Officer at dusk along this line.   "A" & "B" Coys.
    on the Southern portion & "C" & "D" on the northern.   "B" & "D"
    Coys. will push out covering parties at 11.30 p.m.   Coys. will
    start moving forward to this assembly position at 11.30 p.m.
    ABSOLUTE silence must be maintained throughout and NO smoking will
    be allowed between 11.30 p.m. and ZERO hour.   "B" & "D" Coys.
    will find a guide for "A" & "C" Coys. respectively.
    Reports that Coys. are in position to be sent to Bn. Hd. Qrs. at
    PILL BOX I.15.c.8...

8. BARRAGE.   The Artillery Barrage will commence at Zero on the line
    I.16.d.0.8. - I.22.b.0.3.   It will remain stationary on this
    line till ZERO + 4 when it will commence creeping at the rate
    of 100 yds in 5 minutes.   After every 500 yds. there will be a
    six minute halt - when the barrage reaches the line of JASPER
    DUG-OUTS i.e. immediately in front of the Bn. final objective.
    It will halt for 15 minutes to allow the 1st. BORDER Regt. time
    to pass through. All Coys. will move forward from assembly

                              (1).

(2).

position as soon as the Barrage admits, opening out to correct distances as they move forward.

9. TWO Stokes Guns will accompany the Bn. and will be carried forward on Pack Mules. They will move close up behind "A" Coy. If ammunition is not previously all used they will be prepared to fire on JACKDAW TUNNELS on reaching the Bn. objective in order to assist the 1st. BORDER Regt.

10. INFORMATION. Coys. must send back to B.H.Q. short reports i.e. "Objective reached - all well" immediately they reach their objectives. These will be followed later by rough maps of dispositions and Coy. Hd. qrs.

11. CONSOLIDATION. On reaching Objective Coys. must at once re-organise and take up positions in depth - gain touch with flanks - consolidate.

12. Bn. SCOUTS. A group of 8 scouts will be attached to B & C Coys. They will advance with Coy. Hd. qrs.. Their duties will be to keep in touch with the situation and on reaching objective, 2 will be sent back to B.H.Q. to report. The remainder will keep in touch with 1st. BORDER Regt. after they have passed through, and will keep B.H.Q. informed as objectives are taken.

13. All ranks must be warned that no man is allowed to accompany wounded to the rear or escort prisoners except with a written order from an officer. Battle Police will be detailed from Bn. H.Q. and names of all stragglers will be taken.

14. AID POST. will be at B.H.Q., which at Zero hour will be at I.16.c.2.7 and will later move forward to about I.17.c.7.1.

15. SIGNALLING. As soon as the Blue Line is reached the Signalling Officer will lay a line from B.H.Q. to about I.17.c.7.1. - Communication with Coys. forward of this point will be maintained by wire and Lucas Lamp. A Brigade visual Station will be established on the S.E. corner of YPRES Ramparts.

16. DUMP. A Brigade Dump is being formed at I.9.d.15.05 and will contain :-
        200 boxes   SAA.
        1000   L.G. Magazines (filled)
        200 Tins   Water
        150 Boxes No. 36 Rifle Grenades.

17. AEROPLANES. Flares will be lighted and tin discs shewn by front line troops only when called for by contact planes. The signal for flares is a succession of A's on the Klaxon Horn or the firing of Very Lights.

18. The following will be carried on the men.-
    6 Rifle Grenades per Rifle Grenadier
    2 Bombs per man less L.Gunners and Rifle Grenadiers
    1 Aeroplane flare per 2 men (to be kept in tins)
    2 Tin discs per Section
  170 Rounds per men except L.Gunners and R.Grenadiers
    25 Shovels per Company
    2 S.O.S. Rockets per Platoon.

Copies to   (Signed) T.V.D. DICKINSON Capt.& Adjt.
1-4 A-D Coys.   9 Bn. South Wales Borderers
5 O.C. 1/Border Regt.
6 I.O. T.M.B.
7 I.O. & Signalling Officer.
8 Intelligence Offr. & O/C. Command
9 File.

CONFIDENTIAL.

WAR DIARY

OF

2nd. BATTALION

SOUTH WALES BORDERERS

FROM. 1.10.18.   TO 31.10.18.

VOLUME No. 45.

Army Form C. 2118.

WAR DIARY
or
INTELLIGENCE SUMMARY.
(Erase heading not required.)

October 1918.

Place	Date	Hour	Summary of Events and Information	Remarks and references to Appendices
GHELEVELT	1st		Bn: remained in Camp in Brigade Reserve - Capt: G. Edmond rejoined Bn: took over Command of B Coy. - 2/Lieut P.Davies in Command of A Coy.	
N. of GELUWE	2nd	5.0 pm	Bn: moved up to take over left Sect. of Divisional front line relieving 2/13 R. Fusiliers - dispositions as per Map A - light quiet - Casualties - Major A. 2/Lieut: F.O. Nicholas wounded & 6 O.Rs. Relief complete 11.45 pm.	
	3rd	10.0 pm	Bn: relieved by 26th Bn: R. Fusiliers (41st Divn) - relief complete 11.20 pm. Bn: on relief returned to former lines at GHELEVELT.	
WESTHOEK	4th	2.30 pm	Bn: moved by route march (2 miles) Bn: accommodated in deep dug-outs (Abro Corps) D Coy: in Shelters - 2/Lieut: R. Jones joined Bn: from 5th SWB	
"	6th		Coys re-organised completing deficiencies in Battle Stores etc - Bn: issued with Leather Waistcoats - C.O. I.O. & 1 officer per Coy; reconnoitred route from Camp to DADIZEELE.	
YPRES	7th	2.0 pm	Bn: relieved by 1st Honourable Regt on relief reached to YPRES & went into Billets	
"	8th	9.30 am	Inspection of Billets by Commanding Officer - Coys proceeded with completion of Battle Stores.	
"	9th	10 am	Bn: inspected by G.O.C. 2nd Corps.	

Army Form C. 2118.

WAR DIARY
or
INTELLIGENCE SUMMARY.
(Erase heading not required.)

Instructions regarding War Diaries and Intelligence Summaries are contained in F. S. Regs., Part II. and the Staff Manual respectively. Title pages will be prepared in manuscript.

(1)

Place	Date	Hour	Summary of Events and Information	Remarks and references to Appendices
WESTHOEK	10th	1.30 p.	Bn. moved out of YPRES & returned to WESTHOEK, reoccupying same positions as on the 4th inst.	
KFEGHEM	11th	1.15"	Bn. moved off in two battle order. - Coy. Cmdrs. A. Lieut. Fearby - B. Capt. Esmond - C. Capt. Dutton - D. Capt. Drury.	
		3.15"	Arrived KEIBERG - Hot dinners served.	
		5.0"	Bn. moved off - at about 5.30 pm. Bn. was held up by hostile counter barrage. Bn. bivouac'd overnight. - Dispositions as per Map A.	
	12th	4.0 am	Active hostile shelling around BAD'ZEELE.	
		5-6 pm	C&D Coys employed on cutting gaps in wire along BECQUE and MOORSHEAD FARM. Patrol from B Coy. found LEDEGHEM church unoccupied.	
		11.0 pm	Projectile gas attack - slight hostile shelling in retaliation. Casualties 50 Rs wounded.	
	13th	2.0 am	Situation Quiet	
	"	5.0 am	Patrol from B Coy. reached SWANSTON × ROADS, producing active hostile movement.	
	"	2.30"	Heavy hostile shelling of BAD'ZEELE	

Army Form C. 2118.

WAR DIARY
or
INTELLIGENCE SUMMARY.
(Erase heading not required.)

Instructions regarding War Diaries and Intelligence Summaries are contained in F. S. Regs., Part II. and the Staff Manual respectively. Title pages will be prepared in manuscript.

Place	Date	Hour	Summary of Events and Information	Remarks and references to Appendices
LE DOULIEU	12th	5.0 p.m.	Heavy hostile shelling due to a projected gas attack on our front on the Right Division.	
		6.0 p.m.	Bn: relieved by 9/Royal Fusiliers — on relief Bn: withdrew to jumping off trench immediately west of Bn: H.qrs. (SINNER FARM).	
	14th		See App: 1 " Map A.	App: 1 Map A
	15th		Casualties on 14th 1. O.R. killed & 9 wounded.	
			" 15th 28 O.Rs killed, 130 wounded & 5 missing. Capt. R. Dudey	
			killed & 2/Lieuts H. Jones & G. Smith wounded	
SALINES	16th	12 noon	Bn: relieved by 2/Leinster Regt — on relief Bn: moved back in to billets around G 9 C central.	
	17,18, 19th		Coys re-organised their platoons & made up deficiencies — 2/Lieut Glover took over command of A Coy — 2/Lieut Gitts took over command of D Coy. — 2/Lieuts Green & 2/Lieut King joined Bn: from 2nd Battn — Bn: killed at	
	20th	12.30 p.m.	Bn: moved off at 200x interval in order A-B-C-D-H.qrs — Bn: killed at Camp.	

WAR DIARY
or
INTELLIGENCE SUMMARY.

(Erase heading not required.)

Army Form C. 2118.

(4)

Place	Date	Hour	Summary of Events and Information	Remarks and references to Appendices
STACEGHEM	21st		Hoga 2.8 (Majr) & Lightening farms – all Coys in billets by 6.30 p.m.	
	22nd		Bn: Remained in Billets.	
		10 a.m.	Bn: moved off as Reserve Bn: in Bde. – Started around Area I.26.C and	
			T.33.a where dinners were issued	
		5.0 p.m.	Bn: moved off again to Relieve 1/KOSB & 1/Border Reg' in Front Line – Dispositions	
			See Map B. – Relief complete by 10.20 p.m.	Map B
O.11	23rd	2–3 p	Hostile artillery & MG activity from our Right	
			Hostile artillery vy Active	
		7.0 p.m.	Bn: relieved A–B & D Coys by 10th Queens & C Coy by 36th R. Fusiliers (4th Div).	
			Relief complete 11.20 p.m. Bn: on relief withdrew to STEENBRUGGE in fields.	
			Account of operations from 20/23rd Oct: attached. Casualties 1 OR killed 1 wounded. O/fs, 2	
STEENBRUGGE	24th		Bn: checked Battle Stores. 2/Lieuts Gloag & McPherson proceeded on leave. Lieut T.N. Wheldon	
	25th		Bn: bathed – All outstanding kit is such as Burials, Battle Police etc rejoined from Team.	
			rejoined Bn: Lieut-Col Raikes proceeded on heart. 2/Lieuts Major & T.R. Jones rejoined	
	26th		Bn: parade 9.30 a.m. 2/Lieut Pritchard Hamtramp went on Course	
	27th	7 a.m.	Bn: moved by hand Route to MOUSCRON Area (9 miles) – all Bn: in billets.	

Army Form C. 2118.

WAR DIARY
or
INTELLIGENCE SUMMARY.
(Erase heading not required.)

Instructions regarding War Diaries and Intelligence Summaries are contained in F. S. Regs., Part II. and the Staff Manual respectively. Title pages will be prepared in manuscript.

Place	Date	Hour	Summary of Events and Information	Remarks and references to Appendices
	28th	10.A.M	Bn: moved by route march to ST: ANDRE area (10 miles) All Bn: in billets. 2/Lt: T.R. JONES to Hospital.	
	29th	11 A.m	Bn: parade. G.O.C. addressed Bn: + expressed his appreciation for the good work done in recent operations. Bn:	
			Practice Ceremonial parade. Capt: + Adjt: MWR. Dickinson proceeded on leave. Lt: A.M. Threlkeld, as Adjt: 2.30 p.m.} 2 Lt: Officers attended lecture by G.O.C.	
	30th	11.45.	Bn: Practice Ceremonial parade. Major: A.E. CROWDER rejoined from Hospital. Draft 32 O.R's arrived.	
	31st	10. Am	Brigade Ceremonial parade. Draft 37 O.R's arrived. 2/Lt: C. LEWIS rejoined from leave.	
	31st		Strength of Bn: Officers 45.	
			O.R's 635.	Appx: 3.
			Nominal roll of Officers	

John Longbourne Major.
Commanding 7th Bn: Loyal North Lancs Regt.

Account of Operations 14th – 16th Oct 1917.   ①

1. In conjunction with 9th Div on left and 36th Div on right, the 29th Division attacked at 5:30 am. 88th Bde on right 86th Bde on left 87th Bde in Reserve.
Boundaries & Objectives are shown on attached map.

2. On night 13/14th the Battn was relieved in the front line at Ledgeham by Roy. Irish Fusiliers & moved back to a line of old German trenches in K 5.d. & K.11.c. Hot food, rations & water were issued to the men & all coys were complete & in position by 1.30 am. Bn H.Q. remained at K.12.a 5.8. Pack animals with S.A.A, officers' mess, Sig. equipment & 5 officer chargers came up to Pctanjibrug.
At 4.25 am Enemy opened fairly heavy shelling round Dadizeele & K 11 & 12
At 5.32 am our barrage opened, hostile retaliation was insignificant.
At 7.0 am 87th Bde moved forward. 1/Border Regt in front and S.W.Borderers & 1/R.S. B ? in rear on left & right respectively. The Battn

moved up in the following order. Scouts –
C. D. & B. platoons at 100ˣ interval distance
On passing Zedeghem Station, the mist &
smoke from the barrage was so thick that
it was impossible to see 100 yards. It was
obvious that leading troops must have
got somewhat disorganised & that & howitzer
M.Guns could be heard apparently about
Sovereign Wood & Moorseele.
27ᵗ Bⁿ halted Bⁿ in diamond formation
till situation was cleared up. During the
afternoon it was clear that advanced troops
had reached about G.9 & 14 & Brigade
moved forward hastily about dark. The
Battⁿ went into billets about L.11.a.
Officers & men were very tired, & it was
arranged that everyone should get to bed
as early as possible & not be worried for
orders or rations till as late as possible
the following morning.
Orders were received that 27ᵗ Bⁿ would
continue the attack at 9 am on 16ᵗ
Sp. Bⁿ left Battⁿ Hqrs on n/15/16.
Orders for attack are attached. The sy. Hqrs

being the original Div objective i.e. Red
line in G.12.
At 5.0 am all men were woken up. Hot food
Rations issued & scheme of attack explained to
all ranks.
At 7.15 Bn commenced to move to assembly
position well opened out into lines & waves.
Assembly position was G.7.b.3.3 — G.8.d.3.6
As Bn arrived about 300x short of this line
the Enemy opened the advance & put forth fairly
heavy machine gun fire & Trench Mortars
but no casualties were caused.
The barrage opened very accurately & there
was a brief short ebbing. Coys. moved off at
once & no further news came through
for 2 or 3 hours except what could be gathered
from wounded.
On the left the 9th Division instead of attacking level
with us on the flank, attacked Steenbeck & Bois
d'Steile from the North. This left our left flank
exposed during the advance, hostile M.Gs. near
Steenbeck fired on the rear of D & B Coys after
they had passed & in consequence of
hostile fire from Bois d'Steile D Coy had

to clear the South Eastern portion of the wood
& be contained by the comparatively insignificant parties of the enemy. The 9th & 10th troops
arrived later. Owing to this a gap occurred
between C & D Coys in the front line
& B Coy gradually moved up till all
were in the front line.

The post bn arrived on the objective
Inghelmunster — Courtrai Railway at
11.20 am, with right of C Coy at Q 18 b
1.5 & Left of D Coy at Q 13 b 55.30 i.e
on a front of 850x.

Patrols were pushed forward but Coys did
not advance beyond the line.

Throughout the advance the Division on the
right made slow progress through the
villages of Gulleghem & Heule & hostile M.Gun
fire was heavy on their flank.

During the attack our MG Regt missing with
our own barrage & the enemy also kept
his Artillery barrage almost mixed up with
ours. Consequently casualties were heavy from
shell fire. At certain places, stray hostile
M.Gunners put up a stiff defence but were

run at that last moment.
At 3.20 pm D & C Coys pushed out an
outpost line roughly from H.7.b.40.70
to H.13.a.85.70 + a patrol was sent across
to Cuerne. Meanwhile the 9th Div formed
a Reserve Brigade through which got forward
almost to Steenbeek.
At 4.3 pm the 1/KOSB passed through
& made good the bridges at H.14.b.30.7 –
H.14.B.15.25 – H.15.c.25.75. and
later occupied the bridge at H.16.a.6.0
pushing out posts from H.16 central to
H.21 central.
B.H.Q was established at G.10.d.3.3 +
Coys moved into billets except for outpost
piquets.
From about 2.0 pm onwards there was
practically no shells & no opposition except
from the Courtrai side.
On 16th the Bn was relieved by 2nd Leicesters
& moved back to vicinity of H.Q central

17
10
10   G T Rainier Major
              Commdg 1/ South Borders

Narrative of events from 20th – 2[illegible] October 1918

(2)

1. Bn received orders to be ready to move at half an hours notice from 8.0 a.m. on 20th. 22nd Bn [illegible] crossed the Lys at 8.0 a.m. & the remaining
26 Bn was in support ready to move through
1 & 7th Bn in Reserve
At 12.30 pm the Bn moved off in following
order A. B. C. D. HQ. 6 pack animals with
SAA. 6 pack with Stokes 1 pack Signalling
1 pack officers mess. Lg Gun limbers moved
with Coys Cookers, Mess Cart SAA limbers
~~Bomb~~ Grenade Limber behind the Battn.
The Battn moved via G.9.b – G10 central –
G.6. c & D to cross Rds H.8.b.5.0.
At about 4.0 pm Bn again ~~[illegible]~~ moved forward
& after much delay owing to traffic at Lys
bridge billeted in the area H23 & H29
Bn HQ at H29 a 1 9
21st No move
22nd Bn moved at 10.0 am to area I 26 b &
32 b. in reserve to 1/Border Regt & 1/KOSB
who attacked at 9.0 am. During the day
the Bn waited in this area ready to move at
short notice. Men had dinners & [illegible]
ammunition & following days rations were
issued to the men. At 5.30 pm the
Bn moved forward & took over the
front line from 1/Border Regt & 1/KOSB

3 Coys in front line each with one platoon forward & one in support, 1 Coy in Reserve. Dispositions shown on attached sketch.

Enemy MG's active on the Right Coy front with M Guns throughout the night but quiet on other Coy fronts. Relief took place without incident. Roads were shelled during the night but our front line was not shelled.

23. Bn remained in Outposts — Enemy shelled the front line on Right & Centre Coy fronts heavily for 3 hours during the afternoon & intermittently at other times.

After dark the Bn was relieved as follows:—

A B — D Coys + H.Q by 10th Queens
C Coy by 2 Coys 26th R Fusiliers

Relief complete by 12 midnight.
Bn moved back to billets in vicinity of Steenbrugge.

24/10/18

G. Parker ? Colonel
Comdg ? Bn ?

APPENDIX 3.

NOMINAL ROLL OF OFFICERS 31.10.18

Major	A.B.	Cowburn	M.C.	Commanding.
Capt.	A.E.	Crowder	M.C.	Commanding "A" Coy.
"	G.	Esmond	M.C.	" "B" " .
"	C.F.	Dutton	M.C.	" "C" " .
2/Lt.	J.E.A.	Gibbs		" "D" " .
"	A.W.	Hardwick		Actg. Adjutant
"	B.G.	Davies		
"	J.W.	Mayou		
"	T.J.	Williams		
"	X.	Xxxxxx		
"	T.C.R.	Bromham		
"	F.W.	Hardy		
"	C.J.	Hardy		
"	P.B.	King		
Lt.	G.J.	Greer		
2/Lt.	C.	Lewis		
Lt.	T.R.	Williams		Transport Officer.
"	T.H.	Waldren	M.C.	Quartermaster.
Capt.		Thompson (R.A.M.C.)		Medical Officer.
Rev.	A.K.	Swallow MC(A.C.D.)		Chaplain

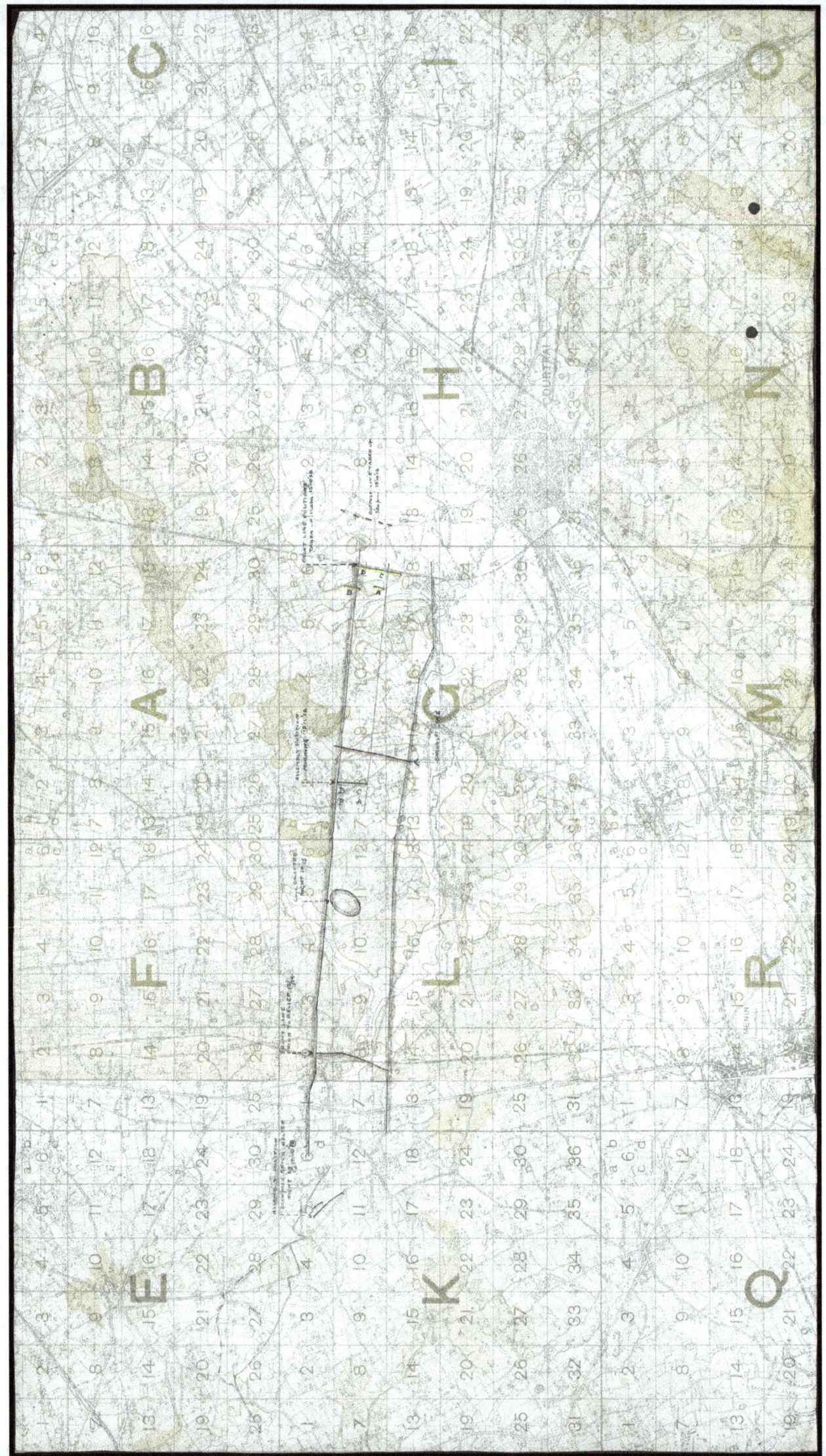

Math

2nd Battn South Wales Borderers

= WAR DIARY =

NOVEMBER 1918.

Army Form C. 2118.

WAR DIARY
or
INTELLIGENCE SUMMARY.
(Erase heading not required.)

November 1918.

Place	Date 1918 Nov:	Hour	Summary of Events and Information	Remarks and references to Appendices
ST. ANDRE.	1st	11-45	Bn: Pastor's Command parade. Transport inspected by Lt: Miller. XV Corps Horsemaster. 2.30 p.m. Inspection Yet: Personnel by Col: Miller.	
	2nd	M.O.	Brigade ceremonial parade - inspection by G.O.C. XV Corps.	
	4th	11.30	Bn: Transport inspection by Lt: Brig.t.t. Furness. 29th Div: Train. Coy.S: Training.	
	5th		— do —	
			by Major Bowland R.W.S. 29th Div:	
	6th		Coy.S: Training. — do —	
TOURCOING.	7th	9.15	Bn: moved by route march to Tourcoing. Bn: in Billets. Capt: A.E.CROWDER to XV Corps from Gun School.	
			2/Lt: C.LEWIS - takes over command "A" Coy. 2/Lt: T.J. WILLIAMS proceeded on special leave.	
	8th	8.30	87 Infy. Bde: moved into support area. Bn: moved by route march to GEUZENHOEK AREA. (Th. A. 2.12) Sh: 29. Bn: in Barns + Billets.	
	9th	1.45	87 Infy. Bde: moved forward. Bn: moved at 1 hour notice to area at O. 32.d. & P. 5. 8.10. Bn: in Barns + Billets.	
	10th	8.30	Bn: moved forward to LILLOA in area E.19. C.3.0. (Nr. 37). 2/Lt: TEGIBBS - proceeding to PARIS PLAGE - for rest.	
			2/Lt: C.J.HARDY took over command of "D" Coy. tentegrant	
	11th	8.30	Bn: assembled at MONTBERNY FARM (starting point) to act as Mourner Guard to 87 Bde: which were ordered to	
			forced into ST. SAUVEUR, area. More orders cancelled owing to signing of ARMISTICE. Bn:	
			returned to Billets. 7. p.m. R.H.Q. moved to E. 26.d.9 w. (Nr. 37.) 2/Lt: T.E.GIBBS returned as duty.	
	12th	M.O.	Bn: moved by route march to F.B.d.3.0. (Sh. 37) Bn: in Barns + Billets. Capt: T.Hardy RAM ops returned from Lake G. Hampshire returned to 87th Fd. Ambulance.	
		1-15	"A" + "C" Coys on working parties, others to make our area.	
	13th	1-0	7 Veterans "B" Coy: + Lt: G.S. Jenkins on R.E. work - in area. M.S. A.M. Clover - N.C. McPherson rejoined	
			rejoined from leave.	

WAR DIARY
-or-
INTELLIGENCE SUMMARY.
(Erase heading not required.)

Army Form C. 2118.

Instructions regarding War Diaries and Intelligence Summaries are contained in F. S. Regs., Part II. and the Staff Manual respectively. Title pages will be prepared in manuscript.

Place	Date	Hour	Summary of Events and Information	Remarks and references to Appendices
		April		
	14/15/(4.S.25		Bn. marched by route march to GHOY. (C.3 central – Sh.36) 7/Lt. Ar. Glover took over command "A" Coy.	
GHOY.	15th		Lt. Col. G.T. Raikes. D.S.O. rejoined from leave.	
			Lt. Col. G.T. RAIKES, takes over command of Bn. The Commander Offr. returned to old Offr. 2nd Lt. + M.C.O.	
			7/Lt. M. Hughes rejoined from leave. Capt. + Adjt. Lt. A.T. Dickinson rejoined from leave.	
	16th	11.30	R.S.M's drill parade. Commanding Officer inspected billets.	
ORLIGNIES	17th	7.0"	Bn. marched to ORLIGNIES – 5 miles – All Coys + HQrs in billets.	
STEENKERQUE	18th	"	" " STEENKERQUE – 12½ " – " "	
"	19th	11.30	R.S.M's parade	
"	20th	12.15p	G.O.C. 27" Bgde presented Army + Divisional Cards to the Bn. Whole Bn. paraded + got clean clothing	
YPRES	21st	8.20	Bn. marched to YPRES – 13½ miles. All Coys in billets. Great Civic Reception in Square. Bn. Living 3 sides of the Square. Burgomaster delivered an address replied to by G.O.C. "O" Bde.	
"	23rd		One Officer + 16 other rank part in the procession to the entry of King Albert into BRUSSELS.	
BOUSVAL	25th	9am	Bn. marched to BOUSVAL – 10 miles. All Bn. in billets.	

WAR DIARY or INTELLIGENCE SUMMARY.

Army Form C. 2118.

(Erase heading not required.)

Place	Date	Hour	Summary of Events and Information	Remarks and references to Appendices
ERNAGE	24"	9.0am	Bn. formed advance guard to Bde. & marched to ERNAGE - 10 miles. All Bn. in Billets.	
GRAND LEEZ	25"	10.30.	Bn. marched to GRAND LEEZ - 7 miles. All Bn. in billets. Following Officers joined Bn. from tour:- 2/Lieut. Ian Bougton, T. Davies, St. John, R. Yeatt. & 60 hourly N.C.Os/men.	
			2/Lieut and Capt Brown A. Coy. Billeted at LFS. CINQ ETOILES.	
"	26.		R.S.M's parade 11.30 a.m. Clean clothing issued. Following Officers joined from the Base. 2/Lieuts. Pn. Priston & R.S. Dunford	
FERVILLE ~~GOSSELIES~~	27"	9.0am	Bn. marched to FERVILLE - 14 miles - dinners en route. Guard of 90O.S.R that FERVILLE on enemy material.	
STREE	28"	9.0am	Bn. " STREE forming advance guard to Bde - 17 miles. Bn. in billets - dinners en route	
COMBLAIN-AU-PONT	29"	"	" " COMBLAIN-AU-PONT - 14 miles - dinners en route. 2/Lt. O'Rourke left behind unable to march owing to bad foots - Bn. in billets.	
WINAMPLANCHE	30"		Bn. marched to WINAMPLANCHE 14 miles - Bad streets - greatcoats dumped and Bn. in charge of 2 men.	

Strength of Bn. on 30" Nov. 30 Officers 558 O.Ranks

2/12/18

G.T. Raikes Lieut/Colonel
Comdg 2/Welch Regiment

LIST OF OFFICERS.

Lieut. Col.	G.T.	Raikes	D.S.O.	Commanding.
Major	L.B.	Cowburn	M.C.	2/1/Command.
Captain	W.V.D.	Dickinson	M.C.	Adjutant.
Captain	A.E.E.	Whitworth	M.C.	87th Brigade.
"	C.F.	Dutton	M.C.	Conndg. "C" Coy.
"	G.	Esmond	M.C.	" "B" ".
"	A.N.	Glover	M.C.	" "A" ".
"	J.E.A.	Gibbs		" "D" ".
Lieut.	T.R.	Williams		Transport.
"	W.G.	Jones		"B" Coy.
"	G.J.	Greer		"C" Coy.
"	~~A.E.~~	~~Crowder~~	~~M.C.~~	~~G.I., I.G. School, XV Corps.~~
2/Lieut.	P.B.	King		"D" Coy.
"	A.W.	Hardwick		A/Adjutant.
"	B.G.	Davies		Intell. Officer.
"	J.W.	Mayou	M.C.	"A" Coy.
"	~~T.J.~~	~~Williams~~		~~"A"~~ "
"	M.	Hughes		"A" "
"	C.	Lewis		"A" "
"	T.C.R.	Bromham		"B"
"	N.C.	McPherson		"B"
"	F.W.	Hardy	M.C.	"C"
"	~~C.J.~~	~~Hardy~~	~~M.C.~~	~~"D"~~
"	A.J.	Pritchard	M.C.	M.E. "D"
"	W.N.	Douglas		~~KEX~~ ~~"D"~~ "C"
"	C.H.J.	Brown		"D"
"	~~W.T.~~	~~Jones~~		~~"D"~~
" "	J.	Davies		"B"
"	D.T.	Johns		"C"
"	W.J.	Millard		"B"
"	C.W.	Worsley		"A"
"	R.	Yorath		"C"
"	R.G.	Dunsford		"D"
"	A.B.	Priston		"B"
Lieut. and Q.Mr.	T.H.	Waldren	M.C.	

November 30th/18.

29th Div.
87th Bde.

WAR DIARY

2nd BATTN. SOUTH WALES BORDERERS.

DECEMBER

1918

Army Form C. 2118.

WAR DIARY
or
INTELLIGENCE SUMMARY.
(Erase heading not required.)

December 1918

Instructions regarding War Diaries and Intelligence
Summaries are contained in F.S. Regs., Part II.
and the Staff Manual respectively. Title pages
will be prepared in manuscript.

Place	Date	Hour	Summary of Events and Information	Remarks and references to Appendices
STAVELOT	1st	9.30a	Bn. marched to STAVELOT, 14 miles, via SPA. Dinner at FRANCORCHAMPS	
"	2 & 3		Bn. trained in field - Coys. have at disposal of Coy. Cmdrs. for cleaning up etc. - 4 Stretchers in these two days repaired 100 pairs of boots.	
NIDRUM	4th	9.30a	Bn. marched to NIDRUM - 16 miles. Passing en route for Dinner the Belgian - German frontier Was crossed at 10.20 am Trevis Yeges Regt. band. - Very cold.	
MUTZENICH	5th	"	Bn. marched to MUTZENICH - 14 miles. Bad billets. Burgomaster arrested for having a dump of Rifles Ant. placed soon afterwards. Dinner en route	
NIDEGGEN	6th	"	Bn: marched to NIDEGGEN 15 miles - good billets. Dinner en route. 2/Lieut Scrimgeour	
VETTWEISS	7th	10.30	" " VETTWEISS 7 " " " 2/Lieut. Williams TS	
			+ 3 ORs rejoined from leave.	
KIERDORF	8th	9.	Bn: marched to KIERDORF 12½ miles	
KÖLN.	9th	7.30.	" " " KÖLN. 12½ miles. Whole Bn: billeted in Large School	
(Suburb of) COLOGNE	10th		AD Corps proceeded into COLOGNE and took on duties of guarding the WHARF, RAILWAY & ordinary Traffic bridges. Remainder of Bn: engaged on cleaning up. A. B & Hqrs had baths.	
	11th		Corps engaged on cleaning up - New clothing drawn from DADOS.	

Army Form C. 2118.

WAR DIARY
or
INTELLIGENCE SUMMARY.
(Erase heading not required.)

Instructions regarding War Diaries and Intelligence Summaries are contained in F. S. Regs., Part II. and the Staff Manual respectively. Title pages will be prepared in manuscript.

Place	Date	Hour	Summary of Events and Information	Remarks and references to Appendices
COLOGNE	12"		Ord. Corps athuwed Hd./and remainder of Bn.	
	13"	9.30	Bn: marched to BERG GLADBACH 12 1/2 miles via the Slubs of COLOGNE – marched	
			Past the II Corps Commander Saluting. From Western end of HOHENZOLLERN BRIDGE	
BERG	14"		Bn. in good billets.	
GLADBACH (PAARCHEID)	15"	9 a.m.	Bn: marched to BURSCHEID 9 miles. Good billets.	
BLEIDING	16"	9 a.m.	" " PALEIDING HAUSEN 11 miles. C Coy. did advance Guard to Bn.	
HAUSEN	17"		Bad billets. Lieut. Hardwick v Mayor left for UK in charge of Colour Party proceeding to Capt. Bowen	
"	18"		Bn: furnished a daily guard at PREYERS 15'+ 12 m.n.	
"	19"		A HQ v HQrs. moved into better billets on REMSCHEID – ERINGHAUSEN Road.	
"	20"		Whole Bn: tallied treated bath clean clothing.	
"	21"		Lady of Corsals Day + Draft of 63 arrived from 29th Div. Brigton Camp – Capt. A.E. Corder	
			and 2/Lieut. G. Quinrood joined. Latter on 1st appointment.	
"	23"		Battalion Educational Classes Started under Capt. A.E. Corder.	
"	24–28"		Educational classes – Drill parades – Kit Inspection	
BURSCHEID	29"		Bn: marched from REMSCHEID – 14 miles.	

Army Form C. 2118.

WAR DIARY
or
INTELLIGENCE SUMMARY.

(Erase heading not required.)

December 1918 (3)

Place	Date	Hour	Summary of Events and Information	Remarks and references to Appendices
BURCHID	30 + 31		Educational Training – Brig parade. Numbers demobilized up to including 31st Dec. 87. Strength of Bde. on 31/12/18. 30 officers, 624 O.Rs. List of officers attached.	

R. Rochut
Lieut-Colonel
Comdg. 97 Swabian Brigade

2nd South Wales Borderers

Rank	Name	Award
Lt. Colonel	G. T. Raikes	D.S.O
Major	A. B. Cowburn	M.C.
Captain	W. R. D. Dickinson	M.C.
"	C. F. Dutton	M.C.
"	E. A. Crowder	M.C.
"	G. Esmond	M.C.
"	A. N. Glover	M.C.
"	J. E. A. Gibbs	
Lieut.	G. J. Greer	
"	W. G. Jones	
"	J. H. Waldren	M.C
"	J. R. Williams	
2/Lt.	B. G. Davies	
"	F. J. Williams	
"	M. Hughes	
"	C. Lewis	
"	R. G. Grimwood	
"	N. C. McPherson	
"	J. Davies	
"	W. J. Millard	
"	A. P. Priston	
"	F. W. Hardy	M.C.
"	W. N. Douglas	
"	D. J. Johns	
"	R. Gorath	
"	P. B. King	
"	A. J. Pritchard	M.C.
"	C. H. J. Brown	
"	W. J. Jones	
"	R. S. Dunsford	

APPENDIX........

2nd. SOUTH WALES BORDERERS.

```
Lieut. Colonel.      G.T. Raikes        D.S.O.
Major.               A.B. Cowburn       M.C.
Captain.         W.V.D. Dickinson       M.C.
    "                A.N. Gaover        M.C.
    "                C.F. Dutton        M.C.
Lieut.               G.J. Greer
2/Lieut.             N.C. McPherson
    "                  J. Davies.
    "                T.J. Williams
    "                  M. Hughes
    "                R.G. Grimwood
    "              T.C.R. Bromham       M.C.
    "                W.J. Millard
    "                A.V. Priston
    "                D.T. Johns
    "                C.J. Hardy         M.C.
    "                A.J. Pritchard     M.C.
    "              C.H.J. Brown
    "                R.S. Dunsford
    "                C.W. Worsley
```

OTHER RANKS.

477.

31/1/19

SOUTHERN (LATE 29TH) DIVN
87TH INFY BDE

2ND BN STH WALES BORDERERS
JAN - APR 1919

To O.I.C.

CONFIDENTIAL.

WAR DIARY

OF THE

2nd. BATTN.,

SOUTH WALES BORDERERS.

FROM 1919 TO

1st January — 31st January.

VOLUME NO. 16.

Army Form C. 2118.

WAR DIARY
or
INTELLIGENCE SUMMARY.
(Erase heading not required.)

Place	Date	Hour	Summary of Events and Information	Remarks and references to Appendices
BURSCHIED	1919 Jan 1			
		2.15	Lt. G.F. Bound MC & 11th Batt. instructing classes. Lt. C.F. Stocks MC. returns from leave.	
			Lt. Bicks to 11th Doultrington (Nurses)	
			Lt. O'Rourke to 11th " " " Colour Party. ended the 11th Batt. concerts nights for	
			dropper M.O. course introduction from 11th. Lt. T.R. Jones. approved from Hospital.	
		6 pm	Commanding Officer returned to the Mess. no Soldiers	
		7 pm	Rev Baxter (temporary) farewell dinner arranged by the M.W. Thomson. Lt. G.F. Bowes	
			Commission. pt. farewell for recipients by Rev. Commissioner to 11th M.O. farewell to Capt. C.E. Anthony	
			Certificate MC. MC. Ransome to A.I.C. (January MC. Lt. Thompson etc. to Brittany MC. to Thursday MC.	
			the D.C.M. introduced to Dr. Mills. introduce to 16. O.R.s. letters and parcels introduced. Major H.S. Corkhead	
			proceeds to 11th on leave.	
		9 am	Commanding Officer to Brigade. Conference into Army Commander.	
		10 pm	R.S.M. Lying listeners to Bn. on sheeting of next Regt." letters to Redwig House & recipitation by T.P.R.	
			Lt. C.F. Dutton MC. proceeds on leave. Lt. A.L. Price takes over command "C" Coy.	
11		4.15	Lt. O.B. King & 245 O.R.s. to 11th demobilisation. Lt. W.M. Douglas on leave & Repatriation.	
12			the McNulty proceeds draft consisting of near Mr.	
13		10 am	Divisional Baxter RN. lectured to Bn. on "In marked Vr Mr. Lt. J.H. Matthew. MC. proceeds on leave MK.	
				Lt. T.R. Williams takes over sittler Q.M.

Army Form C. 2118.

WAR DIARY
or
INTELLIGENCE SUMMARY.
(Erase heading not required.)

Instructions regarding War Diaries and Intelligence Summaries are contained in F. S. Regs., Part II. and the Staff Manual respectively. Title pages will be prepared in manuscript.

Place	Date	Hour	Summary of Events and Information	Remarks and references to Appendices
BURSCHIED	Jan 16	1.15 pm	1919. Mr: J.R. Jones & R. Jenkin to UK demobilization.	
	" 16		Capt: McLancter M.O. proceeded leave to UK.	
	" 19		Major J.C. A Tittley proceeded leave to UK. H/Capt. H. G. Ashcroft taken over Command D/Coy. of 17/ft force proceeded on leave to UK.	
	" 20		Capt: E.G.M. Kirwood M.C. (att. 29ᵗʰ Div) T/UK. demobilization.	
	" 21		Mr: B.S.P. Davies proceeded UK. soft demobilizing leave.	
	" 22		Burial of Offr. T.O.R. maker refused cut with her. Buy observed on a Transport. H/t T.R. Brechan M.C. returned from leave.	
	" 25	10.30	Mr: Mortomer Smith Returned to Br. on "Manoeuvres" to Ireland dated 22/1/19.	
	" 26		Lieut. 109 Jones with 1/t Hopgood M.C. proceeded to UK soft demobg. leave. H/t T.R. Brechan M.C. also took command "B" Coy.	
	" 27	10.30	Mr: T.P. Young returned to Br. on "Finding & Joining Plantain". Lieut T. Williams to UK demobilizaton soft demobng leave. Mr. Mcindoe M.C. rejoined from leave. Mr. Davies taken over transport. H/t R.C. McKenzie taken over utrsa OM.	
	28ᵗʰ		Lieut Rw Hardrisk proceeded on leave. – 1st Bn. bathed also exchange of clean clothes.	
	29ᵗʰ	9am	Pam Rode march – 14 kilos – 1st Bn Colours to UK for armistirgation	

Army Form C. 2118.

WAR DIARY
or
INTELLIGENCE SUMMARY. (3)
(Erase heading not required.)

Instructions regarding War Diaries and Intelligence Summaries are contained in F. S. Regs., Part II. and the Staff Manual respectively. Title pages will be prepared in manuscript.

Place	Date	Hour	Summary of Events and Information	Remarks and references to Appendices
BURSCHEID	30th	9	Army official photographer visited Bn. Took group Bn. photographed on parade with Colours (uncased) - Capt. C.F. Battin no proceed on leave to UK.	
	31st		Strength of Bn. 20 officers + 477 ors. (Roll attached) Elementary Education Classes have been held daily throughout the month — average daily attendance 60.	

W Parsons Lieut. Colonel
Cmdg. 9/Snake Borderers

WAR DIARY
or
INTELLIGENCE SUMMARY.
(Erase heading not required.)

Army Form C. 2118.

Instructions regarding War Diaries and Intelligence Summaries are contained in F. S. Regs., Part II. and the Staff Manual respectively. Title pages will be prepared in manuscript.

Place	Date	Hour	Summary of Events and Information	Remarks and references to Appendices
			BAR to M.C.	
			Capt. (A/Major) D.H.S. SOMERVILLE M.C.	
			Lieut. (A/Capt.) C. MUMFORD. M.C.	
			The Military Cross.	
			Lieut. E.S.W. COOKE.	
			The Military Medal	
			No. 9346 Sgt. KEY.A.R. 18905 Cpl. RICHARDS.T.	
			25148 C/Shan.T. 19342 L/Cpl. AKERMAN.T.	
			25902 L/Cpl. KNIGHT.A. 29143 Pte TAYLOR.E.C.	
			40760 Pte STARR.H.	

CONFIDENTIAL.

WAR DIARY

OF

2nd. BATTALION

SOUTH WALES BORDERERS

FROM 1.2.19 TO 28.2.19

VOLUME No—

Army Form C. 2118.

WAR DIARY
INTELLIGENCE SUMMARY.
(Erase heading not required.)

February 1919

Instructions regarding War Diaries and Intelligence Summaries are contained in F. S. Regs., Part II. and the Staff Manual respectively. Title pages will be prepared in manuscript.

Place	Date	Hour	Summary of Events and Information	Remarks and references to Appendices
BURSCHEID	3rd		Capt G. Bernard MC rejoined Bn. from leave to U.K.	
	4th		Whole Bn. bathed & reissued with clean clothes.	
	5th		Bn. route march – 14 kilos. Lecture on "Round the World in No Time" by "M".	
			Hatfield in the Cinema Hall at 2.30 pm.	
	8th		2/Lieut. A.N. Douglas rejoined Bn. from Agricultural Course at BONN.	
	9th		2/Lieut. R.G. Grinrod proceeded to COLOGNE on Equitation Course. Capt Gitts rejoined	
			Bn. from leave to U.K.	
	10th		Lt Col Glasbrook relinquished command of the Bn.	
			Lt. Major A.B. Cockburn M.C. took over command of the Bn.	
			Capt Goodall MC proceeded on 14 days leave to UK	
	11th		Whole Bn. bathed & reissued with clean clothes. Capt W.O. Dishworth proceeded to take over	
			duties of Asst. Adjutant to Deputy Adjt. after leaving the duties of Adjutant.	
	12th		Bn. route march 12 kilos. Capt C.F. Potts M.C. proceeded to U.K. for Demobilization.	
	13th		2/Lieut Ainslie was rejoined Bn. from leave to U.K.	
			Lecture in the Hotel Esplanade by Lieut Bowman on the Cinema Hall at 3 pm.	
	14th		Coll. Goodin M.C. proceeded to U.K. Accidentally attended unofficial meeting.	
			Lieut Worseley proceeded to U.K. on two months leave pending reopening the Bn.	

Army Form C. 2118.

②

WAR DIARY
or
INTELLIGENCE SUMMARY. February 1919

(Erase heading not required.)

Instructions regarding War Diaries and Intelligence Summaries are contained in F. S. Regs., Part II. and the Staff Manual respectively. Title pages will be prepared in manuscript.

Place	Date	Hour	Summary of Events and Information	Remarks and references to Appendices
BORGGHEM	15th		First to arrive overseas.	
	16th		2 Lieut B.G Davies rejoined the Bn. from leave to U.K.	
	16th		Col Rhodes D.S.O. visited the Bn.	
	17th		Lieut B.G Davies proceeded to BERG GLADBACH in charge of lorries for woollen vest.	
	18th		The whole Bn. bathed and issued with clean clothes.	
			Lecture by Lt Col. Stephens D.S.O. to all officers in Cinema at Bornheim at 11.30 a.m.	
	19th		Bn. route march 12 Kilos. 5.15 p.m. Bn. whist drive followed by concert by	
			Bn. concert party — THE FIVE FRATERNISERS	
	20th		2 Lieut B.G Davies returned from BERG GLADBACH	
	21st		2 Lieut Harwood returned from leave to U.K. and took over command	
			of C Coy.	
	21st		1st XV Soccer match V 1st R.S.F. lost 1 – 3.	
	22nd		Col Rhodes rejoined Bn from 86th Bde.	
	23rd 24th		Maj P Parker O.B.E. proceeded to U.K. on leave.	
	25th		The whole Bn. bathed and was issued with a clean change.	
	26th		Rugby XV visited 1st Bn at EVSKIRCHEN and won 14 – 3. Bn Route march 10 Kilos.	

Army Form C. 2118.

WAR DIARY
or
INTELLIGENCE SUMMARY. February 1919

(Erase heading not required.)

Instructions regarding War Diaries and Intelligence Summaries are contained in F. S. Regs., Part II. and the Staff Manual respectively. Title pages will be prepared in manuscript.

Place	Date	Hour	Summary of Events and Information	Remarks and references to Appendices
BURSCHEID	27th		Bn. visited by escort party of "Hussars"	
	28th		Escort in Cinema Burscheid at 2.15pm by Capt Lloyd R.A.F. on work of a Reconnaissance Squadron. Band "Jazz" Band provided to pass Eq "H.M.S" at SASSENEM	
			Strength of Bn. 24 off. 472 O.R.	
			Arthur Stratham Major	
			Comdg. 2nd Bn. South Wales Borderers	

2nd. SOUTH WALES BORDERERS.

Major.	A.B.	Cowburn	M.C.
Capt.	A.N.	Glover	M.C.
"	G.	Esmond	M.C.
"	J.E.A.	Gibbs	
Lieut.	G.J.	Greer	
"	W.G.	Jones	
"	T.H.	Waldren	M.C.
2/Lieut.	A.W.	Hardwick	
"	N.C.	McPherson	
"	J.	Davies	
"	B.G.	Davies	
"	T.J.	Williams	
"	M.	Hughes	
"	T.C.R.	Bromham	M.C.
"	W.J.	Millard	
"	A.V.	Priston	
"	F.W.	Hardy	M.C.
"	W.N.	Douglas	
"	D.T.	Johns	
"	C.J.	Hardy	M.C.
"	A.J.	Pritchard	M.C.
"	C.H.J.	Brown	
"	W.T.	Jones	
"	R.S.	Dunsford	

----------ooOOoo----------

OTHER RANKS.

472.

Army Form C. 2118.

2nd Bn. the South Staff Bord[?] Regt[?]

WAR DIARY
or
INTELLIGENCE SUMMARY.
(Erase heading not required.)

March 1919

Place	Date	Hour	Summary of Events and Information	Remarks and references to Appendices
Bucquoy	3rd		Lieut W Rogers the S/Leary RA stat[?] at Rugby 21 battle and staff 7 22 OR.	
	4th		Arrived from 10th Bn RWF	
	5th		The whole Bn bathed and were present with clean clothes.	
			The Bn C March Division. Lieut D. Ihles proceeded to Cologne in [?] to [?]	
			T. Army Leave Scheme. "Papillon" Concert party entertained Bn at 6pm	
	6th		Party of 15 OR left for UK for Demobilisation	
	7th		Party of 10 OR left for UK for Demobilisation.	
	8th		The Bn v Concert party versed Bn. Divisional football Officers v ORs 4-0	
	9th		Lieut M. Hughes left Bn for duty with D.R.I & W. Cologne. Final of Divl football	
			Competition won Fost 4 KOYLI at Fres GuadRieu - Bn were in train	
			to see match.	
	11th		Lecture by Lieut Quen Habford on "Local and Industrial situation" at 11am in	
			Cinema BURSCHEID Whole Bn billed and were present with clean clothes	
	13th		Paid[?] a visit a/light Anker Burnet[?] 2Lieuts W A Douglas (Oving[?]) J A Ysemiant	
			2 Lieut[?] Rd Duvie, Beg Duns[?] Ly Ihles and GR left to join 6/ of the	
			Gd Bn 1st Division	

Army Form C. 2118.

WAR DIARY
or
INTELLIGENCE SUMMARY.
(Erase heading not required.)

Month: March 1919

Instructions regarding War Diaries and Intelligence Summaries are contained in F. S. Regs., Part II. and the Staff Manual respectively. Title pages will be prepared in manuscript.

Place	Date	Hour	Summary of Events and Information	Remarks and references to Appendices
BERGISCH	March 13th	11 am	Draft consisting of 2 Lieut. a/Capt. Edwards F.G. and 2 Lieuts. L.G.R. Bromham &c &c Lieut. Hardy, W.L.F. F.P. Hardy, M.C., A.M. MacGuale & Lieut. M. Hopkins and 65 O.R. Surgeons. W.B. to join 32 nd the 1/W.B. at Dieringen.	
		2pm	Draft consisting of 2 Lieut. a/Capt. H.L. Pytke and 2 Lieuts. A.H. Printer W.A. Gay, H.A. Green, J.W. Leigh, T.B. Lodge, L.J. Tuttle and 121 O.R. left for that W.B. to join 58 th Bn W.B.	
	14th	7.30 am	Draft consisting of Lieut. W.G. Moir Stuart L.H.Y. Cross and 121 O.R. proceeded to U.K. for demobilisation	
		3pm	Advance party of the Railway Bn 60th Divn arrived at Bergisch G to take over.	
	15		Lieut. Col. A. Hislop D.S.O. returned from leave to U.K.	
			Draft of 114 O.R. (demobilised men) proceeded to U.K. via Ostend, en route to disposal Zeebrugge etc.	
	16th		50 th Bn Devonshire Regt arrived at Bergisch to take over.	
MULHEIM	17th		Bn. withdrew 7 th Bn S.W.B. S.D.R. moved by train to Mulheim en route to Cologne	
COLOGNE			Lt. Col. L. Hackett D.S.O. took over duties of Area Commandant Mulheim	

Army Form C. 2118.

WAR DIARY
or
INTELLIGENCE SUMMARY.
(Erase heading not required.)

2nd Bn. The South Wales Borderers

March 1919

Place	Date	Hour	Summary of Events and Information	Remarks and references to Appendices
MAYEN	24th		All Yeoman R.O.M.B. ceased to be attached to the Bn and proceed to the 87th Bde Hd Quarters	
"	30th		Draft of 170 O.R. left for U.K. for demobilization	
"	31st		Major A.B. Cowburn M.C. and 2 Lieut Pritchard M.C. proceeded to U.K. for demobilization. Lieut & Lt. Col. Baldwin M.C. proceeded to join 87th Bde H.Q.	
"	31st		as a volunteer for the Army of Occupation, the cadre of the Bn entrained	
"	31st		for Dunkirk en route for U.K.	

J.P. Rankin Lt.Col.
Cmdg 2nd South Wales Borderers

Index No.......

Cadre

Lt. Colonel G.T. Raikes   D.S.O.
Lieut.   G.J. Greer
  "   A.W. Hardwick
  "   N.C. McPherson.

Other Ranks.

46.

Army Form C. 2118.

2nd Bn. The South Wales Borderers Cadre

WAR DIARY
or
INTELLIGENCE SUMMARY.
(Erase heading not required.)

April 1919 Month and Year

Instructions regarding War Diaries and Intelligence
Summaries are contained in F. S. Regs. Part II.
and the Staff Manual respectively. Title pages
will be prepared in manuscript.

Place	Date	Hour	Summary of Events and Information	Remarks and references to Appendices
DUNKIRK	1/4/19	01000	Cadre of Bn arrived at DUNKIRK	
	2/4/19	6.30	Cadre detrained and marched to "A" camp where the whole cadre was bathed and received clean clothing	
	4/4/19	13.50	Cadre embarked for U.K. on S.S. Golden Eagle	
DOVER	4/4/19	17.30	Bn arrived at DOVER and entrained for LONDON arriving at 9.30 pm. Bn billeted in LONDON for night	
BRECON	5/4/19	17.30	Bn entrained at 11.45 for BRECON arriving there at 17.30. Bn detrained into Depot S.W.B. at 18.10 hrs. Bn marched into South Wales Borderers.	

C.M. Radice Lieut Col.
Cmdg 2nd South Wales Borderers

List of Officers
Major a/Lt Col G.T. Raikes D.S.O.
T/Lieut A.M. Grist
T/Lieut A.W. Hardwick
T/2Lieut N.C. McPherson a/Lt 16 WR

On His Majesty's Service.

www.ingramcontent.com/pod-product-compliance
Lightning Source LLC
Chambersburg PA
CBHW080825010526
44111CB00015B/2610